I0830736

THE GRAND TOUR DIARIES OF WILLIAM GUISE

THE GRAND TOUR DIARIES OF WILLIAM GUISE

FROM LAUSANNE TO ROME

*His Journal from 18 April
to 31 October 1764*

---

edited by

PAUL & JANE BUTLER

THE HOBNOB PRESS

First published in the United Kingdom in 2022

by The Hobnob Press
8 Lock Warehouse
Severn Road, Gloucester GL1 2GA
www.hobnobpress.co.uk

British Library Cataloguing in Publication Data
A catalogue record for this book is available from the British Library

ISBN 978-1-914407-30-7
Typeset in Adobe Garamond Pro 11/14 pt.
Typesetting and origination by John Chandler

For Anselm Guise and the Guise family

CONTENTS

PREFACE

The Grand Tour Diaries of William Guise

William Guise, later Sir William Guise, 5th Baronet of Elmore, travelled in Switzerland and Italy in 1764 and 1765 in the company of Edward Gibbon, the historian. Guise kept thorough journals of his travels from when he left Lausanne in April 1764. The first two journals are stored in the archives of Elmore Court, Gloucestershire, which was his family home. Despite their historic and cultural interest, there has been no full transcription of these journals apart from some references to them in Bonnard's edited diaries of Edward Gibbon[1].

There are two volumes, of 318 pages and 83,000 words in total. The front page of the first journal was annotated by W. V. Guise in 1860 indicating that they had been returned to the family nearly 100 years after they were written. The second journal stops abruptly whilst Guise was still in Rome, indicating that there may well have been other journals. It is known they travelled on together for many more months through Italy and back into France before Gibbon cut short his 'Grand Tour' at Lyons and returned to England, with Guise following later.

The story behind their 'rediscovery' is of some interest. We (Paul & Jane Butler) were searching in the attic of Elmore Court for any documentation which might throw light on the building of a 'Roman' mausoleum in St John's churchyard, Elmore. According to Howard Colvin, this is the "earliest building in Western Europe in which the baseless Doric order is at present [1991] known to have been used."[2] – with such orders being a key indicator of the birth of neo-Classicism. The mausoleum exists, but in a ruined state, and the current owners of the mausoleum – the Mausolea and Monuments Trust – were trying to see if it could be restored. We could find nothing which related to the building of this mausoleum, but we did find these two 'precious'

---

1 Georges A. Bonnard ed., *Gibbon's Journey from Geneva to Rome: His Journal from 20 April to 2 October 1764* (1961)

2 Howard Colvin, 'A Roman Mausoleum at Elmore', *The Georgian Group Journal* (1991).

journals. 'Precious' is the word used by Bonnard in his editing of the Gibbon Grand Tour diaries. He managed to consult the diaries in 1961 at Elmore Court. Since that time, there has been no reference to the diaries. Edward Chaney tried to find them as part of research he was doing into Gibbon and William Beckford. He visited Elmore Court in 1994 but Sir John Guise was unable to locate them.[1]

The aim behind publishing these diaries has been to allow the reader, academic or amateur, to read and enjoy them, as we have done. It is not a full scholarly editing of the diaries, which cover many themes which will be of interest to many different groups. As well as the expected comments on the statues, pictures and other works of art which they saw, and on which Guise offers succinct comments, Guise also refers, sometimes quite extensively, to military matters and fortifications; to the political and governance issues of the towns of Northern Italy; to travel and lodging issues – all this apart from the light it throws upon Gibbon and his travels in Italy. We have kept our editing to brief footnotes mostly about the people that Guise met, interspersed with illustrations where relevant. We hope that, by publishing these diaries in this format, it will allow those with specific interests to mine the diaries for their particular concerns – and in the meantime simply to enjoy reading them.

Biographical note on Edward Gibbon and William Guise

Edward Gibbon

Edward Gibbon wrote The History of the Decline and Fall of the Roman Empire in six volumes between 1776 and 1788. According to Gibbon, "It was at Rome, on the fifteenth of October 1764, as I sat musing amidst the ruins of the Capitol, while the barefooted friars were singing vespers in the temple of Jupiter, that the idea of writing the decline and fall of the City first started in my mind"[2]. At that time he was on the Grand Tour with his friend and close companion, William Guise, whose diaries are recorded here, and which cover this period. The diaries, so useful to Bonnard in his annotation of the Italian Journal of

---

1   Edward Chaney, 'Gibbon, Beckford and the Interpretation of "Dreams, Waking Thoughts, and Incidents'", *The Beckford Society Annual Lectures 2000-2003* (2004).

2   This famous sentence comes from Sheffield's editing of Gibbon's Autobiography. In Gibbon's *Memoirs of my Life*, edited by Georges A. Bonnard, it is referred to thus: "In my Journal the place and moment of conception [of Decline and Fall] are recorded; the fifteenth of October 1764, in the close of evening, as I sat musing in the Church of the Zoccolanti or Franciscan fryars, while they were singing Vespers in the Temple of Jupiter on the ruins of the Capitol".

Fig 1 Edward Gibbon, Florence, 1764

Gibbon, therefore provide a fascinating commentary on the travels of Gibbon which were so influential in the conceptual preparation of his great work.

Gibbon was born in Putney, Surrey (now London) in 1737 and died in 1794. An erratic education led him firstly to Magdalen College, Oxford, where he converted to Roman Catholicism. As a result of this, he was despatched to Lausanne and the care of a Protestant minister, Mr Pavilliard, in 1753 and stayed there for five years. It was here that he converted back to Protestantism and where he completed his European classical education.

He returned to England in 1758 and stayed for five years. It was in this time, in 1761, he published his first work: *Essai sur l'étude de la littérature*.

He arrived back in Lausanne in May 1763 and gradually made preparations – intellectual and practical – for a Grand Tour to complete that part of a gentleman's education. His financial circumstances were however precarious and it is doubtful if he could have contemplated such an extended visit if he hadn't found an agreeable companion. This person was William Guise whose financial circumstances were stronger than Gibbon's and with whom he could thus share expenses. Guise had been staying in Lausanne at M. and Mme Crousaz de Mezery's pension in the rue de Bourg since October 1762. Gibbon arrived there in May 1763, so by April 1764 they were well acquainted, and evidently good friends. In a letter to his stepmother in June 1763, Gibbon describes Guise as 'a very sensible well-bred man'. They were both aged 27 as they set out in 'great harmony and good humour' in April 1764 and parted more than a year later in June 1765. In all this time it seems likely that every day was spent in each other's company.

William Guise

Family

William Guise was the son of Sir John Guise, 4th baronet of Elmore in Gloucestershire. The Guises had been living at Elmore Court since the 13th century. Their fortunes varied over the centuries but survived the civil wars of the 15th and 17th centuries, and prospered, relatively, as members of the landed gentry after the Restoration and the upheavals of the later 17th and early 18th centuries. The Elmore baronetcy was created for Christopher Guise in 1661.

Fig 2 Elmore Court, 2021

There were three succeeding baronets, all Johns, before William assumed the title in 1769.

William was born at '30 minutes after 4' on the 26th July 1737. The precision is thanks to a footnote in the 'Memoirs of the Family of Guise of Elmore Gloucestershire'[1] written by Sir Christopher Guise (1617 – 1670), 1st baronet of Elmore and Sir John Guise (1678 – 1732), the 3rd baronet. At the end there is a page written by Sir John, the 4th baronet and William's father, with a note detailing the births of his four children, including William, whom he called Billy. William was the youngest of the four. His brother was John ('Jackey') born 28 April 1736; his sisters Jane ('Jenny') born 4 January 1733-34 and Elizabeth ('Betty') born 16 December 1734. John died in December 1755, Elizabeth two months later in February 1756. In June 1770, Jane married Shute Barrington, Bishop of Llandaff and then successively of Salisbury and Durham. Jane died in 1807 aged 73 and her husband in 1826 aged 91. There were no children by this marriage. William died on 6 April 1783, unmarried and with no children. The Elmore baronetcy became extinct at that time, but was in effect revived as the Highnam baronetcy in the same year by a distant cousin who was his legatee, John Guise of Highnam.

Whilst William did not marry and therefore had no immediate family, he was connected with a range of other family members and contacts in Gloucestershire and elsewhere. Amongst his elder relations: William Guise of Abload's Court, an estate the other side of Gloucester from Elmore. He was a distinguished orientalist with an 'immense' reputation as a scholar and a detailed knowledge of Arabic, Hebrew, Syriac and Aramaic as well as Turkish, Samaritan, Persian, Ethiopic and Armenian. He died of smallpox in 1683 aged just 31. His son John (born 1682) succeeded him and became both a general and one of the great art collectors of the 18th century, with virtually all his collection going on his death in 1765 to his Oxford college, Christ Church, where it forms a major part of the current Christ Church Gallery.

He was thus a member of the landed gentry class who via his estate and his connections were part of the governing elite of the country.

Education

Little is known of his early education. His great great grandfather Christopher at the age of nine or ten was "sojourned in an honest house [in Wotton under Edge] where our dyett and all thinges else were of the playnest but holesome".

---

1   G. Davies, 'Autobiography of Thomas Raymond and Memoirs of the family of Guise of Elmore, Gloucestershire', edited for *The Royal Historical Society. Camden Third Series, Vol XXVIII* (1917). Reprinted by the Leopold Classic Library.

William would either have been similarly sojourned or he would have been home schooled via a tutor; or he could have gone to a local grammar school in Gloucester. It is unlikely that he would have gone to a more distant school such as Westminster or Eton, which was however where his future brother in law, Shute Barrington, was educated. Wherever he went, he would have been educated in the basics of Latin and Greek.

Guise matriculated at Queen's College Oxford on 5 July 1754, aged nearly 17, and was awarded an MA on 29 October 1759. Not all sons of noblemen (a classification which generally included baronets) found it necessary to take a degree, so one must assume that Guise attended to his studies reasonably assiduously. He is also on record as being admitted (as the 'second son of Sir John Gyse, baronet') to Lincoln's Inn on 6th June 1755. Law was essentially self-taught at this time: pupils would attend the law courts or read the law in barristers' chambers and private lodgings. As the second son, he would have been expected to find a living for himself, and the two principal civil occupations were the church (for which he would have needed the MA from Oxford), or the law, which is where attendance at one of the Inns of Court would have been essential. However, his elder brother died 6 months after he was admitted to Lincolns Inn, so the assumption would be that his 'occupation' would be to succeed his father to the title and estates and all the privileges, obligations and opportunities consequent upon this. Having some familiarity with the law would however also have been of help in the family business of being an MP.

Life and career

Again not much is known about his life after graduation. There is a fine portrait of him painted by Allan Ramsay in 1761 – "one of the most beautiful of all Ramsay's portraits of male sitters"[1]. Guise would have been 23 or 24 at the time. Ramsay was the leading portraitist of his age, at least until Reynolds. In 1761 he was appointed 'one of his majesty's Principal Painters in Ordinary' along with John Shackleton. On Shackleton's death in 1767, he became the Principal Painter. Having a portrait done by such a distinguished painter was a very visible mark of the standing of the family in the country.

We next hear of him in Lausanne where he had come, according to Gibbon, in October 1762. Guise went to Lausanne "partly for the sake of learning French and partly, or so it seems, to get over some disappointment in love"[2]. Lausanne played a significant part in the education of many English gentlemen,

---

1   Alastair Smart, *Alan Ramsay 1713-1784*, Scottish National Portrait Gallery (1992), p 133

2   Georges A. Bonnard, ed., *Gibbon's Journey from Geneva to Rome: His Journal from 20 April to 2 October 1764* (1961), p vii

either as a continuation of their university life; or post school, providing them with the opportunity to learn French and understand something of the Swiss Enlightenment. It had the advantage as well of being Protestant rather than Catholic. In Gibbon's case, his first stay there (1753-58) was specifically to cure him of his recent conversion to Catholicism, which was effected by Christmas 1754. Gibbon's second stay in the town was very much a learning opportunity before embarking on the Grand Tour of Italy. It was presumably much the same thing for Guise. Gibbon's comment on Guise is revealing:

We have some English here; most of them raw boys just escaped from Eaton. Mr. Guise—I do not reckon him in the number of them. He is about my age, has seen a good deal of the world, & without being a profound scholar is far from wanting either parts or knowledge. As far as I can judge of him he seems to be a prudent worthy young man. If I can go into Italy with him I should like it extremely.[1]

They set off for Italy in April 1764 and their diaries record their daily activities until the end of September, in Gibbon's case, and the end of October in Guise's. It is probable that Guise continued to write his diaries, but they have been lost.

Guise and Gibbon travelled together for 14 months in total. They parted in Lyons where Gibbon returned directly to England, arriving at the end of June 1765. Guise returned two months later in August of that year. He succeeded to the baronetcy four years later in 1769 and became the MP for Gloucestershire in August 1770 until his death on 6 April 1783, aged 45. He appears only to have spoken twice in the House of Commons, on militia affairs, on 25 April 1780; and in favour of sending a relief fund to Barbados on 24 January 1781.

He was unmarried and had therefore no direct heirs when he died. In his will, dated 21 March 1783, he left the bulk of his estate to his sister Jane Barrington and his distant cousin, John Guise of Highnam. With William's death, the Elmore baronetcy became extinct, but was in effect reinstated in the same year as the Highnam baronetcy. The Highnam estate was later sold, and the Guise family re-adopted Elmore Court as their seat.

Transcriptions issues

We have kept the spelling as exactly as possible to that in the diary – that is, we have not corrected for obvious errors or for idiosyncrasies of spelling. It is in

---

1   letter to his stepmother 7 December 1763.

fact remarkable, bearing in mind that spelling was not really standardised until after the introduction of dictionaries (Johnson's was published in 1755), how few spelling 'errors' there are. None of the words which we spell differently today cause any problems with understanding the text.

Similarly, we have kept capitalisation exactly as in the text. Guise's use of capitals was not always consistent. In some case it may have been to give emphasis; in others, he simply used a capital since it was a proper noun (commonly capitalised) or if not, for no obvious reason. Equally, from our point of view, it is sometimes difficult knowing what word is capitalised or not – the letters C, M and W pose particular problems and there may be occasions when we have got it wrong.

The same comments can be made about punctuation. We have left it exactly as Guise has written. It is more idiosyncratic than it would be today, and it is not necessarily internally consistent. But nowhere does it affect the sense of what is written, and it provides a good example of how an original script would have been seen at that time.

Sometimes the paragraph lengths as written down by Guise are very long and modern usage would break them up, but we have kept them as set down by Guise.

Guise used superscripts as abbreviations fairly commonly. Most are obvious, but sometimes he used y^t for 'that', y^n for 'than' and y^e for 'the', which may not be immediately obvious. We have kept abbreviations as they are in the text, but with the 'dot' after the final superscripted letter rather than below. Ampersands (&) and 'ands' are as in the script.

Guise used footnotes in his Journals which appeared at the end of the relevant page. We have generally placed them at the end of the day's entry, except where the entry is very extensive where they appear at the end of a paragraph. They were generally written as 'a', b', etc. Because their new position does not correspond to the pagination of the original diaries, we have altered them – for example, from 'b' to 'a' - where necessary, so they make current sense.

We have kept the names as written by Guise. For places, if it is not completely clear, we have put the current name in square brackets immediately after the name as written by Guise. The identity of the artists mentioned is generally easily ascertainable. Annibale Caracci, for example, has several variations of both first name and surname, but it is always clear who it is.

Guise headed each day entry in his diary with sometimes just a date (28th) but more often with a date and place: 'day/date/month – place', so "Tuesday 24th July – Florence". We have used this format for each day. In the second of the two volumes, Guise took to using a marginal heading on occasions. We have italicised these headings at the beginning of the section to which the heading refers.

Long sections of Latin – generally copied by Guise from another source – have been translated, courtesy of Stephen Chambers. These sections are indented and a point size smaller than the main text has been used. Single sentences, and the occasional use of French, have been kept as they were written.

We have used footnotes where some elucidation may be useful. They generally refer to people and provide some context to his travels. Our principal sources have been the Oxford Dictionary of National Biography and Ingamells[1].

Acknowledgements

We thought that the diaries were important and Bonnard obviously thought so. But our academic backgrounds did not really allow us to come to a firm opinion on this matter. We have however been incredibly fortunate in being able to show the first rough drafts of our transcriptions to our friend and distinguished art historian, Christopher Lloyd. Not only was he kind enough to read them, he also provided a resumé of the reasons why they should be published, which went much further than the 'art historical' route, important though that is. Christopher also put us in touch with an equally distinguished historian, Edward Chaney, an expert on the Grand Tour, Edward Gibbon, William Beckford and on many other cultural aspects of the period in question. He had tried to find the dairies in 1994 (see above) and was consequently pleased that they had now been found. His opinion of their importance reinforced that of Christopher Lloyd's. We are also indebted to our publisher, John Chandler of the Hobnob Press. John's encouragement and expert advice on how to move from a typescript to the finished product has been invaluable and we are extremely grateful for his friendly expertise.

We would also like to acknowledge the help that Gabriel Sewell, the Librarian at Christ Church, Oxford, provided in chasing up references to some of the people Guise met; and Stephen Chambers who kindly translated those sections which were written in Latin – thank you both.

---

1   John Ingamells ed., *A Dictionary of British and Irish travellers in Italy 1701-1800* (1997)

78:

Saturday
21st

July. Florence

We have as yet been obliged to see a great many very indifferent things, to be able to find out something worth notice; This Morning we were more than made amends for the bad things we had seen in the Corridores, by the many very valuable, and indeed inestimable things, we found in La Camera detta la Tribuna; This room is of an Octagon form, the light comes in by a Cupola in the Top, and several small windows round the sides. In the middle of the Room stands an Octagon Table of Florentine work; at some distance from the Table are six large Statues, behind them against the wall several smaller ones; upon a shelf about 6 feet from the ground a great many small pieces of Antiquity, and Busts, and round the wall above this a great many valuable Pictures: There is a kind of Alcove filled with different pieces of work in precious stones, and on each side of this is a kind of Closet filled with valuable things of various sorts. In speaking of these things I shall content myself to mention only those that are most unattable or at least pleased me the most. —

At entering the The Octagon, the first thing that must strike the Eye, and draw the attention of every one, is that master piece of Sculpture, the Venus de Medicis. I am afraid to attempt giving any description of her, as I am very well convinced, how impossible it must be not only for me, but for any one, to confer a tolerable idea of the Beauties and Perfections of this Statue.

La Tribuna

Venus de Medicis

Fig 3 diary page July 21st, 1764

THE GRAND TOUR DIARIES OF WILLIAM GUISE

Wednesday 18ᵗʰ April – Lausanne to Geneva

The best manner of going from Lausanne, or Geneva to Turin is by voiturier: That is, by makeing an agrement with a Person to take you there, for a certain sum he paying ev'ry expence between the two places. Mʳ. Gibbons,[1] and I agreed with one, to provide us with a Carriage for our selves, one for our Servants and to pay ev'ry expence on the road (except foreign wines) and to receive of us at Turin the sum of twenty one Louis d'ors neufs. He was to take us there in eight days from Lausanne. It may be easily done in seven.

Sorry to quit a place where I had past eighteen Months, in a very agreable manner (mais plus faché de quitter una personna[2] que toutes les autres ensemble) I set out for Turin with Mʳ. Gibbon. Messrs de Mezzery, Cap. Seigneux, Mʳ. Murray and Cap. Willamoy came as far as Geneva with us. Mʳ. Gibbons and myself went to take leave of Mademˡᵉ. Tarsenak, as we passed through Morge. She is daughter of the Bailiff, and had spent some time at Lausanne. An agreable Girl. We got to Geneva in good time, and all supped together.

Thursday 19ᵗʰ April – Geneva

This Morning after having taken leave of Mʳ. de Mezery &c Mʳ. Gibbons and myself went to see the publick library shewn us by a Mʳ. Pittey, I beleive. It consists of three Rooms, one of which is very large. This library which was began only about the beginning of this century, has at present about 30,000 volumes, and as it has been formed in an age more enlightened and by more learned men than most of the very old library's have, it has the advantage of being composed of none but very good Books. We were shewn a Latin Bible in manuscript, which appears by a writeing at the end of the Book to have belonged to a bishop who lived in the year 1115 but the Bible by the difference of the writing, which is more square and the letters sharper, is beleived to be of

---

1   Sometimes there is a final 's'; occasionally it is spelt as if French – 'Guibon'.
2   Person unknown, presumably a close female friend

the Year 900 or thereabouts. In S^t. John I saw the passage of the three witnesses, which I remember to be omitted in a very old Bible I saw at Berne, as well as in some others. Secondly, we were shewn some Sermons of S^t. Augustine of about the 6th. century, written upon a sort of Papirian paper, which was certainly very tender, as the leaves, 'tho all double, are very much harmed and torn. Thirdly, a curious Tablet of Philip le bel, made of wax upon wood. The characters are very obscure. Mon^r. Cranmer, professor at Geneva, has explained them, and given a Copy of its Contents, to the Library. I wish I had had time to have read it as those things certainly give an idea of the customs and manner of living of the times they were wrote in. Fourthly, a Buckler in Silver that the Antients hung up in the Temples as a votary or offring. By an Inscription upon it, it appear'd, to be about the time of Valentinian. It is about 15 inch. In Diametre. Fifthly, a Tooth of the Narval, which seemed to be about 10 Ft long, runing to a point, wth. a ring winding round it from top to bottom. There is a plan of Geneva remarkably nicely delineated and several pretty good paintings. We dined to day at Lord Mountstewarts,[1] with Col: Edmonston who travels wth. him: Lord Abingdon[2], & Mr^s. Vivian who is wth. him. M^r. Chaloner, and M^r. Beckford.[3] We went f^m. hence with Ld. Mountstewart, to see the paintings of Mon^r. Hubert, who paints very prettily but excels in cutting out likenesses in paper, vellum &c. A very good likeness of the handsome Mad: Jennings: a bad one of L^d. Abingdon. We supped this Evening at Ld. Mountstewarts, where we found an addition to the Company at Dinner, a M^r. Turner (son of a sugar boiler we were told) & a M^r. Vollet. L^d. Mountstewart, is a young man of a very amiable Caracter, very affable, & good-natured: a handsome Figure. He has been alwais particularly Civil to me & never more than to day.

Friday 20th April – Geneva to Anecy [Annecy]
We left Geneva this Morning, continuing our Journey for Turin. We dined at Corsel [Cruseilles] a very poor place & bad Inn at about 3 ½ L: from Geneva: from hence we went to day as far as Anecy three-and-a-half Leag: farther, where we lay. The road is hitherto very stony and hilly, & we came only a foot pace. Anecy is a small Town, indifferently built, capital of Savoy, Genevois: Many of the windows of oyl paper. We found some of the King of Sardinias Dragoons quarter'd here in the Castel. We met with a quartermaster by accident, who shewed us the Castel. It is a very large building; the walls very thick, but the

---

1   Lord Mount Stuart (1744-1814), later 1st Marquess of Bute, son of John Stuart, 3rd Earl of Bute (prime minister of Great Britain 1762-63), aged 19 at this time
2   Willoughby Bertie (1740-99), 4th Earl of Abingdon, aged 24. He became a distinguished composer and music patron
3   William Beckford (1744-99), aged 19. Heir to large estates in Jamaica. Cousin to William Beckford of Fonthill Abbey fame.

place not capable of much defence. There is room in the Castel for about 2000 Men: it is much out of repair. By a Muster Role he shew'd us, we saw how compleat their Troops generaly are, a Squadron consisting of 450 men, never having been for many years, under 430 & 40. Their pay is very low, and as the Quartermaster told us, not enough to support a man without the assistance of his Familly. They give each Dragoon about 5 louis at inlisting.

Saturday 21st April – Anecy to Chambery

Leaving Anecy about 7 o'clock this Morning we went 4 L farther before dinner, as far as Aix [Aix-les-Bains]. Here are hot sulphurous Baths, much frequented. I saw three different Springs: two of them much hotter than the other: the hottest I guess to be about the warmth of the little Bath at Bath. There is one place where they told us people bath themselves, but it is quite open & does not appear very proper for it. After Dinner we went to Chambery about 3 L from Aix. The road from Anecy here is better than that of yesterday. The country from Geneva to this place is undoubtedly hilly & raither barren, but has not so poor an appearance as Savoy is generally imagined to have. It seems thin of people, but those one sees are better cloathed, and do not seem so miserable as in many parts of France. There are some small Vineards, & fields of Corn which looked very well. Chambery is the Capital of Savoy proper, and where the Council for Savoy assemble. The Town is pretty large. There are two Streets of a good weadth & length, but the houses seem old, & bad built. The windows chiefly of oyl'd papers.

Sunday 22nd April – Chambery to Aigues-belles [Aiguebelle]

We went to day as far as Aigues-belles, 7 L: from Chambery. 3 L: from this last, lies Mont Malinson. Of the strong fortifications there were formerly, there are at present no remains. This last day was very tiresome, the road being very hilly and stony, except about a L: out of Chambery, which is a good raised Causeway. The Country begins to be more mountanous and barren.

Monday 23rd April – Aigues-belles to St Michel

At near a League from Aigues-Belles the Mountains contract and one enters into a valley which leads you quite to the Foot of Mount Cenis; We went 4 L: this Morning which brought us to La Chambre, where we dined. It is a very poor, small place, and affords nothing for my Pen; however an agreament made there between Mr. Gibbons, and myself will most probably remind me of it; and a thing we did there, 'tho uninteresting at that time, will one of these days become much more interesting to both.[1] At 4L: from La Chambre is S[t]. Michel, where we lay to night. Between these two places lies S[t]. Jean de Moriesme [St-Jean-Maurienne], a pretty village being in a valley, with a fine Piece of raised Causeway for about a mile, leading to it. That part of Savoy known under that name, begins there. The road during this last Stage is mostly very bad, cut in the Side of the Mountain, and in many places spoiled by great pieces of Rocks, which by the continual thawing of the Snows, are separated from the Mountains above, which in many places are so undermined, that they appear as if they would fall down upon you. We found 190 Men employed in clearing away part of a Rock, that had fallen into the road a few days before: Asking those men if they received any pay for their labour, one of them told us, that they should not have so much as a pinch of Snuff, if we did not give it them. But that if they neglected doing it the Marechaussee would soon oblige them to do it. This Place is very dirty but did not prove a nest of Robbers as it had been represented to us.

Tuesday 24th April – St Michel to Lanebourg [Lanslebourg]
Leaving S[t]. Michel early this Morning, we went no farther than 3L: to Modena [Modane] before dinner, and arrived in good time at Lanebourg, a poor village at the Foot of Mount Cenis. The road from S[t]. Michel to Modena is a continual ascent, and very indifferent: From Modena to this place it is much steeper, but better in other respects. – People at this place are obliged to have their Carriages taken to pieces, and carried over on mules, as the Mountain begins close to the village. – – – – –

Close to the Mountains' Foot we Lan'bourg found
Hid by the Snowy Alps, which rise around
Where near five (a) Months deprived of Phoebus' Rays,
A Poor, laborious People pass their Days.

    (a) The Sun does not shine upon it from November 'till the middle of March

The road from the begining of the valley to this place is very remarkable, & pleasing. The River Arc, which rises in the Mount Cenis, runs down it, the water often falling in Cascades made by the uneavenness of the ground, & great pieces of Rocks fallen from the neighbouring Mountains. The Road winding from one side of the valley to the other, one often crosses the River

1   An intriguing reference, but it is not known what was the nature of this agreement or what they did there. The agreement ('contrat') is mentioned by Gibbon but with no further information about it. It is not referred to subsequently in either's journals.

upon Bridges of one or two arches, & well built. These, with the great heighth of the Mountains, hanging in many places over the road, and broke in the most scaggy & frightful manner, cover'd too with old Fir Trees & Snow, form the most extraordinary and Romantick[1] views. -

The whole of the road from Geneva here, tho bad, is as good as can be well expected, considering the hillyness of the Country, and that a great part is made on the Sides of the Mountains, which are continually breaking and falling into them: One plainly sees that the King of Sardinia is desirous of having them pretty good, by what is done already, & one may hope that will be still better. The part of Savoy we have come through, is very thin of People, but they do not seem so poor or miserable, as might be expected from, the little employment they have a great part of the year, from the small part of the Country fit to be cultivated, and from the high taxes they pay.

Fig 4 crossing the Alps, 1755

Wednesday 25th April – Lanebourg to Susa

We left Lanebourg about 6 o'clock this Morning, myself mounted on a mule, my Friend Gibbon, being no great Jockey prefer'd a Chair. – This Chair is,

1   Gibbon also calls this view 'romanesque'/romantic, perhaps an early use of this word for these landscapes

only a Seat made of Rushes & Cords, placed between two long poles: It has a low back & arms to it: Their is a board between the two poles for to support your feet & prevent their hanging down. They are light, & well contrived for carriing. You take 4 or 6 men, who change at fixt distances, and carry you an amazing pace. From Lanebourg to La Ramasse which is near the highest part of the Mount Cenis is a League; the hill is pretty steep and, one should not be able to go up it, without winding very much. This Side of the Mountain is cover'd with snow from about 4 to 6 or 8 Feet deep: Where we went was a narrow path made by the Mules: It was exceeding slippery, having frozen hard in the night. La Ramasse is the place where people comeing down on this Side, commonly make use of a small kind of Sledge, in which they come down in about 10 minutes. You have a man in it with you who guides it and stops it easily by means of a Chain & stick on each side. The plain begins here, and continues two small leagues, to La Grande Croix. A little way from La Ramasse, we saw where a few days before there had been an avalanche, or great quantity of Snow which breaking from the side of the Mountain, is forced down by the wind, and becomes so large that it often covers the plain 8, 10 or 12 Feet deep. They dont happen often on this Mountain, but when they do, inevitably bury ev'ry thing, that is so unfortunate to be in its way. My Muliteer told me very unconcern'dly, that they alwais provided themselves with a large piece of bread, least they should have occasion to live under the snow two or three days. People have been taken out after 4 days living under the snow. A League from la Ramasse is La Maison de Postes, where the chairmen commonly stop to rest themselves. We bought some excellent Cheese here, made upon the mountains which we sent to M. de Mezery. About half a L farther is the Hospital. A curate lives here, and people who by the badness of the weather are obliged to lay on the mountain, are well taken care of here. Half a L from hence is La Grande Croix, the place for getting into the Sledges for going down to Novalese [Novalesa]. The Mountain, we were told, is very beautiful in Summer. It bears the finest herbage, and is cover'd with the most beautiful flowers. About half way the plain of the right hand, is a large Lake. Great numbers of Cattle are drove in the summer to feed on the plain round it. At the same time you see the tops of the neighbouring Mountains cover'd with snow. All these things I can easily imagine may make this Scene, at present so dreary, very pleasing. The Lake is above a L: in Circumference; It abounds with large Trouts and other fish. It was now froze over and cover'd with snow, so that I could only see where it was. There are great plenty of hares and pheasants on the Mountain in Summer. Lord Abingdon the last summer past more than a Month at the Curates, on purpose for hunting.

At la Grande Croix, I quitted my mule, and went in a Chair to Novalese which is 2L farther. The road is so very stony, uneaven, and in many places so steep and full of holes, that it would be dangerous to go down on a mule. About a Leag: from La G: Croix is Terriera. My Chairman stopt here, and I took notice that this place can not well be upon a level with Lanebourg, as M[r]. Keysler[1] thinks it is. I think it must be considerably higher, as the descent from La G. Croix to this place is not near so rapid, or long as the ascent from Lanebourg to La Ramasse. On the left hand of this place is Mount Rochemelon [Rocciamelone], beleived to be the highest Mountain of the Alps. On the Top of it there is a Chapel, where Thousands of people climb over Ice & snow, to hear Mass which is said there ev'ry year, on the fifth of August. There superstition or Devotion however, often costs them very dear, as many of them are commonly lost or frozen amongst the Snows. There is a Glaciere; or Mountain cover'd with snow that is never thaw'd, not far from it; but it is not so high as M[t]: Rochemelon. A L: from Terriera is Novalese, where we arrived at about half an hour after Eleven o' clock, having been about five hours & half in comeing over the Mountain, of which we staid half an hour at the post house. We found almost all the Snow on this side the Mountain thaw'd. The Mountain is not near so steep as on the other side, but from its uneaveness and roughness, is much more disagreable. I had but two men to carry me, but 'tho I crossed over some of the steepest and worst places, they never made a false step, 'tho they went very fast. I fancy that the road is much better than in the time of M[r]. Keysler as wc were never obliged to get out of our Chairs, tho the road winds very much. Neither did I see the place he calls, Le pass de Simble. The weather was as fine as possible, and except for an hour early in the Morning we were raither too hot than too cold, the sun shineing all the time.

The pay of a chairman from Lanebourg to Novalese is no more than 50 sols per man, or about half a crown English which is certainly too little considering the distance & hardness of the work. Indeed they commonly get something more from the people they carry, which they well deserve. I cannot say that they are easily contented. One of M[r]. Gibbon's chairmen asked him for something for having carried his sword & cane, and for having lent him a pair of Gloves, tho he had already given them a Guinea above their pay. It is not so surprizing when one considers how many of them there are, and how little they have to do. At this time there were more than 120 at Lanebourg, & 150 at Terriera, and at Novalese, who have nothing else to do but to carry

---

1 Keysler, J.G., *Travels through Germany* [etc]; 2nd edition 1752; English translations 1756 and 1758, London

for seven months in the year. We dined here and set out afterwards for Susa, which we reached with ease in an hour and a half. The road is a little rough, otherwise very good.

[A gap of 7 pages. No entry for 26th so presumably WG left these pages to be filled in later. Gibbon records that they dined at 'St Amboise' – San Ambrogio di Torino – and slept at Turin 'after a journey of seven days from Geneva'.]

Fig 5 Map of Northern Italy, 1796

Friday 27th April – Turin

Hearing that M[r]. Pit,[1] our Minister, was to set out for England the next day, we wrote to him desireing to wait upon him, and to be presented at Court before he went from Turin. He came to us in the afternoon and told us it had been impossible to do it as it was the Kings birth Day and it was necessary to

---

1 George Pitt (1721-1803), later 1st Baron Rivers, aged 42. He was the Envoy-extraordinary to the Kingdom of Sardinia at Turin.

have our names given to the King the Day before. But that he had spoke to the Count Very, Minister for the foreign affairs, who promised to mention us to the King, and that Monsieur Dutems[1], British Charge d'affaires, in the Abscence of M[r]. Pit, would present us. M[r]. Ponsonby[2], Son of the Speaker in Ireland, Ld Berkeley:(a)[3] Cap[t] Atkins who has the command of two ships, one of 50, and another of 36, which the King of Sardignia bought of us & M[r]. Dobson Governor to Ld Baltimore (b)[4] came to see us. In the Eveng. we went to La Promenade, w[ch] is nothing more than part of the road between the Rows of Trees just out of Town, where they go ev'ry Evening to shew their Carriages.

(a) [no note]
(b) Ld. Baltimore would not make us the first visit, as all the other English did.

Saturday 28th April – Turin

We went to see Count Very, who received us very Civilly, offer'd to serve us: had heard of us from Ld Mountstewart.

Sunday 29th April – Turin

Dined with Baron Wolfe.[5] He is of a German Family that has been long settled in Russia: an uncle having left him a very considerable Estate. He has settled himself in Hampshire. After Dinner, Mon. Dutems presented us to the Marquise de St. Giles. She keeps a constant Assembly, where foreigners are alwais taken to as soon as they come to Turin.

Sunday 30th April – Turin

M[r]. Gibbons and myself takeing a walk about the Town this Morning could not help makeing some observations on the Rue de Po: named from the river which runs a little without the Gate at the Bottom of that Street. It is much the noblest Street I ever saw, and so well proportion'd we thought it worth measuring. The length of the street is 2042 English feet, the weadth between the piazzas 53 ft +1/2: distance of one arcade fm. another 14 ft, Breadth 14,

1   Louis Dutens (1730-1812), aged 34. Amongst other achievements, he collected and published the works of Leibnitz whilst at Turin.

2   William Brabazon Ponsonby (1744-1806), later 1st Baron Ponsonby, aged 19.

3   Frederick Augustus Berkeley (1745-1810), 5th Earl of Berkeley, aged 19. His seat was Berkeley Castle, 14 miles from Guise's residence at Elmore Court. He succeeded to the earldom when aged 10.

4   Frederick Calvert (1731-71), 6th Baron Baltimore, hereditary Proprietary Governor of Maryland. Aged 33.

5   Possibly the nephew (and heir) of Baron von Woolff, the distinguished German philosopher and key figure in the German Enlightenment

Heigth about 24. The Arcades continue from one end of the street to the other, on each side. At the end next the Gate they open in a large semi circle wch we did not measure. The Houses are all built of Brick: three story's high, beside the Arcades which seem raither too high for the height of the houses. It is much the finest and best proportion'd street I ever saw.

From hence we went to the Church of the Carmelites in La place de St Carlo. It is a very neat Church but there is nothing remarkable in it except a very large statue of St Therese. She is represented as overcome by the appearance of something. Her surprise is well expressed and the drapery seems very well done.

Monday 1st May – Turin

We took a view this Morning of the Jesuits Church [SS Martiri], and of La Consola [Basilica Sanctuary of the Consolata]. They are neither very remarkable. The paintings in Fresco which are pretty good, and the Pillars and other ornaments in Marble of the Country, make it neat and pleasing, 'tho nothing more. La Consola is reckoned much finer, but I cannot say I saw any thing that was very strik'ing. The manner it is built in is the most particular. It is properly two large Chapels together. One of them has a Dome. They are prettily but not ritchly ornamented.

We went this Evening to see a Comick Opera at the little Theatre, which tho small in comparison of the other perhaps, will nevertheless hold a thousand people. The form is round, and very pretty. The sides divided into small Boxes which are alwais bought for the Season by particular people so that ev'ry one else is obliged to go into the Pit. Women never go there.

Tuesday 2nd May – Turin

M^r. Moula[1] & the Baron Wolfe went with us to see La Superga. This Church which it is said the late King began pursuant to a vow he made during the Siege of Turin, is built on one of the highest hills near Turin, at about four English miles from the town. It was from this hill that Prince Eugene and the King took a view of the French Army. The ground where the Church stands was near 30 ft higher than at present. The entrance is a very handsome Portico: the Pillars are very large and handsome, but it is a shame to see of how bad stone they are made as there is not one of them that has not a great number of pieces of stone let into it. There are two Towers, one at each end. The Cupola is supported by eight Corinthian Pillars of an immense size & height, made of a blue grey marble.

---

1   Frédéric Moula, travelling companion to Baron Wolff.

From the Ground to the top of their Base seem'd above 7 Feet. The smaller Pillars which are above these and support the Dome more properly are of red Marble, & seem too small for those below. Within the Cupola is a Gallery near a 100 paces round. In the Centre of the Roof in a Circle are the following words: "Victorius Amadeus Rex, anno salutis 1626". Without the Dome are three Galleries, one above another. To the uppermost are about 320 steps. From this one discovers a most extensive and beautiful view. I was told that Milan may be seen from it. The Altars are very handsome. In the back part of them some good pieces of Sculpture in Marble. There are some pretty good paintings. In a little Chapel on one side is the tomb of Victor Amadeus who is buried there. A vault is intended to be made for Royal Family – Behind the Church.

Wednesday 3ʳᵈ May – Turin

Haveing been told by Mʳ. Dutems that the king[1] had been told of our intention to be presented, we went this Morning to Court at about eleven o'clock. A Custom was long ago introduced at this Court by some Noblemen that none but, Peers or Sons of Peers should be presented to the King in his Closet or inward Chamber, but in one of the Rooms through wᶜʰ. he passes when he goes to Mass. It was at the door of one of these that Mʳ. Dutems presented us: as we had the misfortune not to be Lord, Count, or Marquis, without which a man is not much esteem'd at Turin. His majesty is very short and little, and looks very old. Altogether he is as mean, and un-kingly a Figure as I ever saw. He stopt about a minute or two, & asked us from whence we came and where we were going. We could not be presented to the rest of the Family to day, but just saw them comeing from Mass: shall say nothing of them now, as we are to be presented to them Sunday: nor of the Palace as we intend seeing it Monday.

Thursday 4ᵗʰ May – Turin

We went after dinner wᵗʰ. the Bⁿ. Wolfe & Mʳ. Moula to La Venerie [La Venaria Reale], one of the King's Palaces about an hour out of Turin. It is an extensive building, of brick, in many parts much broke and damaged. None of the sides very regular. That next the Orangery is the best. We were first shewn into a large salloon (the guard Room) which is large & very high, where is the Duchess and many other ladies painted on horseback in hunting pieces. They are but very indifferent. From thence going through the King's apartement you see all the Kings of England, of France; the Austrian Family and that of the

---

1   Charles Emmanuel III (1701-1773), Duke of Savoy and King of Sardinia from 1730 till his death. Aged therefore 63 at time of visit.

Kings of Sardinia. All very indifferent. After passing through this apartement which is handsome we came into a very handsome Gallery which, I stept, and beleived to be about 100 yards long, and a very good weadth. It is very little ornamented at present, but intended to be, <u>when the King can spare the Money</u>. From this, we were shewn into the Duke & Duchesses apartement, which consists of four or five small rooms for each, that are furnished in the most elegant and pleasing manner. The bed chambers are hung with a Green and White Silk, some pictures over the Doors, the frame of a light small gilding as are the cornishes and base and mouldings of the rooms. The cabinets, are of Japan, Black and Yellow, and the ground of one a beautiful Red. The Furniture of this apartement wch. is throughout the same pleased us so much that I wish to remember it. There are several other Rooms, that are not very remarkable in themselves, nor for what is in them. There are many statues but no very good ones. A Sleeping Cupid, not bad. Leaving these we went into the Church [Sant'Uberto], wch. joins to it. It is an elegant building, is well ornamented, and has a handsome Dome. In the four corners beneath it are 4 very large statues of 4 Saints. The largest altar is a good piece of work. Over some of the others are several paintings by Conca, Ricci and Beaumont. One in particular representing St. Sebastian, and St. Rock by Sebastian Ricci is a very good piece. From hence we went to see the Stables which are long and wide, and which they told me will hold 290 horses. I counted near 200. Many English ones. We were next shewn the Gardens, which are pretty extensive but laid out in a very bad manner. The walks are almost all of gravel, planted on each sides with hedges, and Trees cut regularly. I saw a great number of pheasants, Hares etc. The King commonly passes about one Month of the year at this place, and keep his Court Sundays.

Friday 5th May – Turin

The Royal Museum furnished sufficient employment and amusement for this Morning. This repository of Antiquities and Curiosities has not been began to be made but within these three years, and it is surprising how large and good a Collection of the most rare and valuable peices of Sculpture, Statues, Busts and things relateing to them, of Precious Stones, Medals and Antiques of evr'y kind are to be found already in this place. We were shewn them by Monsr. Bartoli,[1] Antiquarian to the King, who has shewn not only his love for these things, but his taste and learning, by the order and manner of disposeing them, having placed ev'ry thing according to the time they existed in. Beginning

---

1   Giuseppe Bartoli (1717-88), professor at Turin University from 1745 and 'antiquaire royal' to the king.

with the Heathen Gods he has put them according to their rank placeing between each the particular Simbols and attributes belonging to them, and marks or whatever served to distinguish them. After these are things that belonged to the Antient Romans, and other nations at the same time existing, all distributed in a manner that they serve to explain each other, and assist you in remembering them: – The little time one has to see so great a variety, makes it almost impossible to recollect them all, besides if one could it would take near a Folio. – Some of the most remarkable things were, first. at the top of the room a very good piece of Bass-relief in several divisions. The Middle one represents Jupiter, Juno and Venus. Several of the others represent the Birth and education of Bacchus. In another part of it one sees the Olympick Games. This last part is broke, and there only remains at present part of the horses, very near the Pillar on which the Prize was put and which appears plainely was a vase. Just by the horses is the figure of a man, by which the horse next it, seems much frightened. Secondly, a small statue of the Athenian Minerva, which is as beautiful, and as curious a piece as ever I saw. The head, hands, feet, and all of the body that is uncover'd is of black touchstone. The Drapery of a most beautiful, Transparent, Oriental Aliblaster. They value it much from beleiving it to be like that that was in the Temple at Athens. In her right hand she holds something much like what we call a Truncheon on her breast plate, the Medusa's head and in her left hand a Shild with a thunder Bolt embossed upon it. Thirdly, a very beautiful figure of Apollo the same size as the last. Fourthly, a small figure of Ajax in biass. He is represented in a sad, pensive posture, with several dead things which he had killed at his feet. M^r. Bartoli shew'd us the passage relating to him in Sophocles, and his attitude in this little Statue, answers exactly to the description given of him there, after the Shield of Achilles had been adjudged to Ulysses, and in his fury he had killed so many things in the Camp, but became afterwards melancholy. This piece is much valued, & very justly. Fifthly. The Discus used by the Romans. It is made of a Granet Stone, is flat, about an Inch thick; the edge done entirely round with Iron. On one side is a hole for the Thumb and on the other a place for about 4 fingers. It is by no means heavy. Sixthly. An ossuarium, or earthen vessel, <u>under and in which</u>, they formerly put their bones. I say, <u>under & in which</u> as they put them first into an earthen pot not very large (at least this was not). This pot has two close covers, the first is small and is just the Size of the Mouth of the Pot, the second is a little larger and made to fit to a Rim of the pot which is turned round it. This pot is put under a large cover made likewise of Earth, which is full as high again, and as big again round, is close at the top and drawn up to a point or pretty near. I saw two of these ossuarii, and an urn in which they put the Ashes. They were found near Turin. Seventhly. Some little figures in Brass which were found in Sardinia. They were intended to represent Soldiers as is plain from their having Bows & kind of Quivers. Nothing can possibly be worse formed or more coarsely made than these figures, nor nothing can show more plainly the little progress, the Arts had made amongst them. The bodies are extremely long, and evr'y part very much out of proportion. They are much like the figures one sees in some very old Chinese paintings that are in this Cabinet. Eighthly. Four little earthenware Lamps brought from Arabia. By the figures marked on them it is plain they belonged to some Christians. On one of them is a Cross, on another a Dove, on another a Ship, on a Fourth a Fish. On asking M. Bartoli how he explained the last to be an emblem of our Saviour, he shew'd us a passage in St. Augustin where there are the following words which explained it Ιηδγς Χριδτος θηγυος, σοτερ. the first letters of which words (if I have wrote them right) being put together make Ιχθυς, or piscis, and which appears still more clearly by the following words, which I don't recollect. Ninethly; a Tripod of Brass. It is about 3 feet high, made with pieces which go across from the top of each leg to the bottom of the other by means of which they made it stand higher or lower. There are kind of hooks at the top. Tenthly. A ThunderBolt which had certainly belonged to some very large Statue from the size of; being as near as I can guess about 2 1/2 Feet long, an inch thick. There are an innumerable number of other things, perhaps more curious relating, as well to the Mythology of the Antients, as to the Custom of the Romans, Grecians, Egyptians, and other nations, and wch. is impossible to remember, or if I could to set down here.

From these we went to the Meddals, which are kept in the same Chamber, and of which he told us he had actually, near 60,000, in which there can be no doubt M^r. Bartoli must have exaggerated very much. M^r. Gibbon was much surprised at his saying it, as he had seen those of the King of France which are but 50,000 and take up a space much larger than these could supposing they were all arranged, which indeed they are not one quarter. Of Roman ones, he has all the Consular and Imperial Families in Silver, besides a great many Grecian, some Egyptian, of all which I cannot recollect many particulars, both for want of more time to observe them, as well as memory to retain the number of things we have seen there. Amongst the Faustina's I recollect seeing one or two on wch. we saw Augusta & not Diva Faustina, by wch. it is plain it was struck in her lifetime. We did not see a great many Gold ones. Those that we did were many of them valuable. We were shewn several brass Otho's, which M^r. Bartoli beleived to be the work of some modern hand. He has a great number of Brass and Copper Medals, which he had not then examined.

Out of this Chamber we were shewn three more, one of which is for natural curiosities, another has statues and marbles, and a smaller on one side is filled with Egyptian antiquities only. There is a very large Mummy, and several Busts and Statues. Before the house is a very large and handsome Court, round which is a Collonade, the Pillars, and Arches of which are light and handsome. On the walls are placed, or raither let in many antient Inscriptions, and between the Arches, are many pieces of Pillars, & Altars. M[r]. Bartoli has disposed these things as well as the rest with a great deal of taste, and Judgment.

Saturday 6th May – Turin

We went to Court this morning and were presented to the Duke[1] and Duchess of Savoy. The Duke is of a middle size, pretty well made, thin, not handsome, but has a sensible look. He is now in his 38th year. He asked us several questions, but seem'd raither timid, w[ch]. we were told he is. We were afterwards presented to the Duchess, who is far from handsome. There were no other Ladies except some of her maids of honour. We went from hence to the Chapel, where all the Court came to hear Mass. The Chapel is handsomely ornamented in respect to the Altar, and some marble pillars, tho nothing otherwise extraordinary. Here is a good band of Musick, w[ch]. plays constantly. I, as well as my countryman wth. me, knelt down at the elevation of the host, out of conformity, & decency. There were a great number of people, particularly Officers at the Dukes, and many more than we had seen at the Kings, who they say is very jealous of his son. I cannot help takeing notice of the state and good order, one sees at this Court. The Kings attendance is really grand. In three handsome Rooms one passes through to that where the company see the King, our first the Swiss, secondly a great a number of Footmen, and last the Pages who are all the Sons of the Best Families in the Country all very handsomely dressed. It is impossible to see more order and decency than is observ'd in every respect by evr'y one at Court.

In the Afternoon we went to the place where the Kings Archives are kept. It consists of five large handsome rooms on a floor, besides some smaller, and ten of those large rooms are filled wth. those writeings. It was here M[r]. Bartoli, shew'd us the Famous Tabula Isiaca, that was taken from Mantua when it was sacked and pillaged. This Egyptian table is looked upon as one of the most antient pieces existing. It is made of a kind of brass or copper. There are many Figures and Caracters, which are of Silver very nicely inlaid. The

---

1   Vittorio Amedeo (1726-96). Styled since birth as the Duke of Savoy. In 1773 he became King Vittorio Amedeo III on the death of his father.

Principal Figure in the Middle represents Isis. On one side is Apis, under the shape of an Ox. Priests &c all round. In a Room within this we were so fortunate as to see the much celebrated Manuscript of Pyrrhus Legorius, which consists of 30 volumes in Folio. Three or four and twenty of these volumes, are an Historical account as well as Geographical, of Italy and the Ancients, explained by Inscriptions, Statues, Buildings, Medals, and other monuments of antiquity all examined, copied and drawn out in the most exact and faithful manner with his own hand. Three or four more of these volumes are composed of Medals only, one volume an explanation of all the abbreviations found in the Inscriptions, and on the Medals, and another filled with drawings of Figures and buildings. Every Inscription seems to be taken with the most trif'ling exactness, and ev'ry Medal and Figure drawn equally well. One sees plainly (as much as we could judge by what we could see in the little time we had, & by what M[r]. Bartoli told us) that it is all done by one hand, and what must certainly serve to shew the fidelity of the author, is that in several places where there appears to have been a letter wanting or any small defect, he has wrote over, Sic, to shew that the fault was not in his Copiing, and in ev'ry respect it appears to have been the fruits of his own Travels and Studies, set down with all the truth possible. -- There are many pages that are vacant, and that it is plain he intended filling up, as one sees on the top of them the place of which he intended to write, and often Medals drawn on the margin. It is wrote in Italian, the greatest part on a Blue paper, the rest white; In a pretty good caracter. The Medals are very nicely drawn, as are the buildings. There are the ground plans of several houses. This inestimable work has been a great many years in the possession of the Dukes of Savoy, and I <u>was told</u> that they gave above 14,000 Sequins for it, but this is by no means certain. M[r]. Bartoli has read them, and gave us great hope that we should see one of these days a considerable part of them in print.

Sunday 7th May – Turin

The Palace found employment for us this Morning. The first Room we were shewn was a very noble guardRoom. Out of this we went into a long and handsome Gallery where there are some very large Pictures by Paul Veronese, Bassano &c. One of Queen Sheba before Solomon, by the former, appeared to me very good. This Gallery conducted us into the Queen's appartement, which consists of 4 or 5 Rooms very magnificently furnished. The furniture all very ritchly adorned with Gold or Silver. Out of this apartement we came into a Gallery which leads to the Kings Apartement. This Gallery is very handsome. In it there are a great many pictures; some very good. One of

Charles first by one Myten a scholer of Vandyks, in full length; a very good piece. His three children, by vandyk: the colours remarkably good. The head of an old man: Rembrandt. A David; full length, by Guido: a very fine piece. The Satyr Marsias Skin'd by Apollo by the same. The Satyr finely done. The Apollo not finished. The Kings apartement is very handsome, & convenient tho not so magnificent, as the Queens. Passing through it, one sees many pretty good pictures. Amongst them one cannot help remarking, the four Elements in four separate pictures, by Albani. The colouring, expression, and design of these pieces are excellent. A Sick Woman by Girard Douw. I remember sight of a form of expression and beauty of Clair-obscure, that one seldom meets with. Two small pieces, representing the heads of two Children in one, and of

Fig 6 Teatro Regio, Turin, 1752

one in the other. I think by Skedoni, admirably done. A lamp burning, & the light striking on the head of a person: admirably done by a Flemish Painter. These Chambers which are very numerous, are filled with Pictures. A great many by Teniers, Pietra di Cortona, Solemini, Vanderswerf, & Pannini. This last has drawn the views of, and from, Tivoli. A great number of Flemish paintings: by Gerard Douw, Vowermens, Van Astade, and Breughel, and many others, a great number of which may be said to have great Beauties. Their is a Closet which is entirely hung with Mineatures, by Ramelli: most of them very well done. This closet is besides much adorned with Glass & Gilding. The Cielings are chiefly painted by Daniel Sticken, Beaumont &c: not remarkably fine in my opinion. After we had seen the Palace, we went to take a view of the Great Theatre, to which the court passes by a colonnade which reaches from the Palace to the Theatre. At the upper end directly opposite the Stage is a large and handsome Box or raither canopy for the King & Royal Family. The part of the House for the Company is undoubtedly very spacious, and grand. It is supposed to have room enough for about 3000 people. But the part which struck me the most was the Stage, which is by far the most spacious ev'ry way that I ever saw. As we saw it only by day-light, it did not appear so advantageously as it does by night when it is lighted up, and filled by the Scenery, which we are told is very fine. This is reckon'd the Second if not the best Theatre in Italy.

Tuesday 8th May – Turin

In order to see the Citadel it is necessary to have an order or permission from the King, which M^r. Dutens having got for us, we went this Morning to see it. We were first conducted to see the subterraneous works. After going about 100 yards as near as I can guess, we came to a spacious opening, called the Casemate which is the place where the Soldiers lie in time of a seage. This is bomb proof. From hence we passed by a long gallery to another of these Casemates: besides these, there are Casemates for the horses. From these we were shewn three Galleries one lower than another, the lowest of which is 150 feet under Ground. These Galleries pass under all the outsides works, quite without the Citadel. It is from these that they make their Mines, when they find the Enemy makeing any works near them. It is so contrived by means of walls, that they can spring a mine to blow up one part without damaging the Gallery close adjoining. There are little Rooms which they call patty's over some part of the Galleries, from which they can let down Iron doors, and at the same time throw down fire and combustibles so as to suffocate the Enemy if they get into the Galleries . Out of the Galleries there are ways that go above a mile from the Citadel, into the great roads that lead to the City, and others that go only to the Gates. All these works appear, and we are told are as well, as strongly built as is possible. They have wells in the Casemates, and some other parts, as likewise Oven and other conveniences in case of a seage. After having pretty well examined all the under Ground works we went over the ramparts, from which Captaine Curchaud, who accompanied us explained the outworks &c. First beginning from the Citadel are, the Bastions or angles. Under these are the Case mates. The part between the Bastions is called ye Curtain. Next to these is the Great Ditch, beyond the ditch come the Demi Lune and Counter Guard. The Demi Lune serves to defend the Bastions, and the Counter Guard, the Curtain. Then comes the second Ditch, defended by the Glacis, and the outermost part of all is the Cover'd way which is a parapet of earth raised to protect the Soldiers at first. The Galleries run under and beyond all these works so that the besieged can undermine all their works and prevent their approaches (a). At the last siege of Turin the French had come as far as the great ditch. The present Governor is the Comte de Briquerarche to whom we made a visit after dinner. In the Evening we went to the Opera where there were about 50 people. From thence we went to M: St Giles, where we amused ourselves as well as people do, where they do not understand the language the company speaks, nor the game they play, and the standers by are makeing their court to some Lady, or have not politeness enough to speak to strangers. M: de St Giles (tho very polite) was engaged at a party of Tarrow. M: de Prier wth. her Gallant, & some officers talking together.

(a) About 5000 would be sufficient to defend this Citadel. The Famous well M^{r}. Keysler speaks of is now much ruined. We were shewn the place where Micha the pioneer sacrificed himself to save the place.

Wednesday 9th May – Turin

We went this Morning to the Museum. We found Monsr. Bartoli there, who took us immediately into the Room, where the Egyptian antiquities are kept, and there shew'd us the Bust which has caused so much dispute between him & M^{r}. Needham.[1] By the form of the Bust, the dress of the head and general appearance of it, it seems to me more like a Roman or Grecian Statue than an Egyptian one, as it differs too very much from any Egyptian one I have ever seen, and from any that are there. There is a bust placed by it which they do not pretend to be Egyptian but is of the same marble and differs in nothing except the Caracters, of which there are none on the latter.

1   John Turberville Needham, 1713-81, who adduced the bust as that of Isis with the symbols being hieroglyphs. Comprehensively disproved by Bartoli and others, including Winckelmann.

We compared it with the draft M[r]. Needham has had taken of it, and which we found not be taken by any means exact. This Bust is supposed by M[r]. Needham to be that of Isis: the caracters cut in it he beleives Chinese.[1] M[r]. Bartoli beleives it to be a modern work. After Dinner we accompanied M[r]. Wolfe &c to see the Manufactures for tobacco, cards, paper and working of the lead in thin sheets for putting the Snuff in. These all belonged to the King. The buildings for it are very extensive, and handsome. They have been began but about six years since. The Tobacco is first sowed in Boxes like our hot beds, and covered over on nights till they become strong when they are transplanted on the field adjoining. The whole of these Fabricks seem well contrived and very substantially finished. I could not inform myself of many particulars I wanted to know, as the person with us (M[r]. Mattey[2]) did not know much of the matter.

Thursday 10th May – Turin

We were presented to day to the Princesses of Savoy and the Duke of Chablais.[3] The Eldest princesse is about 36 years, the other two are each a year younger. They received us not only with all the polit'ness but ease and affability possible: We stayed with them near a quarter of an hour during which time they talked to us with the greatest freedom. They seem'd glad of an opportunity to speak to us: and one may beleive it without vanity, as they can seldom converse with any, except some few of the Court, and never stir out but to the Opera wth. the King in the winter, and to ye Promenade in the Summer. The Duke of Chablais is about 29. He is of a pretty Figure, and genteel address. He received us very politely, & asked many questions. (a).

L[d]. Berkeley, M[r]. Ponsonby, Wolfe &c dined wth. us to day. L[d]. Berkeley talked much about M[r]. Berkeley[4], and of his having promised him to give up the L[d]. lieutenancy to him as soon as he should be of age.[5]

(a) He is the Kings favorite and to whom he gives all he can, & even more than to the Duke of Savoy, who has hardly what is necessary

Friday 11th May – Turin

We spent this Morning wth. M[r]. Bartoli, who read us part of a Dissertation he has composed, setting forth his having been ill used, by M[r]. Needham,

---

1   In fact, hieroglyphs but, Needham thought, very similar to Chinese characters and thus shared a common provenance.

2   Mr Matti/Mattè/Mattei was the son of the Engineer (Macchinista) to the King of Sardinia.

3   Benedetto Maria Maurizio, 1741 – 1808, the youngest child of Charles Emmanuel III.

4   Norton Berkeley, 1717-70. He claimed the abeyant title of Baron Botetourt in 1764, probably at some time after this conversation.

5   He became Lord Lieutenant of Gloucestershire in 1766, aged 21.

justifying his opinion in respect to the Bust of Isis, and proving it to be in all probability a piece made in Italy, as they find Marble exactly the same as that of the Bust; and as the Caracters upon are different from those which M[r]. Needham compared them to, and as those which he had found like them in the Chinese Dictionary at Rome had been alter'd by the Chinese Interpreter, who explained them to him. By what I can find, M[r]. Bartoli is much more knowing in antiquity, and more able to judge of these things than M[r]. Needham.

In the Afternoon we went to see the Arsenal, having had an order for it by the means of M[r]. Dutems. We were shewn it by the Count of --- . We were first shewn the small arms, of which he told us there are about 100,000 new, not counting any old ones, or those in constant use. They appeard to be strong, and well made, but raither heavy. The expence for each Musket about 12 livres Piedmontese. We could not learn the number of Cannon, but we saw a great number, and they make new ones constantly. The largest for 32p: the others 16. 8. and 4 pounders. There is a remarkably well invented machine for boreing them drove by water, wth. which they bore a piece of 32 in a little more than two days; a smaller one in 24 Hrs. and in 12. I am not good enough Mechanick to give a proper or good description of this Machine, of which I took much notice. Near it is a lever, which is fixed to the top of a kind of pillar, which by means of screw rises, and falls and by w[ch]. they move the Cannon wth. great ease from the Machine by w[ch]. it is bored, off & on. Being laid in a horizontal direction, the Canon is turned round, by the force of the water driving the Machine on w[ch]. it lays, at the same time the piece of Iron (w[ch]. is flat & pointed) by which it is bored is continually forced forward against it, by means of an Iron Screw which one sees below the Bar, that enters the Canon. We were shewn near the place where they cast the Canon and manner of doing it. They begin by forming the Mould round a piece of wood iron the size of the intended Canon. The first coat is what they called (sweet or suit), and round this is formed the real Mould of clay about 3 or 4 Inches thick as I guessed it, when this last is well formed, the inside coat of Tallow is melted away, and the piece of wood taken out. The mould is then left 'till it is pretty dry & hard and then bound round wth. Iron hoops. After being properly hardened it is removed to another place where there is a large pit into which, by means of pullys fasten'd over, it is let down, and held perpendicularly. The Pit holds about 4 of them. The spaces between them are filled up wth. sand, so as to confine and prevent the mould from moveing. Being thus placed the Metal is run into them, and the canon when formed is drawn out by the same pulley that they used to let down the mould. This, 'tho no great matter, being all I could learn about it. I think worth remembering, least I should have no opportunity of learning any more. But nothing deserves more to be taken notice of & remember, than the building intended for the Arms, Artillery &c, &c. It has been already began about five years, and is not very much advanced, owing to the Kings prudence, & economy, who for this, as well as his other works, lays by, a certain sum of Money ev'ry year, which he never exceeds. The Sum commonly employ'ed for this use is about 4 Thousand pounds a year. The building when finished (a) will form a very handsome Square*.

(a) An officer told us it would be hardly finished under 20 year more.
(*) A kind of open Gallery is to run round the inside of the Square, equal wth.
the first floor, for putting the arms out, when needful.

The different sides of this Square will be employed for containing the Arms, for founding & planeing the canon, for lodging for the Governor and officers &c&c. One side, which is intended for the small arms is near finished. It will make one long & large Gallery, capable of holding 100,000 small arms, which will be placed in piramids separate from each other. Each piramid containing arms, and ev'ry other thing necessary to fit out, and equip a single Battalion, for the Field, so that a person walking through this Room and counting the Piramids, can immediately tell how many Battalions the King can compleatly arm. He is likelier to want men than arms. Behind one side of the arsenal they intend making barracks for the soldiers. This Arsenal will certainly be a very handsome building but the thing concerning it perhaps the most worthy of notice is, the hands by whom ev'ry individual part of this work is done, and to be done. There is alwais a Battalion of the Artillery lodged there, by whom ev'ry single thing is done. It was one of that Regiment that invented & made the Model for it, and no one man that Is not of the Regiment is ever suffer'd to do the least thing about the Building. This certainly does honor to the King, who at the same time he keeps his men employ'd, is saving so much Money. But in this as well as ev'ry other part of his Government, ev'ry thing is done with equal order, economy and Judgment. Ev'ry thing here seems well contrived, and indeed equally well executed.

There is a person there who has began to make some China of which he shew'd us some Cups & little pieces: not very fine. We were afterwards conducted into a Room, where we were shewn some fossils, minerals & amongst the latter several pieces of Marble & stone containing a considerable amount of Gold. These have been found in the valley d'Aouste, where there are Mines, from which the King draws annually about 200 Marks, or 80 pound weight. They find also considerable quantities of Silver, Copper &c. We were shewn here also several pieces of Christal, of which there are considerable quantities in the Alps. From hence we went to make our Visits of Adieu: Mess.^r: my lord Berkeley, Ponsonby (a), Atkins, Wolfe & Moula supped wth. us this Evening and thus we spent our last day and Evening at Turin.

(a) A sensible, pretty young man. He received an account to day that he would certainly be chose member for Cork.[1]

The City of Turin is much the most regular, and indeed takeing it altogether the handsomest I have yet seen. The Streets are all built in straight lines; each Street that crosses another, makeing a right angle. The houses in each street, being all of an equal height, and built in ev'ry respect the same, have a good effect. There are several Squares: that called La Place du Chateau, & La Place de S^t. Carlo are very handsome. Round the latter are arched piazzas of a fine height, and breadth, and which continue the same all down each side the Rue de Po.

The outside of the Palace is not very remarkable. There is a large Court before it. From the door of the palace one sees in direct line, over the palace Court, la place du Chateau, down la rue neuve, over la place de S^t. Charles, to La porte neuve. The front of the palace of the Prince de Caringnan is very handsome. There are many very handsome streets, but the most remarkable are La Rue de Po, & la rue neuve. There four Gates, La Porte de la Venerie, wch. is also called porte de la victoire & de la Tour, Porte des Suisses, porte Neuve, and Porte du Po. By means of an engine on one side of the Town they can let water into all the Streets very easily. The Streets are well paved wth. small stones and kept very clean. They count between 70 & 80 thousand Inhabitants at Turin.

But nothing requires the Attention of Traveller so much as the order, and economy with which everything relating to the Government and Court of Turin, is conducted. In the first place the King does a great deal of business himself, and looks into that of evr'y person with the greatest Strictness, so that he is never cheated by Ministers, Treasurers, paymasters, & other Officers. He spends every year a certain Sum, towards strengthening some of the places, and passes in or near the Mountains of which there are La Brunette, Fenestrelle, Demon, Exile and some other I don't recollect at present; or else in carrying

---

1   William Brabazon Ponsonby was elected the member for Cork in 1764 and became a prominent member of the Irish, and then the British, House of Commons.

on some Manufacture, Publick building, or in the encouragement of arts, and different parts of learning. It is easy to Imagine how much Æconomy must be necessary for to do all these things, when one considers that his whole revenues don't amount to above 20 Million of livres or, about 1 Million of pounds Sterling, and indeed it is amazing how he can support himself, much more make the figure he does, when one knows how little other Courts can do with that Money. The King, tho' perhaps a Bigot as they say he is, must undoubtedly be allowed to be very Clever, and of an uncommon understanding. Being old he can not have so much attention to the Army as may be necessary, for wch. reason his Troops are certainly far from being very good, and he is very saving in respect to all kind of advantages that may be made by Officers, he is not much loved by them. Indeed they complain most heavily of the Service, which most certainly in respect to pay, and advancement is very bad.

The Duke of Savoy is most generally loved. Ev'ry one allows him to be very sensible, and Clever. The Officers love him very much, and say that he understands military affaires very well.

I shall say one word of the Inhabitants of this place. Ev'ry one almost that is not of the bourgeoisie, is Noble. One cannot walk the streets without running against a Marquis, a Count or some one that calls himself a Nobleman. This Set of people are perhaps in General the proudest, and meanest that exist. If a person has not a Title, 'tho he be ever so ritch, or of ever so good and antient a Family, they will hardly spake to him. When a Foreigner comes into the Town, the first thing they ask, is if he is a Nobleman, if not, he has but a poor chance of receiving much civility from them. This has been often proved by the little attention they have paid to some of our Ministers, who have been only commoners. M^r. Pitt even, they say has experienced this, very much. There chief concern is makeing as much outward shew as possible, while in their houses and private life they live in the meanest manner. If one may judge of the Society and of their assemblies by one I was in at Mad: de S^t. Gilles, they are very disagreeable, as the Men I saw there had not the politeness to speak to us, but talked constantly Piemontese; and the Women were either engaged at Tarow or with their Chichisteaus [cicisbei]. This is a general complaint of all Foreigners. The Nobility never admit any of the Bourgeoisie or people that happen to be engaged in any business, 'tho of better Families than themselves, into their Assemblies of any kind.

Account of the King of Sardinia's Forces given me by Captain Curchod of the Regiment of Montfort

	Battalions	Compans :	Men & Off:
Les Gardes	2	10	1108
Monserrat	2	10	1108
Savoye	2	10	1108
Piemont	2	10	1108
Fusiliers	2	10	1108
Saluces	2	10	1108
La Marine	1	10	554
La Reine	1	10	554
Sardaigne	1	10	554
	(15)	(150)	(8310)

Each battalion is composed of nine Company's, of 56 men each, of what they call, Factionnaires, or Battalion men, and the Company of Grenadiers of 50 men. Each Company has 3 Officers; 2 Serjeants, 4 Corporals, 1 drum, & 1 Fife. Each Regiment is worth to its Colonel about 5000 Liv:Pr:.Ann; a Captain receives 1500L: a Lieutenant 650, and a soldiers pay is 3 Sols and his bread pr: Diem.

Foreign Troops in his pay

	Batt:	Comp:	Men: & Off
Eastern, German	2	6	1008
Breme, Dit Swisses	2	6	1008
Souter "	3	4	1500
Taharnan "	3	4	1500
Fatio "	1 ½	4	750
Sprech "	1 ½	4	750
Meyer "	1	4	500
Montfort	2	9	1008
	16	(41)	(8024)

The German Regim^t: have 84 men pr: Company. The Swisses have 125: pr Co, 4 Officers: 4 Serg^{ts}; and 8 Corporals. The Colonel of a German Regiment has 18000 Liv. pr ann: & a Captain 2000. The Colonel of a Swiss Regim^t; has from 12 to 15000L: pr ann: Cap^{ne} about 5, or 6000. The Colonel of the Reg^t: of Montfort, has about 10,000L: pr Ann:, Cap: 1500, pay of the German soldiers for 5 days 20 Sols & Bd: Swisse: 22 ½ & Bd: Montfort 19 & Bd. This last Regiment consists of men of all nations, and was given originally by Q: Ann:

Dragons:	Squadrons	Compan :	M: & Off:
Dragons du Roy	5	2	450
" de son Altesse	5	2	450
" de la Reine	5	2	450
	(15)	(30)	1350
Cavalry			
Piemont Royal	5	2	450
" de Savoy	5	2	450
	(10)	(20)	(900)
Artillery	Batl.ˢ	Compan :	M: & Off:
	2	16	1440

Gardes du Corps & Company's: Piemontese, Swisses, & Sicilien

Total of the Infantry   16334

Dit.   of the Cavalry   2250

Dit.   of Artillery   1440

                                   20,024

Besides these the King of Sardinia has ten Battalions of Sixty men each, whom they call Provincials. They are a kind of militia: are exercised at two seasons of the year, ten days: Receives 1 Sol per day throughout the year, & are clothed once in three years: In cases of necessity he arms the Peasants, and by that means can easily have an army of 60,000 Men; as was the case in the War of the Year 1740 &c.

Saturday 12ᵗʰ May – Road to Milan fᵐ. Turin

We set out this Morning about eight o' clock for Milan, and went to day no farther than Novarra [Novara] which is five postes from Turin. There is nothing very remarkable on this part of the road: one passes through Civassio [Chivasso], Vercelli, and some other little places: the former of these is the largest of any hitherto. There are a great many little Rivers which one either fords, or passes over by a bridge made of two boats joined together. Where the River is wider there is only one, in which you are ferried over. The Country is very flat, particularly near Novarra, within a few leagues of which the grounds were at this time cut very much in small ditches, and almost cover'd over wᵗʰ. water. About half way from Turin there are some very large open plains cover'd with a kind of heath, and resemble much to our commons in England. The Country seems very fertile, & pleasant, cover'd wᵗʰ. Rye and different kinds of Corn, all very forward. The Doria & Sturia [Stura di Lanzo] are the most considerable of the Rivers one crosses. Novarra is the first of Town one comes to on the Milanese: it belongs to the King of Sardignia: is fortified, and at this time is Garrison'd by one of his Majesties foreign regiments: comeing in late and setting out early next Morning we did not see much of the town neither did we hear of much to be seen.

Sunday 13th May – Novara to Milan

Leaving Novara early this Morning we continued our Road for Milan, where we arrived about 12 o'clock. About a league out of Novara, we crossed the Ticino or Tezin (a pretty considerable River) in a Ferry boat, and about a League farther we came to Bufolery [Boffalora Sopra Ticino] the first Town in the Milanese belonging to the Queen of Hungary. From hence to Milan is raither more than two posts. The Country from Novara to Milan is very flat, but otherwise very pleasing, cultivated and fruitful (a). Being arrived at Milan we went to the Three Kings, which is a pretty good Inn, but dearer than that at Turin. I went in the Evening to the Theatre to see an Italian Comedy, or raither to see the Theatre as the Italian Comedies are very bad in General, & as this proved to be. The Theatre is in ev'ry respect handsome, and larger than that at Turin. They say it will hold near 4000 people. The Boxes are very neat and prettily ornamented within & without. Each box is lighted up in the Inside wth. a candle or two according to the Size of the Box. There is a very large box directly opposite to the Theatre (or stage) for the Duke of Modena and Family.

(a). The road from Turin here is very good but the posts are very dear. We paid for the 9 Posts 27 Sequins

Monday 14th May – Milan

We went this Morning to see the Cathedral, which is dedicated to the Virgin Mary. Was I to give a particular account of this stupendous building it would take both more time and place than I can spare, for which reason I shall only endeavour to preserve as good an Idea of it as I can. It was founded in the year 1386 by J[r] Galeazzo Viscomti, first Duke of Milan. He gave a very large mine of Marble, as well as Estate, towards building it, and to forward this amazing work as much as possible he procured indulgences from the Pope for all those who should assist at so Pious an Undertaking. This being once granted, there was no great doubt but there would be enough ready to shew <u>their Zeal,</u> & accordingly all ranks and conditions of people, Men & Women offer'd their Services towards forwarding this Edifice. By this means, it advanced very fast. Yet, although great numbers of workmen have been constantly employed in working about it ever since, it is not near finished, nor likely to be, which is not so difficult to account for, when one knows that the Canons will lose when it is finished, a very considerable estate that was long ago left towards finishing of it. This Church is perhaps one of the most amazing pieces of Gothick Architecture that exists. The Architect seems to have exhausted all his skill in loading ev'ry part of it, with Statues, Busts, Bas-relievos, and other pieces of sculpture. He has tried to frighten the Spectator as much as possible by introducing numbers of large statues which have no visible support.

The Church is ill placed, being closely surrounded on all sides by other buildings. The front, in which is the large door of Entrance, is not near finished: being compleat no higher than even wth. the top of the door. That part is highly ornamented with statues, and other things in Carving. As soon as you come in, you see on each side the Door two very large Pillars of Fine Grey Marble. The body of the Church is divided into three Isles, by two Rows of Marble Pillars which support the vault of the Church. These Pillars are fifty two in number, each of them about 10 feet in Diameter. Between these Columns are hung up some very large, & raither indifferent Pictures Representing the life and action of S^t. Charles Borromeo. A little before one comes to the Choir the body of the Church opens, into two Chapels, one of each side, which are but small, and hardly give it the Figure of a Cross as some say. In each of these Chapels are placed two Colossal Statues of four saints, besides many smaller, and a great deal of Bas-Relieves. Just in the Middle between these two chappels is an opening to let the light into the Chapel in which is preserved the body of S^t. Borromeo. This opening is surrounded wth. an Iron rail, & just over it is the Cupola. The Church is paved with brick, which appears very poor and ridiculous, where every thing else is of Marble. They have indeed began to pave a part of it wth. Marble of different Colors, wch. when finished may be handsome. From this part we went round the Choir, behind which their are two windows of Painted Glass pretty good. There is likewise a much esteemed Statue of S^t. Bartholomy flae'd alive. He is represented holding his skin in his left hand, torn off of his Face, Body & Arms: down to the muscles. The Muscles, Veins and indeed the whole of the body seems perfectly well expressed, but does not see so much expression of pain & torment in the face, as one might expect to do in a person in his Situation.

The most remarkable thing in the Choir are the Prebendaries Stalls which deserve much notice. They are made of walnut tree very finely carved in a basso-relievo, representing the remarkable actions of S^t. Theodoricus, & S^t. Ambrose. Nothing can be more nicely finished than this piece of Sculpture. From hence we went to ascend the Dome to the Cupola, which at present is

132 Brachio high, and when finished will be about 200 in all. The Stairs by which one goes up are of a commodious size, and entirely made of Marble. They are divided into 5 or 6 Flights from each of which one comes out upon a Gallery which commonly goes round the Dome. Round one of these Galleries which may be near half way up, are placed at proper distances 100 Piramidical Columns, which from the quantity of work bestowed on them and the Singularity of their construction are really astonishing. They are twenty Brachio in heigth, and are formed from the bottom to the Top of an immense number of small Pillars, between which are placed statues of a very considerable size, and at the Top of each Column is a very large Statue. Ev'ry part of these Columns are ornamented with carving as much as possible. The windows, and sides of the Dome are cover'd with Colossal Statues of Marble, which you would imagine would fall upon you, being hung against the wall, and not put in nitches. Indeed one sees them better, but then you cannot look at them without thinking yourself in danger. There is no part of the outside hardly that is not adorned with some Bas-relief or other piece of Sculpture in Marble. One of the last flights of Steps is formed in the Inside of a large pillar. On one of the lower Galleries is a Statue as big as life in Marble, of Visconti. Having left the Dome we were shewn into a Chapel which is under the Choir, and where service is performed in winter, from hence we went into the Chapel in wch. rests the body of S^t. Borromeo. The inside of this Chapel is chiefly cover'd with Silver. Some pannels and small spaces are of a Gold Stuff. Round the upper part are eight pieces of Basso-Relievo in Silver representing all the Actions of S^t. Borromeo. Between these are placed as many emblematical figures in Silver of the Virtues &c relating to the good qualities of the S^t. These are likewise in Silver: and altogether wth. the other eight pieces weigh about 6760 ounces. On one Side is placed the Body of the Saint, which is in a Shrine of Christal, set in Silver: that is formed of pieces very fine Christal, about 6, 8 & 10 Inches each piece, which are framed & join'd together with Silver: and altogether make a most beautiful Shrine. The Silver of this is said to weigh about 4000 Ounces, for which reason I imagine the bottom is of massy Silver, 'tho I cannot say I examined it. This was given the Church by Philip the fourth of Spain. Through this one sees the body wch. is cover'd wth. a very ritch Episcopal Robe, of Gold. The face is uncover'd. The Robe is fasten'd upon the Breast by a very large Ruby: on one Finger is a Ring of Oriental Topaz of a very great Size. In his left hand is a Pastoral Crook of Silver, in the head of which are some very fine diamonds: on one side of him lies a Crosiar of Gold, the head of which is almost entirely of Rubies & Diamonds. Over his head hangs a Crown of Gold enritched wth. rubies & diamonds, given by an Arch-duchess of Bavaria.

Upon his breast hangs a Jesus of Gold, on which are many Diamonds over the Jesus is a Crown formed almost of Diamonds. The quantity of Ritches and Precious Stones one sees about the body, is immense, and are chiefly the gifts of people, who hope to save their Souls perhaps by the Intercessions of this saint. This Shrine is cover'd over by a wooden Coffin much ornamented. Having prettily pretty well examined this Chapel, we were still more astonished by the vast treasure we found in the Sacristy. It is impossible to enumerate the great number of Statues, Vases, Cups, Crusifixes, and other things that one finds here made of entire Gold & Silver, besides many of them being inlaid with the finest and rarest Stones. There is a Statue of S^t. Borromeo as big as life of Massy Silver; on his breast hangs a Diamond Crusifix: opposite to him is another Statue (a), the same size in Silver also: near it a Silver one of the present King of Sardignia, given by his Father on the recovery of his Son from an illness: a ring of S^t. Borromeo's containing an oriental Topaz, near an Inch Square. Several small bones, entirely cover'd wth. different sorts of Jewels, in one of which is a Sapphire of an immense size. It is almost impossible to give a good Idea of either the number or value of other things that are kept, here. Here is also a Carton of Raphael; the adoration of the Magi. Amongst all these things, what well deserves notice also, is the work of a Lady called Lidovina Peregrina, who lived near two hundred years ago. She has worked some Altar Cloths in Silk, the figures on which are many of them so well done that one might easily mistake them for painting. Indeed the faces of some of them are painted & do not look so natural as this work. After seeing most in the Inside we walked round the outside, and could not help remarking the ill effect of this manner of building. After evr'y thing that the art of the builder, & Sculptor can afford, is bestowed upon it, the whole has but an odd unfinished look, owing to the Confusion the Multiplicity of ornaments causes, and the unnatural manner of makeing use of them.

After dinner we went to the Citadel, near which we were so fortunate to see the Austrian regiment of Baden Baden, exercising in three different companies. It is a very large Regiment: of 3 Battalions; & about 2200 Men. 'Tho I understand little of Military affairs, I could not help being struck by the visible superiority of these troops to any I have ever seen: their steadiness, quickness, and exactness in all their motions, surpris'd not only me, but my Friend Gibbon, who has been much accustom'd to see different troupes.[1]

(a) of S^t. Ambrose

1 Gibbon served in the South Hampshire militia from 1759 to 1762.

Tuesday 15ᵗʰ May – Milan

We went this Morning to see the Ambrosian Library, which is open and free for anyone, two hours in the Morning; and as many in the Afternoon. Those who chose to go and Study there are furnished wᵗʰ. pen, Ink and paper &c: gratis. 'Tho the Servant that shewd us this library assured us there are near 60,000 printed, and 15,000 volumes in Manuscript, we could not believe by any guess we could give by seeing them, that there are more than about half the number he told us, of either; if there can be so many. Amongst the Manuscripts we saw <u>Rufinus's Josephus</u> written on the bark of a Tree, said by some to be 13 by others 1100 years old. Many of the leafs are much decayed: a Pentateuch written on vellum about 500 years old. There are many others very curious, but not understanding much Italian, and having a Servant wᵗʰ. us, who did not understand much French & otherwise raither ignorant, we did not see so many as we might otherwise.

Near this is an Academy for painting, where students are permitted to come and copy from the paintings &c that are there. In a Room near this are kept the Models & Copies of some of the best Busts & Statues in Italy. Two or three large Cartons by Raphael, much valued. There is likewise the skeleton of a beautiful woman; who directed that her bones should be kept there, to put the living in mind of takeing Care of the Sick, wᶜʰ. which they may be the better able to do from seeing how they themselves are formed. In a Room within this is kept the Collection of Natural Curiosities made by Satella, of which I shall not speak as I had not sufficient time to examine it. In this Room are many good paintings. The four Elements by Breughel a Flemish painter, very well done: the Earth, & Water pleased me Particularly: Besides these four, there are many other pieces of Flours, landskips &c all very good, by the same hand. Many pretty good pictures by Leonardo Vinci, Guido Rheni, and other painters (a). But what is most valued amongst the curiosities preserved in this Room are the Manuscripts of Leonardus Vincius, given to the Library by Galeazzo Areonati, and for which it is said James the first offer'd immense sums. We were shewn on very thick Folio Volume consisting of Mathematical Designs of all sorts; Sketches of Buildings, Figures of people, and great variety on all subjects: Amongst them are many drafts of Bombs in different positions, for throwing different heigths & distances, besides these, designs of Canons of all sorts. The account, & notes upon all these things are wrote from right to left, which cannot be read without the help of a Glass. I took more particular notice of these drawings of Bombs as Mʳ. Gibbon observed, it was the opinion of many people that they were not invented so early as the lifetime of Leonard. Vinci which was about the year 1500: He died in the year 1520 according to Keysler, who is commonly exact.

(a) There is a very pleasing and good head of a woman by Gayetano

We went from hence to see the Church of S[t]. Alexandre, which is more remarkable for the Marble and ornaments which are fine, than for any thing in particular: There are many Pictures in it of a middling rank. Besides this we saw to day the Churches of S[ta]. Maria della Victoria, S[ta] Maria Pres San Celso, & S[t]. Lorenzo. The first of these is a very neat small church; The Pillars & Pillastres are painted to represent white Marble. Here are some good Paintings. In particular an Assumtion, the Apostles looking in the Tomb, by Salvator Rosa: there are two more one on each side the great Altar piece: one S[t]. John in the Desert, by Francesco Mola: The landskip part by Gasparo Rossino: opposite to this a S[t]. Paul, they thought by Salvator Rosa. There is a convent for women joining to this, the door of which being open I happen'd to step about a yard within, before one of the women saw me but who immediately called to me to retire. S[ta]. Maria Sans Celso. The front of this Church is very fine, entirely of Marble. It is very much ornamented with Statues, Bas reliefs & other pieces of Sculpture. The Pillars, of which there are two Rows one over the other, are of the Corinthian order, over the door on each side, are two Sibbils lying down, well done by Fonzana. At the extremity of the Front on each side are two Fine Statues of Adam and Eve, by Artildo di Lorenzi a Florentin. The Eve is remarkably well done, and a very pleasing Figure. We took notice of a particular manner in which the Serpent is represented, having the Head of a Man, and only the lower parts of a Serpent. He is holding a Branch with an apple upon it in his hand, which Eve is gathering. The Adam is a good figure, but not so well done. The Architecture of the Inside of the Church is very pleasing. There are several Statues likewise, amongst which one of the Virgin in white Marble, is reckon'd a very good one. S[t]. Lorenzo: This church is remarkable for the manner in which it is formed, makeing an Octagon: Four of the Sides are circular: Between them are very large Colums, which support the Dome: The other sides of the Octagon, are made into Galleries. There is nothing extraordinary either, in respect to Painting or Sculpture. Near this Church is a piece of Roman Antiquity: It is a Colonade of Sixteen Pillars; They are fluted all the way up: Their Capitals of the Corinthian order. The Pillars are pretty large, the space between them, rather narrow, except in the Midle, where the space is about double the others, and appears to have been the

Entrance to the building of which these pillars formed the Front. Part of the Cornish likewise remains and appears to have been very plain. We guessed the Pillars might be about 30 feet high.

We took a view also to day of the great hospital, which is a very large, handsome building: It is formed round a Court, round which is a Colonade, the Pillars of which are all double, and the Arches very light & pleasing. The windows and upper part of this building are much ornamented, and the whole has a very pleasing effect. There is besides at Milan a foundling hospital, and another called the Lazaretto, or what we call a Peste House.

Wednesday 16th May – Milan to Borromean Islands

We set out at four o'clock this Morning to see the Borromean Islands, situated in the Lago Maggiore (a). We went in our Chaise to Cesti [Sesto Calende], a small Town about 30 Miles from Milan, and upon the River Ticino or Tizin which runs out of the Lake. We hired a boat at this place to carry us to the Islands, which are about fifteen miles up the Lake.

(a) These Islands are three in number. One of them called Isola Bella, belonging to a Count Borromeo, of the same Family as the S[t]. of that name. Another called, Isola Madre, belongs to his uncle. The third is called l'Ille des pecheurs.

We likewise provided ourselves here with some eateables, as they told us the Inns on the Islands, were very bad. Our boat was row'd by five men, one of which managed two oars. One goes two or three mile in the River Tezin, before one enters the lake, which does not become wide for some time. The weather unfortunately being very bad, obliged us to have a Cover to our boat, which prevented our enjoying the beautiful prospect which we expected to have of the sides of this Lake. The wind too blowing hard against us, made us between 4 & 5 hours in going there, so that we did not get to the Isola Bella till past 6 in the Evening. We landed on a flight of steps which come down to the water, the same side, as the small houses for the Fishermen are of. This is not the place where the Count & Family land. There are a pair of stairs for them, on the other side the Island. Those where we landed, bring one into a Court before the Offices: on one side are the Stairs, which bring you into the Palace. A very large, and wide Staircase of Stone, leads you to the Apartments on the first Floor. The first Room one comes into is a very large Square kind of hall. From this you pass to a suit of Rooms some of which are very large. Several of them are bed Chambers. There are two Rooms larger & handsomer than the rest, one of them is a long Gallery, in one side of which, there are doors for going out upon a wide Terrass. At one End of this Room is the Door by which they go into The Gardens. This is called the Dancing Room. The other is likewise a long Room, at one end of which is a bed in an Alcove: at the other, two windows. The floors throughout the Palace are of Brick, and the walls of common Plaster whitewashed. These have certainly a very poor look, especially when one sees at the same time a great deal of Gilding and finery about the rest of the Furniture. That is not however much the case here, as the Furniture is all very old, and does not appear to have been ever very ritch. The white walls indeed do not much appear, as they are chiefly cover'd with pictures. Many of these Pictures I beleive are well done, but without being at other end of the Palace. In the Middle (I beleive between the old & new apartments) they are likewise building a large theatre, and a Room joining to it.

We went from hence down to the Ground Floor, where there is a suit of 5 or 6 Rooms, which pleased me more than all the others. They are in the manner of a Grotto: only instead of shells, the Walls, Floors, Pillars &c are made of Stones of Different Colours, which are so well disposed as to have a very pleasing effect, and look much like mosaik work. From some of these Rooms, one has a most delightful view of the lake & adjacent Mountains. A large Room contiguous to it, is designed for water works. The weather was not quite proper at this time for these kind of habitations, nevertheless it was easy to conceive how pleasing it must be in the heat of Summer.

After having seen the palace, we attempted to take a walk in the gardens: but the rain was so very heavy, that it obliged us to run to shelter after having taken one turn, without getting a better idea of the place, than if we had not went into it. We got into a very vile hut, which they told us was the best Inn on either of the Islands, so that we were very glad to accept the offer the man that shew'd us the House, made us of a Bed in the Palace. We accordingly went there, and were shew'd in to a very good Room, where a fire was prepared for us. The Man who had the care of the Palace, appearing a sensible man, we asked him several questions about y^e. Counts Family. He told us that he married a Daughter of the Duke of Bracciano: one of the best families at Rome. He has seven Children, 6 daughters & 1 Son. He commonly spends about 6 weeks, in the Months of June & July, at the Isola bella. The rest of the year he is either at Milan or at a large house he has not far from it. He has two Brothers, & an Uncle. The Count was at this time at Milan. Our landlord was very civil to us, & provided us with two very good beds.

Thursday 17th May – Borromean Islands
The Weather this Morning was not so clear as we could have wished, but

however did not prevent our seeing the Island very well, 'tho the prospect of the neighbouring Mountains was not so perfect. This Island, by what we could inform ourselves, or by what we could guess of its size is near half a mile in circumference. It is much longer than wide, and in form may be said not be unlike a pyramid except that the Middle is something wider than the extremities of its ends. The north end which is the widest is entirely occupied by the palace: A narrow space on one Side is filled with a number of small poor houses: the opposite side is chiefly employed in different walks & a Grove, and the South end is formed into Terraces, of which there are ten, rising one above another. The Middle consists chiefly of a pretty large parterre. From the palace, are a flight of steps which lead to this parterre, on which are planted many Lemon and orange Trees, and many other things, which are not disposed wth. much taste. There is formed against the Terraces a very handsome piece of Rockwork. On the Top is a very large Figure of a Unicorn, and on the outsides are Statues & obelisques by turns, which have a very good Effect. On each side of this Rock Work are a flight of steps, by wch. one goes on the Terraces, each of them make a most delightful walk. They are raised about 9 or 10 feet above each other, and become less & less to the Top, where is a space of about 40 or 50 yards, surrounded wth. a Balustrade. It is paved wth. Stone, and round it are placed several large Statues. Under this pavement is a reservoir which catches the rain, & furnishes water for the Rock Work, I mentioned before. The Walls of the Terraces are cover'd cheifly with Lemon Trees, wch. at this time carried the largest fruit I ever saw. On the Corners are placed Statues and Obelisks alternatively. The disposition of these Figures, one above another, the walls being cover'd with so fine Trees, and the Singularity of it altogether, with the prospect from the Terraces, has the most pleasing effect imaginable.

The keeping these terraces in order, and the wooden Cases with which all the Lemon Trees are cover'd in the winter, costs an amazing sum of money. But this must be trifling in Comparison of the Expense of makeing this part of the Garden. It was originally nothing but a bare rock, so that they were obliged to bring all the Earth, and ev'ry thing else necessary to form such an enchanted place. From this part we went to the side of the Island, where are the Groves. We came first into an orange Grove, the trees of which are extreamly large and beautiful. Beyond this is a kind of Terrass towards the water; the other side of which is a kind of Arcade under which is designed to be made a Grotto, beyond this you come into a larger Grove of Laurel and different sorts of Trees. In one end of this Grove is a water work, which makes a small cascade, & besides throws the water through the Trees in a walk that is cut amongst them, and likewise forces it up through some holes in the Ground, which form a number of little fountains that cross one another, in falling: In the other end of the Grove is cut a Wide Walk, one side of which forms a kind of Amphitheatre, and which <u>the Gardener told us was for acting Pastoral Opera's</u>. You go up some steps out of this, which bring you upon the large parterre or Area, that makes the very Middle of the Island. One is surprised to see the very bad & small houses that take up the greatest part of the other side of the Island, in a place where so much pains & Art has been used to beautify the greatest part: especially when a trifling expence might make them raither an advantage, than a dissight, wch. they are at present. The sides of the Island are mostly wall'd down to the water edge, and indeed a considerable part is vaulted under. In some of these I beleive are kept the Gondelo's, of which the Count has commonly 3 or four. The Mountains of different heights, the tops cover'd with fine woods, and the sides with vineards, and small houses interspersed, and the sides of the Lake, on which you see Polonza, Intra, Isella and several other small Towns, afford a most beautiful prospect from the Island: Isola Madre & L'Isle des Pecheurs which are not far distant, help to improve it. These together with its own beauties, make the Isola bella a most delightful spot; nevertheless, 'tho it pleased me extreamly I cannot say it answer'd entirely to the expectations I had of it, from the account I had heard & read about it.

After having taken as good an Idea as we could of this Island, we went to Isola Madre, which is about a Mile distant from it. This Island appears to be nearly circular. The sides down to the water edge are mostly rough rocks except one side which is walled up, and where there are stairs for landing. On one side of the Island there are six or seven Terraces raised above each other, the walls of which are cover'd with beautiful Orange & Lemon Trees. Near one end is built a large house, which does not appear worth much notice on the outside; no more than they told was the inside worth the trouble of examineing. The other side of the Island is cover'd with Groves down to the Water Edge. The Middle too consists chiefly of a Grove of large Cyprus, Olive and other trees, which serve for a Shelter to the pheasants, Guinea Fouls, & others, of which here are great numbers. Isola Madre undoubtedly is not near so much indebted to art as her neighbour, nevertheless it does not want for beauties, and had a little more art and expence been bestowed upon it, I think she might have had no reason to be Jealous of her Rival. She is situated in a wider and pleasanter part of the Lake, the prospects from here are more pleasing, and she is considerably larger: We rowed round this, as we did likewise round the other. This took us a quarter of an hour, the other ten minutes, and by the quickness of our going we beleived the Isola Bella might be near half a Mile, & the Isola Madre near three quarters of a Mile round. From hence we had an excellant view of the other Island, which appears very beautiful. Isola Madre belongs to an Uncle of the Count who possesses Isola Bella.

In going from the Islands we found nearly the points of view from which M^r. Keysler took his Drafts of them and had a good opportunity of comparing them together. In respect to the view of Isola bella, he has really been pretty exact 'tho I think his draft gives one an Idea of the Terraces takeing a larger spot of Ground than they really do. I am sorry I cannot say he has observed his usual exactness in respect to the Isola Madre. He has shew'd indeed a manifest partiality for the Mother, and has flatter'd her most grossly. Instead of all the fine Palaces & buildings one has described in the Draft he has given of it, one finds nothing more than one very indifferent house.

We were told that the Lago Magiore runs 15 Leagues beyond the Islands amongst the Mountains. There is no doubt of its going a very considerable distance farther, but I can hardly beleive by what one may judge from Maps & other accounts, that it extends so far as we were told. We were so fortunate as to have much finer weather in returning from the Islands than in going there so that we had the pleasure of being convinced of the truth of the discriptions one reads of the beauties of the Environs of this delightful Lake. The Lake may be between two & three Leagues over in the widest part. Its sides are uneaven and winding. On both sides the eye is continually struck by some different objects of Villages, Country houses, or the remains of some old Town or Castle. Above these, rise hills of different heights, the rugged sides of which are cover'd by vineards and Summer houses: Rising above these one sees some of the smaller Mountains, whose tops are cover'd with the most beautiful wood: and still beyond these (in a clear day) may be discover'd Mount S^t. Bernard and S^t. Gothard hiding their Snowy heads amongst the Clouds.

Within about a League of Cesti on the right Shore, one discovers, Arona, a small Town belonging to Count Borromeo. Within about half a Mile of this Town, and a quarter of one above the Lake stands the Amazing Colossal Statue of S^t. Charles Borromeo.

as we were told......... 35 Braccio.

Heigth of the Pedestal..................25 Ditto

I own I was much surprised at being told it was so high, as it does not appear near so much by looking at it from the Ground: which must I think be a proof of its being well-proportion'd, and indeed 'tho it is of such an enormous height and size it is very far from displeasing the Eye. He is represented in a speaking attitude with the right arm extended. There is no way of getting up the pedestal but by a ladder. From thence for near a quarter of the way up the Statue one is obliged to use a ladder, which brings one to a hole under one of his Garments, at which one may enter, and from thence one may go up into the head by a narrow funnel about the size of a man, by the means of some small Iron bars placed very wide from each other. Having a Strong inclination to see how the inside of the body of this saint was formed, and how his head was fill'd, we got some ladders, which were taken out of a Church just by, and raised with some difficulty. My Friend Gibbon not much relishing these scaleing expeditions, I went up alone: The last ladder was so steep, that I cannot say I liked it much myself: however having once enter'd the body, I was not long before I worked my way into the Head, 'tho I found the passages to it very narrow & disagreeable: The Inside of the body, as high as about the top of the neck is all stone, built (as I imagine) from the Pedestal: to this the statue is fasten'd by barrs of Iron, comeing from it, & fixed in the stone work: A very large piece of Timber, going from the Stone work, and supported by large Iron barrs, runs in to the Arm, that is extended, and helps to support it. The Head is large enough to hold 5 or 6 Men with ease: with my arms at full length I could just touch the two ears: By leaning forward a little I easily sat down in the nose. From several parts of the Head are bars, wch. fix it to y^e. Stone work. As well as I could judge from the head, neck & some other small parts of the sides, this Statue is not made of one single piece of Brass or Copper, as M^r. Keysler says it is, but of Sheets of Copper about 2 foot square each, nailed together: neither can I conceive it could hardly be possible to cast a Statue of this Size in one piece, or if it could have been done, how the Stone work in the Middle could have been worked, up it: much less that the Statue could have been put upon it, if the middle part was done first. I shall not pretend to decide of the Merits of this Astonishing Figure; but yet think I may venture to pronounce it not a very bad one, as we were both of us not only much astonished by its Size, but pleased wth. its appearance altogether. Having satisfied out Curiosity here, we walked down to Arona, where we had sent our boat having landed just opposite the Statue. We got to Cesti in about an hour and set out immediately after for Milan, where we arrived raither late, being near eight hours going there. The greatest part of the road is pretty good: one passes through several small town & villages: The Country seems rich and well cultivated, especially for some time before we came to Milan. The Fields and vineards look'd like Gardens.

We found arrived at Milan during our absence, L^d. Tillney.[1] His nephew (perhaps about 9 or 10 years old, his name I beleive Child), a fine lively boy,

---

1   John Tylney (1712-84), 2nd Earl Tylney. Family name, before it was changed to Tylney in 1734, was Child. He settled in Italy and died, unmarried, in Naples. His heir (but not to the title) was his nephew Sir James Tylney-Long (1736-94) who added Tylney to his name on the 2nd Earl's death in 1784. He was the eldest son of Sir Robert Long.

M^r. Long, Son of S^r. Robert Long, and a Clergyman. It was too late to visit them this Evening.

Friday 18th May – Milan

Regiment of Bade-Bade. We went this Morning to the Citadel in hopes of seeing the regiment of Bade Bade reviewed by a General just arrived, but we were much disapointed to find it was nothing more than a particular Muster of the whole regiment. When we came into the great outward Court of y^e. Citadel we found the regiment formed in a Square 4 deep, quite round the Court. It was impossible not to be struck, by y^e. noble appearance of these Troops, above 2000 Men, all of them very tall and near of an equall height: many of them raither young, and very well looking, their Cloathing perfectly white and clean, their hats very neat and smartly cocked (wth. each a Green bough) their gaters, quite white & well made: and in ev'ry other respect as well appointed as possible. To see the steadiness of these Men, and the quickness wth. which they made all their motions, equally amazed me, and pleased me. It is much the finest Regiment that I ever saw. They only went through 4 or five different manoeuvres, between each of which the General kept them a great while, during which rests it was impossible to see the most trifling motion in any part of one of them. Each company was called over after separately, and the men past one by one before the General, who was in a Tent in the Middle of the Court. The Austrian uniform is mostly white, turned up differently in each Regiment: This is white and blue. They are cloathed only once in three years, yet alwais appear clean, owing to their never wearing their coats except General Field Days, others, only their waistcoats and no Gaters.

M^r. Long came to us in the Citadel and introduced us to L^d. Tilney & his Nephew. We breakfasted wth. them, & stay'd wth. them 'till they set out for Venice. L^d. Tilney is short and fat. I cannot say I saw anything in him that prejudiced me in his favor.

We went after dinner to see two Churches, La Passionne and S^t. Antoine. The former is chiefly remarkable for the goodness of its Architecture; The form of the Church is the most pleasing, and the building the lightest I have yet seen here. The body of the Church wch. is a handsome weadth, is supported by two rows of pillars: About 2 thirds of its Length, before one comes to the Choir, the body opens into a large Circle, over which is a fine Doum.

S^t. Antoine is not near so handsome in respect to its form and Architecture, but is much more ornamented.

The Archbishop was out of Town, wch. prevented our seeing his Palace. We went to see a Manufacture of Christal, of which there is a great deal worked at Milan. The Stone is ground smooth with stones &c. &c. as those kind of things commonly are, & if wanted to be made hollow, they use small diamonds, fined properly. I saw one piece which weigh'd 40 pounds. They saw them, with a smooth saw, made of copper, and some kind of fine powder. They asked me 6 Louis for a very small box, not mounted. There are several other manufactures at Milan, but that of silks is the more considerable.

The Town of Milan is very large, the Streets are most of them narrow, and the houses indifferently built. It is said to contain about 300,000 People. There are a very great number of Convents & religious houses: but I could not learn exactly how many. This Town is spoken of as much the best in Italy for the Society, & for the reception of Strangers: I cannot speak by personal knowledge, as we had no letters of recommendation here, except to a Banker: and we did not try to make an acquaintance, as we intended staying a very little time. The Citadel is a large old building, I beleive not very strong, no more than the fortifications of the town. The Country round Milan from the Alps, to pretty near the Pirenees, is the flattest and evenest I ever saw: It is subject to be often overflewn, from the rivers which come, or receive great quantities of water from the Mountains.

Saturday 19th May – Milan to Pavia

We began our Journey this Morning for Genoa, which is about twelve posts and a half from Milan. At about a post and half out of Town we turned a little out of the road to see La Chartreuse de Pavie. The Façade of the Church belonging to this Convent is the most extraordinary piece of work I ever saw. It is in the Gothick manner, and ornamented in ev'ry part with very curious, and fine Sculpture. It is impossible to give a particular account of it without writeing it on the Spot: and almost as impossible to form a good Idea of it, without seeing it. About a Foot above the Ground is a row of Medallions, on which are represented the Heads of many Roman Emperors & others; Above there is a Row of Basso-relievos, setting forth pieces of history. Between these rise some Pillastres, which pass likewise between the first Row of windows; on the top of the pilasters are placed four Statues on each. Just below the Second windows is a Gallery supported by a Row of Pillars, and very near the Top is another Gallery, supported by more pillars. All these different parts are very ritchly ornamented with sculpture. There is a portico before the door of the Church. In the inside against the Sides of the Portico are several different pieces of Basso relievos, on which are represented many things relating to the foundation of this Church & Convent. The infinite number of Figures, houses Trees, and other objects cut out with the greatest nicety in these pieces, cannot be sufficiently admired. The entire Front of the Church, and ev'ry thing upon it is made of white Marble, which 'tho it has not much polish, looks very white and well. Within the Church against the Pillars that support the vault are twelve large statues of white Carrara Marble. On each side of the Church are 7 or 8 Chapels opposite each other. The Pillars on each side of the Altars in these Chapels are of different colour'd Marbles, all very fine; Those that pleased me most, were a kind of clouded yellow, very finely polished: the Marble of these came from near Loretto. The front of the Altar pieces are imatations of painting, made of different sorts of marble curiously inlaid. I took particular notice of one, on which are represented a great number of Flours, birds and other things, which you see through or under the Arches of a Building, all which are done very nicely and naturally. The Convent alwais maintains some workemen mean'ly for these things. The body of the Church is divided from the Choir by some very handsome Iron Gates, that are gilt. In the Choir one is amazed by the quantity of precious Stones, with which the Great Altar Piece is almost cover'd. The rails which run before this Chapel are entirely set round with small pieces of Lapis Lazuli, agates and other stones. In the front and on other parts of this Altar are several fine pieces of Lapis Lazuli, 5 or 6 inches square, one in particular that is still larger. On the Altar is placed a Tabernacle which is at the bottom much ornamented, wth. Lapis Lazuli, Jasper, Amethists, onyx, agates of different sorts, cornelians, Granets and other stones & Gems to an amazing value. On the front of the Altar piece are represented several flowers and fruits made of these diffcrent stones, particularly some flowers made of Amethists, some Cherries of yellowish red Jasper & some olives of a beautiful agate. In a vestry just by, we were shewn a very curious piece of carving made of Sea horses Teeth. It forms the back of an Altar Piece & is the historical part of the Old Testament. The fore Ground of it is to represent three large Arches for a kind of Gate, all the middle part is filled up with small square divisions, which are filled up with the nicest bas-relief; the figures and ornaments of which are all extreamly small & well finished. It may be said to be a very extraordinary & curious piece of work. One sees also a very handsome monument of white marble on which is the Figure of John Galeazzo Viscomti, the founder of the Church & Convent who lies buried just by. They told us he died about the year 1494, wch. appears also from the Inscription just by, if I remember right. We went from hence to see the Chartreuse. Round a very large Square are built the Cells of the Religious, who, if one may judge from their habitation dont live very uncomfortably. They have each of them two apartments one on the Ground Floor, the other one pair of stairs, each apartment consists of 3 or 4 very convenient Rooms. They have besides a very pretty Garden to each Cell. Besides all these, they have a very large Garden surrounded with a high wall. This Garden or raither Park is well planted with trees, disposed in walks &c. Near this place is the Spot of Ground on which was fought the famous Battle of Pavie in 1525 when Francis 1st. was defeated & taken prisoner. By what I could understand from the man that went with us, there are about 50 Monks belonging to this foundation, or raither were originally, & that there are not so many now. Leaving this place we continued our rout through Pavia intending to go as far as Novi, this Evening, but when we came to the Po, about a post beyond Pavia, we found it so swelled (a) that the Common Ferry boat, could not pass, and we did not care to venture our Chaise in a smaller Boat, for which reason we returned to Pavia, hopeing to find a better way. It being late we resolved to lay here to night.

(a) From some rains that had fell during two days before.

Sunday 20th May – Pavia

Being told that the waters might probably be low enough to pass easily the next day, we resolved to pass this, here, for which we were not sorry after, as we had an opportunity of seeing one or two things worth the pains of looking at. In a large Area before the Citadel is an Equestrian Statue of Brass. People are very undecided whether it is intended for Marcus Aurelius, Antoninus Pius, or Constantine the Great,[1] neither shall I pretend to give any opinion about it, 'tho I am surprised that those that are very conversant in the Study of Medals & Statues have not been able to resolve the question. He has on the Roman Vestments. His right arm is held out. I cannot say that I admired the Figure of the Man near so much as that of the horse, which appeard to me to be very well executed: It is raised upon a high Pedestal of modern workmanship. In a Chapel near one of the Churches we were shewn the bones of the French Soldiers slain at the Battle of Pavia. One would beleive that a sight of this kind, could not be very interesting or pleasing: nevertheless from the manner of their being disposed, if they are not very pleasing, they are at least somewhat Curious. They are placed in two vaults, which might more properly be called Grotto's, if one did not know that they were formed of Bones, and I have seen some made of shells, much uglier and more disagreable than these. One of them is particularly well done, ev'ry part of it is made of Bones. In the Sides and ends are made Pillars, niches and different Figures & Shapes; In the Middle of one side is a Nich, in which is

---

1   Opinion still (2021) not decided. It could be of Theodoric the Great, King of the Ostrogoths (471-526); Roman 3rd century AD; or of Emperor Septimius Severus. The statue was destroyed by the Jacobin Club of Pavia in 1796 since it was considered a symbol of monarchy. Replaced by a copy in 1937.

placed a perfect Skeleton of a Man. In the Middle of the Area are two Piramids very artificially made. The bones appear to be put in endways, so that only the Joints appear: The Floor & ceiling is made with the bones placed lengthways, so as to form, Stars, rounds, squares, &c. The Skulls which serve to make the Bases, and besides are disposed in many other parts, with <u>a great deal of Taste</u>, have a very good effect. The other of these vaults is much in the same manner, but not so perfect, or well done. We were much pleased with the novelty & singularity of this extraordinary repository of the remains of those unfortunate Frenchmen. Here is a University where young men are maintained & instructed in different parts of Learning at the Expence of the Colleges. There is more than one College; of one of which Pius the fifth was the founder: There is a very large Colossal Statue of him in Brass placed in the area before the College Gate. The Cathedral is a very large old Building, to which there at present makeing many additions. Pavia is the Ticinum of the Antients, according to M^r. Addison;[1] and took its name undoubtedly from the Ticinum, now called Tezin, on which it is situated. There were at this time more than two Regiments of Austrian troops quarter'd here: Each regiment of two Battalions.

Monday 21ˢᵗ May – Pavia to Campo Maroni [Campomorone]

We left Pavie at four o'clock this Morning, in hopes of getting in the Evening to Genoa: When we came to the Po we found the waters something lower, but not sunk enough to admit of our going over in the Great boat, which obliged us to make use of a small one; however after some difficulties being got over, we landed our Chaise very safe in an hour & a half on the other side; The Po here is a considerable weadth, & very rapid. About a post farther we came to Voghera, from thence we pass through Tortona, Novi, Voltaggio, and Campo Moroni. The greatest part of the Country seems very rich. The fields are well cultivated, and the prospect from the road are very pleasing, particularly from Voghera to Tortona, & so on to Novi. Tortona is not very large: We could see the Castle & some fortifications lying on y^e. left hand. At Voltagio one comes to the Foot of Appenines. As soon as one is out of the Town, one begins to ascend gently, and so continue along the side of a hill between two mountains for about a post: The Ascent is not very steep neither does one go to any great height: The Mountains indeed near here, are not very high, but very rocky & uneaven. The part we came over is called the Bouquetto [Passo della Bocchetta]: At a post from Voltagio one begins to descend, which is done with great rapidity, as the road is all paved, the Hill steeper than on the other side,

---

1   Joseph Addison (1672-1719), author of Remarks on several parts of Italy &c, in the years 1701, 1702, 1703. London, 1705

& the Postilions go a fast Trot or a Gallop: There is a beautiful view from the top of y^e. Bouquetto from whence one discovers Genoa at the bottom of the valley and the sea appears finely beyond it.

Having met with several delays on the road, and finding one of the wheels of our Chaise much hurt by the violence of the Shakeing in comeing down the Hill so fast, we were obliged to lay this evening at Campo Maroni, about a post & a half from Genoa. We found here a very indifferent Town & Inn, for which reasons we left it early in the Morning, and got to Genoa by soon after eight o'clock.

Fig 7 A Prospect of the City of Genoa, 1744

Tuesday 22nd May – Genoa

One has a very beautiful view of the Town at comeing into it. We went immediately to the Sta. Marthe, where we found but indifferent Lodgins, but were obliged to take up with them. We found at this Inn a M^r. Macarthy[1] & his Mother, who came from makeing the Tour of Italy. He came to see us after dinner. We went to see his Mother this Evening, who told us she had been abroad about four years & came only to take care of her Son who was unhealthy: I don't know which is most to be pitied, the Mother or the Son. We went to see our Banker M^r. Lombard and M^r. Gibbon went after to visit a M^r. Celisia[2] who married the Daughter of Mallet when he was Embassador from Genoa to England.

---

1   Unidentified
2   Celesia in Gibbon's journal.

Wednesday 23rd May – Genoa

I received an Invitation this Morn^g. to accompany M^r. Gibbon at M^r. Celisia's.
We accordingly went together. During the Dinner, the Conversation turned
on the extraordinary revolution of 1746, and on the Affairs of Corsica. In
regard to the first he told us that, the Mob were the only cause of its begining,
as well as almost the finishers of it. The Senate came to no resolution 'till
the fourth day, when the Austrians were entirely drove from the Town. They
then declared for the Mob, & supported them. The Government of Genoa
became then very extraordinary. It divided itself into two acting heads, of
which The Mob, formed one, & y^e. Senate the other. The Mob kept a constant
assembly, from which they issued orders relating to things about the Town,
and other home affairs. They order'd some things to be done, and forbid
others, all under pain of Death: They had a hangman setting constantly by
a Gallows, that was erected near a Church, and this officer did not want for
employment. The Senate at the same time continued acting, but without
interfering with the Affairs of y^e. other assembly. They took care of the Foreign
department, sending out Embassaders, concluding treaties, & settling those
kind of things. In this manner it continued for a year, when the Assembly of
the People loosing their Chiefs, gradually decayed, & dwindled into nothing,
without being dissolved by any resolution of their own, or by any order of the
Senate. It is almost equally particular that an assembly of this sort, should be
able to support itself so long, & that as it could, it should end in the quiet
manner it did.

In respect to the Corsicans he said that Paoli[1] is their great support.
M^r. Celesia said he could compare him to no one so well as to Cromwell,
with whose caracter that of Paoli has a great resemblance. Of a Fierce, bold,
undertakeing caracter, with a great deal of dissimulation, & Fanaticism. The
people themselves, are of a bold, unconquer'd spirit, constantly stur'd up &
pushed forward by the Priests, who run about preaching to them in a manner,
fitter to forward, than quiet a Sedition. About four years since the Genoese
offer'd Paoli, the most advantageous conditions, provided he would come over
to them, wch. he refused. The affairs of the Republick are in but a bad way in
Corsica. They have nothing there except Bastia, & some small Fortresses on
the Coasts: They would be glad to get rid of it quite, but of those that would
be glad to have it, they fear the Neighbourhood.

Thursday 24th May – Genoa

Having spent ev'ry day for a great while past, either in Travelling or seeing

---

1   Filippo Antonio Pasquale de' Paoli, 1725 – 1807, a leading figure in Corsican politics for 50 years

places, we were glad to day, to repose not only our Bodies but our Eyes, and accordingly spent it at home. I took this opportunity of beginning to read Entretiens sur les Vies, et sur les ouvrages des plus excellens peintres anciens & Modernes par Mon^r: Felibien.[1] I forgot to mention yesterday, going to the Italian Comedy: The Theatre is small, & y^e. play was very dull.

Friday 25th May – Genoa

We saw this Morning L'Annonciata. It is a very handsome Church, much ornamented, and where there is a great deal of Marble; some of it fine: Over the Door is a very large Picture of the last Supper by I:C: Procaccino: This piece is much esteemed. It is placed in so dark a place, that it is impossible to see it very well; by what I could see, the Colouring seem'd to be very fine, 'tho dark; and the manner strong & bold. We went from hence to see the Jesuits College, which was formerly belonging to the Family of Balbi, and which they say, they got from them by some Artifice: It is a handsome building. There are about forty Fathers. Takeing all the Classes together, they have sometimes near a Thousand Scholars, Sons of Nobility, Merchands &c belonging to the Town. The Library is raither small, and not very remarkable in any respect. There are a few antient Manuscripts. We were shewn a Manuscript of Quintus Curtius in French by Vasque de Lucene a Portugese Nobleman, who presented it to Charles le Hardi: It is very well wrote on vellum, and ev'ry Chapter much ornamented at the Head with paintings relating to the Contents of the Chapter: In the first you see him on his knees presenting his Book to the Duke of Burgundy: He mentions in a short preface, having collected from different Books, the wanting parts of Quintus Curtius. This manuscript is well preserved: Besides these there are, a saint Augustine; and a Quintillian that do not seem very antient. The Person that shew'd it to us was a French Jesuit that had taken refuge here. By his manner of speaking one would imagine that they were the most humble & innocent of men, not deserving the Ill treatment they had met with. We took a walk after dinner with M^r. Celesia: Saw the house and Gardens of M^r. Balbi out of Town: The house appears handsome of y^e. outside, the Gardens are pretty, but what is most pleasing from thence are the Prospects. The conversation turned some of the time upon the Bank of S^t. George, a Society formed formerly during some of the disturbances of the State. It is upon much the same footing as our Publick Funds. For money intrusted to them they do not pay a regular interest, but pay dividends more or less ev'ry year, according to the State of the Bank. They lend the Republick money. They receive sums of Money of particulars, like our bankers. It is at

---

1   In four volumes, published initially 1666 – 1668.

present pretty rich, & has a good credit. We were invited to make a party at Mad. Maineries, Sister to M^{rs}. Celesia; we staid there the Evening & supped at M^r. Celesias. We are as yet much pleased with the behaviour of the Genoese to strangers. They are not only polite, but seem to be glad of an opportunity of pleasing them.

Saturday 26th May – Genoa

Le Palais du Marquis de Balbi, dans la Rue Balbi; was a great amusement to us this Morning. There are in it a great number of very good Pictures, of which I shall only mention a few that pleased me the most. In the first Room beyond the Hall, Andromeda chained to the Rock by Guercio da Cento. The Chief Figure in this seemed to me very well done, & particularly expressive. The adoration of the Magi by Titian, I thought raither imperfect: Seconda Salotta: The Virgin Mary holding our Saviour in her arms, and two Priests on their knees. This is by Titian, much esteem'd. The two last figures, I thought remarkably good. A large Picture of S^t. Francis Seated, by Hannibal Caracci: The Colouring of this is uncommon: It is throughout of one dark, greyish black, wch. is finely varied & shaded; and the Figure is very expressive & good: Not very far from this is another by the same hand, but of which the Colouring is very different, a Venus Sleeping, and two Cupids who are pulling of the Sheet that cover'd her, & looking under. This Piece is full of beauties. The Colouring is beautiful, and all the Figures very natural: The posture of the Venus is not very pleasing as her body is twisted, & her face turned upwards. The two Cupids have both of them an air, fort Mechant. The great difference of these two Pictures, 'tho by y^e. same hand, made me think it must not only be difficult but very uncertain, to know, the Master, by the Manner. S^t. Jerome, with an Angel behind speaking to – Augustine Caracci. Terzo Salotto. A large Picture of S^t. Paul fell from his horse by Michel Angelo de Caravaggio. – S^t. John in y^e. Wilderness by Guido Reni, an excellent work, but I think he has given S^t. John too much the air, of a thoughtless Shepherd. Quarto Salotto. A most beautiful Picture, representing, The Virgin, our Saviour, Saints, Angels & other Figures, By Rubens. The Coulours of this are raither lively, but so good, and natural, most of the figures bold & seemingly rising from y^e. canvas – in short the whole is so fine, that it cant be too much admired. S^t. Jerome in y^e. Desert by Titian; Good; but a small piece. In the Gallery, a small Picture by Corregio of our Saviour, the Virgin Mary & S^t. Catherine. This beautiful little Picture, has all the Charms possible; the figures are Elegant & y^e. Coulours delicate. A Saviour & S^t. John by Rubens, very fine. Small. and Lucrece, by Guido Reni: and a Philosopher by Spanoletto, all very good. There are many others, as good, perhaps better than these; and if they are all originals, as we are opined, it is certainly a valuable collection. They give a printed list of them at going in. – The house is a good one, without being magnificent. From the Street one comes into an Area under the Middle of the House, the Opposite side of this Area supported by Pillars, wch. are continued in a double Row so as to form a Court within. On one side of the Area under the House, are the Stairs, very broad & handsome, which lead to a handsome hall. Here, and indeed, in most parts of Italy, the handsomest Apartments are on the first (a) floor, and not upon the Ground Floor as with us.

(a) au premier Etage

Sunday 27th May – Genoa

We accompanied M^r. & Mad: Celesias to their Country house where we dined wth. a brother of M^r. Celesias only, besides ourselves: Their house is situated about 6 or 7 Miles from Genoa, amongst the Mountains in a very Romantick Situation. It is on one side of the valley, Bozavera [Bolzaneto], or (Polcavera) [Val Polcevera] which runs from beyond the Bochetto, down to Genoa. There is a small River, the Bozavera, that runs down the valley: It becomes often very considerable from the Torrents that come f^rm. y^e. Mountains. Nothing can be more pleasing than the views of this valley in y^e. Spring and Summer. On each side one sees a great number of very handsome Country houses, with little plantations, & Gardens; and the Sides & Tops of the Mountains above them are cover'd with woods, wch. altogether form very beautiful Prospects. The Genoes have several Batteries & small fortifications, upon the Tops of the Hills near here. We return'd into Town raither late. I went to ye Play. Very dull.

Monday 28th May – Genoa

We went this Morning to see the Palais de Marcellino Durazzo (a). This Palace is chiefly remarkable for the richness of its furniture. There are no great number of Pictures. A very large Magdaleine kneeling, & holding the feet of our Saviour, by Paul Veronese is much esteem'd: An Adam and Eve drove from Paradis; by Procacino: seem'd good. Two or three good ones by Van Dick. The Gallery is very handsome & prettily finished: There are seven windows, between each is a Pilastre, wch. is of Looking Glass. The Capitals compleat, & Gilt; on one side of the Pillastre is a Statue, the same between ev'ry Window: One of these Statues, representing a Shepherd is remarkably well done. The Hips & position of the body are very natural: It is made by Parodi, Father of him who has painted the Ceiling of this Gallery. At the Upper end of the Room are two Glasses that almost fill y^e. End. At this end is placed the rape of Proserpine; the Figures are large, the Sculpture pretty good. Over the end windows one each side are two figures, that have a good Effect. The Gallery is much ornamented with Gilding &c: The Duke of York, we were told had a plan taken of it. There are several paintings that we did not see.

In the Jesuits Church which we went to see, are three very good Pictures. Over the great Altar a Circumsition By Rubens. The Figures appear bold & natural, and the Colouring strong & beautiful: Another by the same hand – a Saint cureing those posses'd with the Devil &c is undoubtedly an Admirable piece: An Assumption by Guido Reni, is little inferior to the two others. This is a large, handsome church; pretty much ornamented. We went likewise to see the Cathedral of S^t. Lawrence. The Appearance of this Church is very particular, being Chiefly of black and white marble, placed regularly in Rows. I cannot say it pleased one at all. There are some middling pictures. We looked for an antient Inscription wch. we could not find.

(a) Dans La Rue Balbi

Tuesday 29th May – Genoa

Palais Caregha, Strada Nuova: is a handsome building of Marble. An Adoration by Paul Veronese appear'd to me excellent: The Shading raither dark & uncommon. Rubens in full length by himself, a good picture. Here are many others reckon'd very good. Many that we could not see. Here is one Room very highly fited up & finished: The whole inside is cover'd with Gilding & fine Glasses. From hence we went to the Palace of Giacomino Balbi dans la Rue Balbi: where there are some excellent Pictures; particularly. – Two large Landskips by Rubens. In the Fore Ground of one is a wood, an opening near it in which are Cattle & many other objects; finely done: The lights and shades well observed & y^e. perspective very good. A rainbow over it is well represented. The other a plain, with wood & a variety of Objects: very good. Just by these another large piece by Rubens: seems very good, but raither particular. There are a vast variety of Figures crowded together, which are very bold & y^e. Colouring fine, & appears best at some distance. Two small Pictures of Adam & Eve, very nicely finished by Breughell. The Figures are very good, and the Colours very delicate. But the most remarkable and pleasing to me, is a holy Family: by Rubens; you see our Saviour and S^t. John in a Cradle. Nothing can be more natural than these two Figures; The other figures are very good, and the colouring of the whole delicate and beautiful.

Here are many more good paintings. We went to see Saint Ciro: which is a handsome Church, the Ceiling painted, & the whole much ornamented.

Wednesday 30th May – Genoa

Palais Brignoletti, belonging to the present Doge, in La Rue Neuve is a very handsome, large palace, built of a reddish Stone; There are many good Rooms, tho none very large: The floors are all red brick, in Squares, and small green Squares between each. Amongst the paintings of which here are a considerable number, I thought two or three remarkable good. A S[t]. Sebastian, by Guido. A Christ holding y[e]. Cross by Van-dick. Judith going to give the head of Holofernes to a Black Slave, who stand by her, looking and sloping forwards. The Body of Holofernes appearing partly to hang downwards. The whole of this piece is admirable; but the bloody part from whence the Head is taken, and the Head wth. the blood droping from it are so natural as to be really disagreable. There is another remarkably good Piece by Rubens; the Subject is a little obscure; at least to me. There is a woman with a kind of vase in her hand: Close behind her is a man in armour, who has one hand upon her breast, the other upon the vase; a Cupid is disarming him: In the dark part of the Picture a figure of a man, wth. a Flambeau: In another part a kind of Satyre. The Colouring & execution of this Picture, are very butiful. There is a small apartement upon the Ground Floor very neatly fited up. The palace is not inhabited at present, the Doge being obliged to live during the two years of his employment at a Palace appointed for the Doges: not so good as his own.

We accompanied the Brother of M[r]. Celesia, after dinner to see the Church, and bridge of Carignano, which both well deserve seeing not only from the buildings in themselves but from their being built at the Expence of two private People: The Church was built by Bendinellus Sauli, & the Bridge by his Grandson Stephen Sauli. This Bridge leads to the Church, and is thrown over a deep valley which runs between the town & the Church. It consists of four Arches of an amazing heigth, under which are built many houses of five Storeys high. I went under one of the Arches, which appeared to me, as near as I could guess, by judging from the houses under, to be full ninety foot high; M[r]. Gibbon thought 100. The bridge is long, and of a very handsome weadth. In itself it is an astonishing building, & much more so when consider'd as the work of a single & private person. Neither is the Church when consider'd in y[e]. same light, much less so. It is something in the manner of the Superga by Turin, 'tho infinitely smaller. On each side is a Tower, & in the Middle a Dome, which appears ill proportion'd for the Towers, w[ch]. are too high. The inside is plain & neat; very little ornamented. In the Middle is a Dome: in the

Circle under are four large Statues. Two of them by, Pouget, are very good; a S^r. Paul; & S^r. Sebastien, tied to a Tree. The torment the latter is in, is finely expressed. His body twisted round, and his breast & side thrust forward in trying to give himself some ease, are very natural.

Thursday 31st May – Genoa

I forgot to mention last Monday having received a visit from M^r. Hamilton,[1] an Irish Gentleman, who came on Sunday from Turin, with M^r. Ponsonby. Accompanied by these two Gentlemen we went to see some places on the western coast from Genoa. We stopt first at La Ville Imperiale belonging to the Doria family. Here was nothing worth observing except the Fasade of the house, which is very handsome, being built with a great deal of Taste and Elegance: The Gardens are small, ill laid out, & much neglected. At Sestri, a little farther on, is the house of Ma. Spinola. The house is small, & makes a singular appearance from its great heigth, being upon a Terras, from which one descends on each side by an easy Sloop directly from the house. In the inside there is nothing very remarkable: There's a fine view over the Sea from it. The Garden is chiefly remarkable for the great number of fine orange Trees there are, at present cover'd with Fruit. The next place we came to was Corneliano [Cornigliano], belonging to the Durazzo Family. This is really much the best 'tho not the finest house I have seen since I have been at Genoa. One comes into a large hall on one side of which is a very handsome Stone Staircase: beyond the hall is a very handsome Salloon, which wth. the Hall make the depth of the house. On each Side the Salloon are many very good Rooms. Above stairs there is one very large handsome Room, & on each side a good apartment. The Size, Convenience, and disposition of the Rooms pleased us all much. The Floors are most of them a fine polished Brick, so joined, that they all appear almost like one. The sides of the Rooms plain white ornamented with a slight border &c of Colour'd Stuko: The Cielings are most of them the same. Here are pretty large Gardens, extending very near down to the Sea.

From hence we went to Peggi [Pegli], the house of the Doria's. It is small and indifferent. The Gardens here lying against the side of a hill are capable of being made very pretty. In the lower part are plantations & walks of Oranges & in y^e. upper are some walks cut in a wood; in an opening there is a small piece of water, where there is an Island in y^e. Middle wth. some rock work, from which play'd some water forced into different forms, as one often sees fireworks. By means of underground pipes it plays up through the walks

1   unidentified

under one's Feet; or from y^e. sides. We went no farther than this place which is about six miles from Genoa.

C'est aujourdhui le Jour de l'ascension. Nous avons quitté Turin dans la Dessin de nous rendera a Venize pour etre presents a cette Fete, qui devoit etre fort brillante a cause du Duc de York,[1] qui y est allé. Mais a Milan j'ai changé du plan pour deux raisons. Premierement parceque je ne savois pas assez bien la langue Italienne, pour profiter bien du voyage, et dans la seconde place, pour des raisons Economiques. Le Premiere Mobile commencoit de manquer, et le Plaisir fut oblige de ceder a la Prudence.

Friday 1ˢᵗ June – Genoa

We went this Morning to see the Church of S^t. Philip de Neri. It is but small, but exceedingly ornamented. There is a profusion of Gilding all over it: There are some pretty good pictures by Piola, and a good deal of fine Marbles: The Architecture is not pretty. On one side is a kind of Large Chapel, wch. they call L'Oratoir, where Musick is performed in winter. This is a very Elegant Building, both as to the Architecture, and ornaments. We dined to day with M^r. Celesia. In talking of the Government of Genoa, he mentioned a most excellent institution, they have in it. It is that of Censors, which they call Syndyks, who are appointed to receive the Complaints of all people against all Governors and Magistrates appointed by the State. At the end of the year they go round to ev'ry town and place, to examine into the Conduct of all Magistrates & officers, and the meanest person has a right to lay his complaints, and Information before them. The Doge himself is Subject to be judged by these Syndyks if any one makes a complaint against him. Many Instances have been known of the lowest people getting redress for grevances commited, even by the Doges but continually by oppressions of Governors and other officers of y^e. State. In speaking of the nobility, we were told that ev'ry year, seven Families are proposed before the great Council: Five of the town, and two out of it. It does not very often happen that any one is chosen, but it gives an opportunity of doing it.

Saturday 2ⁿᵈ June – Genoa

The Palace where the Doges alwais live, is a plain, and raither mean looking

---

1   The Duke of York, Edward Augustus (1739-67), second son of Frederick Prince of Wales and brother of George III. For some unknown reason Guise wrote this section in French. It does however echo very closely Gibbon's note on this matter in his diary entry for 18 May: "Notre dessein etoit de pousser jusqu'à Venise pour nous trouver au carnaval que la presence du Duc de York devoit rendre encore plus brilliant; mais notre ignorance de la langue qui nous privoit de mille avantages, appuyè de quleques raisons èconomiques qui se font deja sentir un peu vivement, nous ont fait changer de plan".

building: one comes first into a very large Court: On each side the Door is a very large Statue. One is of Andrew Doria, with an Inscription setting forth his being the Father of his Country & restorer of the Republick; which he is called indeed with the greatest justess. In his younger Days he attached himself to the Service of France: and signalised himself very much ev'ry way, but particularly for his great knowledge in naval Affairs: In the year 1527 he commanded the Fleet of the Allies and was the chief cause of Genoa being taken by the French. Being afterwards much discontent with some slighting behaviour of France towards him, he quited the Service of France, and was employed by the Emperor Charlequint. From this time he formed the design of delivring Genoa, from the French, and restoring its Liberty. He represented to the People that the King of France only wanted to enslave them, to lessen their Riches and weaken their Power, that he would not restore Savone, as he had promised; and by such discourses, and his own generous behaviour, he entirely gained the People over to him; which done, he appeared before Genoa with a fleet of Galleys, landed his men, and made himself master of y^e. Town, without strikeing a Stone; there happening to be but few men in the town, because of the plague, which was very bad at that time.

Having done this Doria would not accept of any Employment: but proposed an assembly of the people, which met and was very numerous. This Assembly named twelve Commissioners who were to form a place of Government, which was accordingly done, and fixed much the same as it is at present, wch. it has continued ever since. This happend in the year 1528. Doria continued serving the State with the greatest disinterestedness, ableness and Bravery 'till the year 1560 when he died in the 93 year of his Life, which he spent with the greatest Glory & honor: He left for his Heir, John Andrew Doria, whose Statue stands on the other side of the Door, and is called the Preserver of his Country. He was Son of Jennetin Doria, who was killed in the Conspiracy of the Count of Fieschi, or Lavagna, in the year 1546.

In this Palace are two very large Chambers, one for the Great, & the other for the small Council. In the largest, round the Sides, are niches, in which are placed the Statues of the Benefactors to the State. There are still several vacant. In the small Council Chambers are three very large paintings By Solimene. One under the Throne, represents the discovery of North America by Christopher Columbus, a Genoese. Opposite to this is, The receiving the Ashes of S^t. John the Baptist at Genoa. On the ceiling The Expulsion of Justiniani from Scio by Soliman. The Figures in these Pictures are very Bold, and the Drawing strong, and easy. But I own I cannot find out so many beauties in them as many people pretend to do.

[page left blank by Guise]

Sunday 3ʳᵈ June Genoa

We dined to day at Mʳ. Celesias, with a Mʳ. Balbi, Mʳ. Mainery and yᵉ. brother of Mʳ. Celesia. We staid there 'till near nine o'clock in yᵉ. Evening, when we went to the Doges, to whom we were presented by Mʳ. Mainery, Mʳ. Celesia being Ill. The present Doge is a Brignoly, about 64 years old. He received us very politely, 'tho with an air of reservedness, & Dignity. His wife was present, and behaved to us in a pleasing manner. Besides other Servants, he is attended by twelve men, whom they call his Pages, 'tho some of them perhaps are 60 years old. They are dressed in a sort of Spanish Habit, with open Sleeves. The employment of Doge does not seem very desirable. The profit of their place is small, as they receive but about 6,000 livres, and spend above 20,000 a year: They are Doge two years, during wᶜʰ. Time, they can not live in there own house, but are obliged to go to the Publick palace, which is a very large building, but not handsome, & unfurnished. They cannot go out of the Town, without the Consent of the Senate, and when they do must be accompanied by them: and never go far. They must not remain in office a quarter of an hour more than the two years: If they do, it is expressly said in some Law that they must be thrown out of Window. They have but very little power, being little more than president in the Councils: Their cheif priviledge seems to be that of, Proposing things to the Senate & Councils, wᶜʰ. is necessary so that indeed it is their fault if any thing contrary to their opinion is done; when proposed they have only one voice like yᵉ. other. The Doges have two hundred men for their Guard.

I have been reading lately the revolutions of Genoa in three volumes; no name.[1] They come as far as the peace of Aix-la-Chapelle in 1748. Genoa one of the first States in Italy that embraced Christianity. Sᵗ. Nazarre preached there about yᵉ. yʳ. 78. They were under the Romans till the invasion of the Goths. When these were drove from Italy, the Romans took it, & the Lombards under the Reign of their King Roharis[2] drove them out, and destroyed the Town almost, in yᵉ. year 638. It went into the hands of Charlemagne about 774, when he drove the Lombards from Italy. He gave it his son Pepin. They were governed by Counts, of whom Ademan was the first: Under him in the war against the Saracens they conquered Corsica, and took possession of it. About the year 888 when the power of Charlemagne in Italy was lessened, they

---

1   In Gibbon's diary, he states in the diary entry for 3 June that 'J'ai achevè l'historire des Revolutions de Gènes'. In Bonnard's note, he states the 'Histoire des Révolutions de Genes' was published anonymously in 1750, and was the first published work of Louis Georges Oudard Feudrix de Bréquigny.
2   Rothari

became independent, & chose Consuls. They afterwards chose a Governor, they called Podestat. About the year 1244 the parties of the Guelphs and Gibelines appear'd at Genoa: The former partisans of the Pope, & the latter of the Emperor. Spinola, & Doria, two very powerful families were chiefs of the Gibelines, and the Grimaldi, & Fiesques, equally powerful, were chiefs of the Guelphs. Genoa was tore to pieces by the ambition of these 4 Men for many years, & afterwards by that of four others. The Montaldo's, Fregosa's, Adorna's and the ....;[1] Bank of S[t]. George took its rise in the year; 1346. First Doge (a) created in the year 1339. They continued very unsettled, and torn to pieces by domestique Factions, or oppressed by the French, the Empire, or whatever power had a mind to conquer them, 'till about the year 1528, when Andrew Doria deliver'd them from under the Government of France, restored their Liberty; and settled the Republick in near the same form it is now. Disturbed only sometimes by the envy of some of their own body, or by the Ambition of some foreign power, they remained for the greatest part pretty free and unconquer'd 'till the year 1746 when they were taken by the Austrians, who made so ill an use of their Conquest, that the <u>people</u> in despair revolted, and deliver'd themselves from the Slavery the Austrians kept them under: They were restored to all their powers & priviledges by the Treaty of Aix-la-Chapelle in 1748, and have remained pretty quiet in themselves ever since.

(a) Boccanegra was his name

Monday 4th June – Genoa
Baron Wolfe & M[r]. Moula came here last night. We dined to day at M[r]. Celesias; and went with Mad: Celesia, and M[r]. Joseph Celesia as far as Vorena, the Palace of M: Lomeliny. It is a good house, but in no respect remarkable; has a fine view over the Sea. The Garden and Wood behind, the house are pretty. Came home; was raither low spirited. The Cause nearly the same, as that of coming here.

Tuesday 5th June – Genoa
We went this Morning to see some pictures at the Abbey of S[t]. Catherine, of the order of Benedictines. There is one representing the Deluge, by Dominicain, that is much esteem'd. The size of the Piece I guess to be about 20 In: by 30. In the distant view, the Arc; a number of Buildings; their tops appearing above the water, and Men and cattle swiming: & nearer to you, are others just preparing to save themselves, undress'd, & undressing, Crying, and expressing great distress.

[1] Left blank in diary

The Shadeing in this Picture, I thought very good; the Colouring fine, but raither dark; the figures distinct & natural, the distances well preserved, except that I dont well see how the waters could be so deep in one part, & there be none in the others, especially as the ground seems pretty even. It is certainly a fine Picture, but I should think hardly worth so much as they ask for it, which is 500 L.S^e. There is a very old picture by Luco Jordano, (I beleive). It is painted upon wood, and I think finely done: The Colouring is good, the Figures bold & natural. It represent S^t. Jerome and two other Saints.

A holy Family by Guido Reni: very well done, and a Crucifixion by Abba Dura [Albrecht Dürer], an exceedingly good Picture. At S^t. Stephens Church, there is a Picture over the great Altar Piece, which is said to be done, the lower part by Raphael, and the upper by Julio Romano. The Lower part is the stoneing of S^t. Stephens; In the upper our Saviour, and some other figures. The Picture seems in General a good Piece; but whether it was done by those two famous painters, is what I wont pretend to decide. It is not impossible, as I beleive they worked together sometimes, & that Julio Romano, was a Diciple of Raphael's.

We were introduced this Evening to a Mad: Pisanio:[1] an agreeable, & pretty woman. She had began to learn English, as many others at Genoa, have. We met a good deal of Company here: amongst others, M^r. Lottinger; he is of Lorraine, has lived much at Florence, and expects to go as Ministre of that place to England. He seems to be a man of knowledge; and agreable. We were received here, with the greatest politeness, and whatever may be the Caracter of the Genoese as for affairs of Business, I must do them the justness to say that they shew great politeness to strangers.

Wednesday 6th June – Genoa

We saw this Morning the Palace of Palavicini, Rue Lomelini. The house is well built and their are some good Rooms. Amongst the pictures, of which there are a good many, we took particular notice of two as better than the rest. One of them I beleived to be a Silenus between a young woman & a man: We thought it much in the manner of Rubens: Done by whom it may, it is certainly a good picture. The other, Diana & her Nymphs, and Actaeon, by Albani. This, tho far from a capital, is nevertheless a very pleasing Picture: The heads of the Women are fine & y^e. Figures easy & natural.

Thursday 7th June – Genoa

The Government of Genoa, consists, of a Great Council, little Council of 200,

---

1   Pesagno in Gibbon's Journal. According to Gibbon, she had learnt English 'dans l'attente du Duc de York'.

Senate of 19, and Doge; Ev'ry one that pays the Taxes regularly, and is noble, has a right, at the age of twenty one, to be of the Great Council, which is of no fixt number, and may be between 5 & 600: The small Council are 200 is chose out of the great: and out of the small Council is formed a Seminary, which is a number of people named by them to be candidates for the Senate: Out of this Seminary the Great Council chuse the Senators when there is a vacancy: and the Senate consists of 20, the Doge included. As each Doge at going out of his office, becomes a kind of honorary member, the Senate commonly is about 23 or 24. No one can be of the Senate, or petit Council, before 27. They have five Judges (a). Two for Criminal, & two for Civil affairs, & a President, who serves for both. They must be all Strangers, and serve only two years. A person of the Town or State, can not, nor never is, employ'd. They have another Civil majestrate, they call Podestat, who must be a Stranger also.

  The Genoese have no great number of Troops; perhaps about 4 or 5000, who are most of them in Towns on y[e]. Coast; or in those they have still in Corsica. They have a great number of arms in the Arsenal; which joins to the Palace: They have at present 4 Galleys: These Galleys carry from 450, to, 550 Men each. The largest w[ch]. has 550, has near 350 Rowers, five on a Bench, which serve them for a Bed, and to which they are chained ev'ry Evening. Each Galley carrys 3 pieces of canon, and a great number of small kind of Swivels. I was on board one of them which has been lately built, and has a Deck to it, and M[r]. Lomelino who built her told me she rows much faster than the others. This was the only one at this time in the Darsena. This is a kind of small port, within the other; The great one is reckoned very unsafe, & much exposed, except the Side next the Town, which is a little shelter'd by the Mole. The English never salute the Town, nor y[e]. Town the English. The Town is surrounded by a double fortification; one just round the town, the other round the Hills that command the Town, to the distance of 2 & 3 miles, and in Circumference make near 15 miles.

(a) They call these the Rota.

Friday 8th June – Genoa

I made this Morning the Tour of these works accompanied by M[r]. Jos: Celesia, and M[r]. Lomeliny commander of the port. We went out at Port Pilley, which is the east side of the Town towards Bisogno. This is much the weakest side of the Town, both in respect to the fortifications, & the situation: It is entirely commanded by a hill they call Madonna del Monte: on which the Genoese have built a Fortress. The farther one goes, the Fortifications become stronger naturally, as one ascends continually on the Edge of a Steep hill, 'till one comes to a place called l'Eperon, which is a great heigth above the Town, & three mile pretty near from it. At this place they erect a Battery which commands a hill called, Les Deux Freres; beyond les Deux Freres, is a very strong place called; Le Diamant. I was surprised here (a l'eperon) to find a breakfast prepared by the order of M^r. Celesia. This is north of Genoa: Not far from l'eperon at the same heigth is a strong place called Mont Morio. From hence one begins to descend, and this whole side is very strong by nature. On this side, I beleive without reach of y^e. fortifications, is, La Misericorde, which commands the valley of Polzavera and a little lower is a strong place they call .... [1]

Towards the bottom are many batteries to defend the Subarbs of S^t. Pietro d'Arena. These fortifications require about 600 pieces of Canon, & above 30,000 Men to defend them around. It is more indebted to nature than art for its strength; they are much neglected, & out of repair. We came in again by the Gate of S^t. Thomas not far from the Lanthorn west side. Genoa is thought to contain, Town & Suberbs near ninety Thousand inhabitants. The Genoese are much tired of having Corsica; there Affairs there are in a very bad way: They are obliged to impose high taxes, to borrow money of S^t. George; It keeps them in distress, hurts there trade, destroys their men, & almost ruins them. They are in treaty at present with France about it: They would be glad to get rid of it.[2]

Saturday 9th June – Genoa

The Town of Genoa makes a fine appearance as one comes in through the Suberbs of S^t. Pietro D'Arena. One sees the Town rising beautifully in a kind of amphitheatre above the port, which is just under it. The Town itself so well built and the number of palaces upon the hills round it, the port full of Ships, & the Sea opening beyond it, has a fine Effect. Many of the houses in the Town are entirely of Marble. La Rue Balbi is the longest & widest in Genoa, and is really handsome: La Rue Neuve is narrower, but entirely full of Palaces, many of them of Marble. The other Streets are all exceeding narrow, and from the goodness of y^e. paving and their neatness, look much like many of the Alleys in London. We took a walk this Evening in the Garden belonging to the palace of Prince Doria: The Palace is a long, plain old building, resembling more a prison than a palace; In the Garden is a fine Terrace, just above the port, & has a beautiful view f^m. it.

---

1   Left blank by Guise
2   Officially ceded to France in 1768.

Sunday 10ᵗʰ June – Genoa

Our design when we came here was to have staid only a fortnight, and went by Sea to Lerice, and from thence taken the post to Lucca, Pisa and Leghorn: to have staid there two or three days, and went on directly to Florence: We had hired a Felucca for 4 Sequins, for this purpose, and sent our Chaise & baggage aboard last Tuesday, hopeing to set out Wednesday Morning; but the wind very unfortunately changing in the night, has obliged us to stay here ever since, flattered ev'ry night with the hopes of its changing, and mortified ev'ry Morning, by hearing that it still continued East.

Monday 11ᵗʰ June – Genoa

The obstinate north east wind still detain'd us here, and as there was no prospect of its changing, we order'd our Chaise and baggage to be brought onshore, resolveing to trust no longer to the winds, but to pass the Bochetto once more, and go by Placentia [Piacenza], Parma &c. We accordingly paid our Patron, half price, and took leave of our Felucca.

Genoa has a very considerable Trade in Silks, Velvets, and some other Stuffs.

Tuesday 12ᵗʰ June – Genoa to Castel Sᵗ. Jeovanni [Castel San Giovanni]

Finding the wind continued deaf to our prayers, and fixt steadily against us, we also continued as steady to the resolution we had taken yesterday, and accordingly left Genoa at 4 o'clock this Morning. We were obliged to pass the Bochetto again, and continued the Road to Milan as far as Voghera where the road to Placentia, turns off to the right: We went to day no farther than Castel Sᵗ. Jeovanni (a), within two posts of Placentia. [Piacenza] The road from Voghera to this place is pretty good, the Country very flat and well cultivated.

(a) In the Duchy of Placentia

Wednesday 13ᵗʰ June – to Placentia and Parma

Early this Morning we continued our Journey, and got to Placentia before eight o'clock. The road continues good and the Country fruitful: within about 1L: of the Town one crosses the river Trebbia, which 'tho in summer, becomes (like many of the rivers here, which come from the Mountains), very large in winter. Here is a plain near yᵉ. river which was the Seat of a Battel between Hannibal and the Romans (a).

(a) In y^e. y^r. 535 of Rome 36,000 foot and 4000 Horse under the command of Tib: Sempronius Longus were defeated by about 28000 ft: & 10000 horse under Hannibal. P: Cornelius Scipio the other Consul had been wounded just before at the Battle of the Tessin.

As soon as we had breakfasted, we walked out to see the Town. In the large Square before the Town House are two large Equestrian Statues in Bronze; and on each side of the Pedestals, two brass Basso relieveos; on the End of the Pedestals, brass plates signifiing to whom they were erected. These inscriptions shew, that one of them, represents Alexander Farnese, third duke of Parma and Placentia, Conqueror of the netherlands &c. &c., and that the People of Placentia put up this Statue out of Gratitude for the many benefits the City had received from him. The Inscription upon the other says y^t. the City of Placentia had erected this Equestrian Statue to Rainuccio Farnese fourth duke of Milan, out of gratitude for his great care in distributing Justice, promoting arts, increasing the number of his people &c. &c. They are both cloathed in the Greek manner; have a loose flowing Robe over their Shoulder, which seems well done. They have both of them a Truncheon in their right hands. That of Alexandre is down; the other is liffted up. The first is much the most esteem'd, and I own I think it the best, 'tho not any great difference. The heads of the men are well done, the bodys may likewise, but they seem to me ill placed. There is a good deal of Fire, and life in the horses; They are in General pretty well formed, nevertheless they have some visible faults, especially in the Legs which are lifted up: It is impossible to see anything worse than the hind one, this is placed forward under the horse, seeming afraid to touch the Ground, and the whole limb so stiff, y^t. you must think him Lame. They are both made by Moca [Francesco Mochi], a scholar of Jean de Boulogne [Giambologna]. We went from hence to the Cathedral where there are some good Paintings. Over the great Altar in the Choir is a good Picture in oyl, by Procaccino. It represents a sick person in a bed: the Colouring seems good, but very dark. On each Side of the Altar are two large Pictures in oyl, by Louis Caracci, and just before these, the Arched part of the roof, is painted in Fresco by the same person. The Ground of this last is a sky blue. Upon it are several Angels in different attitudes, which all seem very natural, and the fore-short'ning (raccourci) excellent: Their is great variety and expression, the Colouring very fine and pleasing. The angels are all very large, but one of them, which is almost Colossal, puts me more in mind of a Hercules, than an Angel, only he has wings. These are fine paintings, and well preserved. In a Chapel on the left hand is a picture of S^t. Martin, by August: Caracci; not very fine. The Cupola is very finely painted in Fresco, by Guercino: It is divided into eight parts, runing to a point at the top of y^e. Cupola. As the Cupola is not large I think those divisions have a bad effect, and make it look smaller than it is. In each division is the Figure of a Prophet, pretty large, and accompanied by several Angels. These pieces appear to me to be admirably well done in ev'ry respect; the figures natural and full of expression, the Colours very strong, but butiful, the lights & Shades well preserved, and the distances well observed: Below this is a kind of Frese, wth. the figures of Children, and below these last some large figures, and story's out of the new Testament. These are all well done, and by the same hand. There are one or two more pretty good pieces, of which I have forgot the names. The Architecture or ornamenting of this Church is, not remarkable. From hence we went to S^t. Augustin, a Church built by Vignola. It is large and handsome, but what pleased us the most, was the manner in which the Chapels are disposed. Instead of being let in, and shut up between the Sides of the wall, they are quite open; and there is only a Row of pillars, which run before them, equal with those that support the Roof of the Church. These have an admirable effect, and make the Church appear much better, lighter, and more pleasing than as they commonly are, when the Side Chapels are buried in the wall: I do not think some other parts of this Church are so well contrived, or built with the same art.

Near this Church is a very large and handsome Convent of Roquelins. There are two or three large Courts, surrounded with handsome Piazza's or Corridor's: At the end of one of these we saw fixed in the walls 30 different Stones with inscriptions that have been found in the neighbourhood of Placentia. I copied one of them from a Stone that may be about 5 long and 3 wide which was as follows.

P. Aufidius L. F. (a) I-I-I-I Vir. I-I Vir
Tr. Milit.Praef. Fab. Sibi et
L. Aufidio C. N. F. Patri et
Fadianae P. F. Matri et
L. Aufridio L. F. fratri I-I-I-I Vir et
Liburniae L. F. Consobrinae
Factum ex testament M-S (b) CIC arbitratu
C. Annisidi C. F. Rufi

(a) May signify Lucii Filius, or, Legum favendorum
(b) signifies: Mille sestertium

Most of the others, as well as this relate to People & Families y[r]. have been buried near this place.

We went from hence to see the Palace, which is built by Vignola. We were disapointed by finding a very large, plain building of Brick, quite unfinished. As the Duke seldom or never lives, or comes here, it is likewise quite unfinished, for which reason we did not take the pains of going into it. The town 'tho not remarkably well built, is nevertheless neat, and looks pretty well, there is one very long, wide street, that looks very handsome, only one of the sides is the greatest part nothing more than a plain wall, and very few houses. The Town is pretty large, but ill people: They told us there might be about 25,000 inhabitants. The fortifications are not very strong.

Placentia is situated upon the Emilian Road (Via Amilia), it became a Roman Colony about the 530th year of Rome: Cremona was about the same time, and both of them were made very strong. M. Livius Solinator, and L: Amilius Paulus Consuls.

After having spent about 4 hours in examining ev'ry thing we could hear of, that deserved our attention, we only staid long enough to dine, and went this Evening to Parma which is five Posts farther, where we arrived in good time, and went to lodge at La Maison de Poste. Nothing can be finer or pleasanter than the road from Placentia to Parma.

If Italy is remarkable for its productions of Art, and the Cabinets, and Gallerys of its Princes for the beautiful works of its antient artists, I think it not much less so, for the Productions of Nature, and the beautiful Pictures, the States and dominions of many of its Princes produce at present. Those of the Duke of Parma, are an example of it. The Fertility of the Soyl, helped by the hand of the Cultivator, offers you the most beautiful Picture of Plenty, and richness. Near the road, and as far as I could see, the Fields are filled with vineards and Corn, that seem in the highest state of perfection. The vines are planted in Rows at a pretty considerable distance from each other; between these is planted ev'ry kind of Grain, which all grow as fine as possible: The country being very flat, and many Rivers comeing from the Po, & the mountains, they have great conveniences for watering the Grounds. The Country appears raither too much inclosed, from the number of Trees, that grow in the hedges and Fields.

I found at the Inn, M[r]. Mercin, and M[r]. Raymond,[1] who spent the winter before last at Lausanne at the same pension with myself. M[r]. Mercin is a Dutch Gentleman of a Considerable fortune in Zealand. He is a very good natured man, but his natural Talents dont appear very extraordinary, as much

---

1   Mersens and Reyman in Gibbon's Journal.

improved; 'tho M^r. Gibbons as well as myself think that Italy has furnished him with a few more Ideas, than he had at Lausanne. M^r. Raymond his Governor, will never help to improve him. I went to the Opera with these Gentlemen: The Opera house is large, and the Scenery very handsome; Neither the Singers, nor dancers very extraordinary. Two Italians and a German pretty good singers. The Duke of Parma was there, but as he was inCog: he sat in a side Box near the Stage, and not in the Front Box.

Thursday 14th June – Parma

We went this morning to see the Cathedral; a handsome building, but chiefly remarkable for the Cupola painted by Corregio. The seeing of this really gave me more pain than pleasure, as one cannot help being very sorry to find so celebrated a piece of this great painter, so entirely ruined as that is, by the wet runing through it. The greatest part of the Figures in the Cove of the Cupola are quite spoiled: there are only about three or four that remain in any degree perfect, and they are considerably damaged. It represented the Assumption of the Virgin. There are some Figures of Saints in the lower part, & in the four Corners that are raither more perfect. Had I not known by whom it had been done, I should not have taken much pains to look for beauties, which I own I searched for almost in vain. In a little Chapel under the Cathedral, we were shewn two Statues, very well worth observation. Tho the work of some common artist (whose name I have forgot) perhaps they might bear being placed near the Statues of some of the more Celebrated. They are the Figures of two women sitting, and leaning upon the monument of a deseased Friend or Parent. I never saw Affliction so naturally expressed, as in the faces and features of these two women. It is almost impossible to see them, without partakeing of their Grief. One of them is weeping, the other appears still sadder, by not being able to releave her Grief by Tears. The Attitudes and drapery are likewise admirably done. Nothing can be more natural than one of them who setting side ways on the Tomb, cross leg'd, & appearing not to have room enough to set firm, supports herself a little by the foot wch. just touches the Ground. In short one would imagine that the Chisel which had been capable of produceing these animated representations of Sorrow, could not fail of succeeding in other works; which they say he never has. We went from hence to S^t. John's Church, where there is a Cupola painted by Corregio, which 'tho perfect in comparason of that we had just seen at the Cathedral, is nevertheless a little damaged by rains or damps. Quite in the Top of the Cupola is Our Saviour, in the lower part a number of saints. The Figures are Colossal, and 'tho at so considerable a heigth appear to me much too large.

The Colouring and shadeing seems lively, strong, and natural, but from the Cupola being raither narrow, & ill lighted and from the great heigth one can hardly judge properly of them. I cannot help thinking it a great pity that so good painters have ever bestowed so much of their art in ornamenting parts of the building so little calculated for shewing their works to advantage. For besides that the light falls upon them is commonly very bad, and the position of the Figures very disadvantageous, it is impossible that the Spectator can hold himself in a manner necessary for seeing them, either for any considerable time, or with any ease and pleasure. So that he must either deprive himself of the pleasure of considering a fine painting, or else put himself to great pain, and almost break his neck, if he does do it.

In a Chapel on the left hand side of this Church are two Pictures by Corregio: They are both good, but one of them appears to me, much finer than the others. That which represents our Saviour dead, the Virgin on one side, and the Magdalene on the other is most admirably done: It is difficult to say which of the Figures is the best. The lifelessness of the body of our Saviour, which is a little raised, and leaning against something; the exstream Affliction of the Virgin, greater than that of the Magdaleine, which nevertheless appears very strongly, are all so well expressed that one is almost in doubt to which one must give the preference.

We went next to see the Great Theatre, built by Palladio; It is in the same manner as the antient Amphiteatres, and certainly much preferable to our Moderne ones both for the Spectator, and the Actor. The Stage I found to be about 50 of my Pace's; The Parterre about 35. The open seats rise round the parterre, and consist of 14 Steps above each other: Above these are two Galleries, the first of which make the boxes, the second quite at the Top serve for the rows of benches that are behind them. These Gallery's are formed of Arches, between which are Pillars, the first of the Dorick, the Second of the Ionick Order. The upper Gallery finishes by a Cornish, wch. runs all round, and over each Arch, is placed a Statue. The front of the Stage is much ornamented; on each side are handsome Pillars and Pillastres, the Capitals of the Corinthian order, and Gilt (a): Just before the Stage are two large Equestrian Statues of Alexandre, and Rainucci Farnese, the latter of which caused this Theatre to be built. The form of it, is Oval.

(a) Over the Great doors, comeing into the Theatre

The whole of this is certainly very well contrived, both for beauty & use, but the Gallerys have the most pleasing Effect: The Arches are well turned

& the Pillars very light and Elegant. This Theatre is also very remarkable for carrying the Sound. A person upon the stage 'tho he does not speak loud, may be heard very distinctly to the most distant part of the Theatre. To be certain of this, one of us went upon the Stage, while the other went to different distances, and we found we heard equally well at the upper Gallery, as at the bottom or middle. I cannot say that there is no Echo, but it is really inconsiderable, and one perceives it less quite at Top, than in the other parts. They told us that this Theatre will contain 15,000 people, but I think one may venture to reduce that number, about the same as the measure of it, which they said was 580 feet in length, and I am very certain, that from wall to wall, it is not 300. The Expence of lighting it is so great, that they never make use of it but upon very extraordinary occasions of rejoycing &c.

After dinner we went to the Academy, where we spent the afternoon in the most agreable manner, in examineing, the antiquities found at Velleia [Veleia Romana], and admireing the most beautiful picture of Corregio's. Velleia, which was the antient name of the Town, is now called Vallera, in the Maps I beleieve, Villora; It is situated about 3 Miles S:E: of Parma. It was a very considerable place in the time of the Romans: We could not learn at present, the exact time of its being lost, 'tho we were told they imagined it to be about the years 102, or 103. The first discovery's that were made of it, were in the years 1745, or 6, that some peasants found a very large Plate of Brass (a), on which is wrote a kind of Contract, by which, Trajan engages himself to provide for a Certain number of Children, that were to be educated in that place, seting forth also how much they were each to have, and the rules of the place. The Caracters are so old, so close together, and difficult to read at first sight, and without being a little used to these things, that we are obliged to trust to the person that shew'd it us, <u>chiefly</u>, for this account. An account of this Inscription has been printed by M^r. Muratori; but so few copies were taken, that we are told it will be impossible to get one. They keep one of them here, but we could not examine it much.

(a) The people that found it being desirous each of them to have a part, broke
it into several parts, but in such a manner as not to hurt the writeing much

Since the finding of this Table, the Duke of Parma, has employed workmen to dig there, who have found the remains of a great many houses, the plans of which are shewn at the Academy.

They have likewise found a great many, Statues, and inscriptions, and many little figures in Bronze; We saw some of them that had bene placed in a large Room (designed for the Library) on purpose to shew them to the D: of York, when he was there. There is a Statue, of Nero when he was young, which seemed to be a pretty good one; It is very perfect but the Arms, which had been broke off, were not put on again, 'tho they have them very entire; Near this was found the Statue of a woman, which they beleive to be an Agrippina: The head and arms of this are wanting, but the rest of it is much the finest piece of Sculpture I have ever seen: The drapery, which appears to have been of a very fine Stuff (a) and is folded round the body very close, is so admirably finished that one sees the form of the body and limbs, perfectly well. Nothing can be more natural or more nicely finished than this figure; and M^r. Strange who had seen it, said, that if the head and arms were equally well done, he should think it equal, if not superior, to any thing he had seen in Italy.

(a) It lies so close to ye. body that it almost appears to have been waisted

We saw two very good little figures in Bronze; one a Hercules; the other, a Victory. There are several stones with Inscriptions upon them, but they would not give us leave to Copy any of them, as the Duke intends haveing an Account of them published: By the help of our memory however, we made a Shift to steal one of them, I beleive pretty exactly, except that I am not quite certain if some more of the words should not be abbreviated. ----

Ti: Claudio Cæsari.

Augusto. Germanico.Ponti.

Max. Tr. Pot.11. Imp.111

Consul. Designato. 111

P: P.

D.   D:

Most of the others likewise relate to the time of Claudius. There are many more Statues, Busts, Inscriptions, and other things that have been found at Velleia, and which are not shewn. They have found a great number of Medals chiefly Bronze, but which they told us were kept at the place, & that we could not see them. The Duke keeps 40 men constantly employed in digging, so that they are in hopes of finding something more remarkable, before they publish an account of it: They are very secret about it at present, so that it is allmost impossible to know half what one should be glad to learn, concerning it.

In this same Room is the Picture I mentioned before. It represents the Virgin, and our Saviour when an Infant; The Magdalene kissing his feet; S^t.

Jerome; and an Angel. One is almost in doubt which part of this Picture to admire the most; but if there is any difference, the figures of Our Saviour, the Magdalane, & the Angel are the most butiful. The features of the Infant are not the most pleasing, but than they are filled with a liveliness, and expression one seldom sees; In the face of the Magdalane one discovers more beauty, sweetness, and innocent satisfaction, than one would imagine could be expressed by painting, and when one looks at the Angel, one sees his joy & happiness represented in the most pleaseing manner; In short the Figures are so natural and full of Grace, the Coulouring so butiful and delicate, and the execution of the whole so admirable, that one can never be satisfied with looking at it, or quit it without regret. This Picture is equally fresh & butiful, as if it was just finished; It belongs to a Church that is just built from the revenues ariseing from an abbey that there was not long since, but the Duke of Parma, without the least right to it, has taken possession of it. Some years since the King of Poland offer'd 17000 Sequins(a) for it, but the duke hearing of it stopt it, just as the Price was agreed upon, and had it put in the Cathedral, from whence he had it removed by a party of his Grenadiers, to the Academy where it is now. One cannot help observing, when one sees this butiful piece, that Corregio was not quite so good a Chronologist as Painter, as I beleive that the Magdalane was not acquainted with our Saviour, when he was an Infant, and S^t. Jerome lived in the fifth Century. However it is impossible to see the Picture, and not forget, or forgive such a mistake, if it was really done by accident. We were deprived of seeing the famous Farnese Library, and Cabinet, as the late Duke of Parma when he went to Naples, took ev'ry part of it with him; so that one must defer that pleasure a little longer. The Duke distributes annually Premiums for the best paintings, drawings, plans of buildings &c; We saw a good many of them here, but no very good ones; An Englishman had the two last Premiums, for the best plans of buildings. We went from hence to see the Dukes Garden, wch. is just by. It is large & handsome, divided into very wide walks, & openings.

    (a) We were told by our valet de place, that he was certain the K: of Poland had offer'd 30,000 Sequins; but it's hardly credeble.

Friday 15th June – Parma

In the Church of S^t. Sepulchre we saw: S^t. Joseph gathering some palm-bows, the Virgin, & the Child, by Corregio. The Colours are weak, and the Figures not near so butiful in my opinion as those of that great master commonly are; however tho it does not please me much, I shall not dispute its merit. There is a good Picture by Annibal Caracci in the Church, des Capuchins.

We saw two or three more Churches, neither remarkable for Paintings, or for the Architecture. The Duke of Parma's Palace is far from being magnificent: – There is one very large handsome Salloon; the other rooms are very good and convenient, and the house altogether would be reckoned very handsome for a Private Gentleman.

The Duke is a middle sized, well looking man; very fond of the French: His subjects I beleive, wish he was not quite so fond of shew, and expensive amusements as he is (a). He has a Son about 13 years of age, under a very able governor. His Daughter is not a year younger, than her Brother. Parma was a Roman Colony, but something later than Placentia. Its fortifications are not very strong. We were told that the Town contains near 50,000 Souls, but I much doubt of it; especially as I see by a map I bought there, that in an account given of them, they are only computed at 25,000. The Duke has three Regiments of Troops; viz: The Guards; Reg[t]. Of Parma and of Placentia. These should make six Battalions of 500 Men each, but by an account M[r]. Gibbon gives me of one the Battalions he saw exercise, they are very incomplete, and bad in all respects.

(a) His revenues are computed at about 150 thousands pounds sterling

[end of first volume]

Haveing examined ev'ry thing we could hear was worth the Attention of a Traveller at Parma, we left it this Evening, and went as far as Regio (a) [Reggio nell'Emilia]. We were fortunate in comeing just at this time, being during the Fair, when the Duke himself comes there, and the best Company from Modena, and the neighbourhood assemble at this place; The D: Of Modena has the power of makeing the Fair last as long, or as little time as he pleases: It holds commonly two Months or longer. It is a great advantage to the Country as there is no duty or Toll, paid for the things that are brought to it.

(a) Regio is two posts from Parma. They reckon about 7 miles to a Poste but they differ very much: some are but 6, others 10 miles

During the time of the Fair there are Opera's, Balls, Redotto's[1] and other Diversions. Comeing here early in the Evening we took a walk in the Fair which is held in a long Street, over which are spread Cloths for keeping off the sun or wet: In a Room on one side, where we went to eat Ice's, we met

1   Ridotto. Casino

a <u>sort</u> of Gentleman, who seeing we were Foreigners, spoke to us in French and proposed going with us to a Redotto yt. was to be to night; but knowing nothing of him, we excused ourselves fm. going wth. him, & leaving him, we returned to our Inn, where, as we were in a travelling dress, we sent for some Bahouts,[1] and Masks, and went to the Redotto, about 10 o'clock. As soon as we came into the Room, we met our new Acquaintance, who soon discover'd himself to be a phisician of Mirandola, come to Regio to speak to the Duke upon Business.

He was of some use to us here, as he told us some things about the place &c, and shew'd us the Duke, and Family who were all dressed just like our selves, except that they wore their masks, & we put them in our hats. There were several of the Princesses playing in mask at Pharaoh.[2] The Hereditary Princess did not.

Dispute between y^f D: of Modena and Son. Our Doctor told us with great pleasure that the Duke and his Son were reconciled; Upon which we asked him, when they had quarrel'd, & the Subject of the Dispute. He told us it was about marrying the Prince's Daughter to one of the Archdukes of Austria. They had promised that she should have the Arch-Duke Leopold, third son of the Emperor, but upon the death of the Second Son, and upon Leopolds being named Grand Duke of Tuscany, the Empress said, that it was not Leopold that was meant, in any other light y^n. as third Son of the Emperor, & that as he was now become the Second, the Princess of Modena must content herself with the Third. The D: of Modena, it is imagined for some profitable reason agreed to it but his Son would not. The Father insisted upon it, and the Son would not consent to it; upon which the Duke confined his Son, and sent his Grand daughter to Milan: He was kept in confinement above two years, 'till at length he was obliged to consent. During his Confinement he was treated in the most cruel manner, in respect to seeing his Friends, and manner of living. I think that this must give one a bad opinion both of the Dukes sense, and principles: the latter indeed are never expected to be very scrupulous in a prince, but one would imagine he should have been glad to have had his Granddaughter Great Duchess of Tuscany. As there was but little Company here, and that that was, play'd at Cards we retired Early.

Saturday 16th June – Regio

We went this Morning to see some Churches. In a Cathedral there is a picture by Annib: Caracci: It expresses our Saviour an Infant, and the Virgin in the

---

1   Masquerade clothes (Bonnard, p 253)
2   A card gambling game

Clouds: below, several Angels, and on each side the figure of a Saint. Cochin[1] speaks much of this Picture, and I make no doubt of its having had much merit; But the Colouring is become so dark and black, and it is in so very bad a light, that I cannot say I saw anything in it very pleasing. A la Capella del Morte there are several pictures wch. I beleive may not be bad; an Annunciation, by Guercino, appear'd to me a very good one: Both the figure of the Angel and of the Virgin are excellent, the Colouring is bright, strong, and natural. This is a pleasing piece, and much the best in the Chapel.

A L'Oratoir de S^t. Etienne: A dead Christ: This is very natural, & well executed; We were told it is a Corregio. In the Church of La Madonna della Giarra [Ghiara], there is a picture by Guercino, esteemed pretty good; another by Leon: Spada, and some paintings in Fresco by Terrini: I can not say I could find any great beauties in them. The Church is much the handsomest, and best built of any here. These are the Chief things we could hear of at Regio.

In the Evening we went to the Opera: The Duke was there; He looks old, & has a very disagreable Countenance. The Theatre is large, and Scenery much varied & handsome. A pretty good Troop of Actors &c, & their dresses very rich. One of the best singers was Giovanni Manzoli,[2] who we are told is engaged to go to England for 1500L per ann and a benefit night, but which he thinks too little. 'Tho he sung well, I think I have heard much better singers: The Opera was L'Ezio. At leaving the Opera we immediately set out for Modena, which is three Posts from Regio. We got there about 3 o'clock in y^e. Morning. The road from Parma to Modena is as good, & the Country as beautiful and Fertile as can be. The Ground at present is loaded with ev'ry kind of Grain: Besides the Common sorts, they have great Crops of Hemp. The Country is very flat so that the views, can not be much varied, but the ritchness of the Soyl furnishes the inhabitants of y^e. country, a prospect more pleasing y^n. hills and vales.

Sunday 17th June – Modena

Library. Getting up very late this Morning, and the weather being hot, we did not stir out till after dinner, when we went to the Dukes Library. We were shewn it by a Jesuit, who has the Care of it at present. It is a very large and handsome Room, and the Cases for the Books, are well contrived, and very well made. They have between 20 & 30 thousand printed Books, besides near 8000 Manuscripts. Of the former we were shewn several English ones, and the Antiquities of Herculaneum: Amongst the latter the Jesuit told us there are

1   Cochin, Charles-Nicholas, *Voyage d'Italie ou recueil de notes sur les ouvrage de peinture et de sculpture qu'on voit dans les principales villes d'Italie*. Paris, 1752 (3 volumes)

2   Giovanni Manzuoli (1720-1782). An Italian castrato. He went to London later that year.

some, very ancient and Curious. We had not time to examine them so much as these kind of things required.

Palace. We went from hence to the Palace, which is a very handsome building: The front of the Entrance, is built with three different orders above each other, and looks very elegant, 'tho it may have some defects, according to the strict rules of Architecture: The Court is very handsome: Two Arcades one upon the other, run round it; The Stairs going up to the Apartments are very wide, and noble. The first Room one comes into is a large Salloon, raither too high; at one end, is a door into a Chapel; and at the other end one goes into a Suit of very handsome Rooms: They are well furnished, but what one admires most are the Pictures of which in my opinion there are many very good ones: It being late in the Evening we resolved to defer the examination of this Collection 'till the next day, when we could see it more leasurely and by a better light. We therefore took a walk about the Town. 'Tho the houses are not finely built, they have nevertheless a very good appearance: The Streets are in general, wide, regular, and many of them have Arcades on each Side. The town is not very large, 'tho we were told that it contains 20,000 Inhabitants. It is fortified; but like most of those in this part of Italy, not able to make any very long defense.

Monday 18th June – Modena

We bestowed two or three hours this Morning upon the Cabinets of the Duke, which is very curious, and worthy the observation of a Traveller. We were first shewn some antique pieces of Sculpture, amongst which I took particular notice of the following. An arm, and hand of the purest white Marble: It is impossible to see any thing worked with greater nicety, with more art, and more naturally than this is; Nothing but the Colour can make one think it the work of art. The Polish and whiteness made me suspect its antiquity, but when ever it was done it does honor to the Artist. Andromeda tied to the Rock, very well executed in white marble. Hercules killing Cacus, and the mouth of a Cave, with one of the Oxen in it, that Cacus had stolen: The figures of Hercules and Cacus, appear to me very natural; The Strength of the first & the fury of the other, are well express'd. Besides these, there are two or three antique heads, that have their merit, I make no doubt. In the Cabinets there are some very large Cups and other things made of single pieces of Agate & other Stones.

In a Case on one side of the room, are several small Grecian and Egyptian figures, and antiquities: amongst which a Cistrum,[1] is the most

---

1   Sistrum – an Egyptian instrument

Curious; it is but small & ill worked. Upon a Stand in the middle of the Room is a very extraordinary Casette, or kind of Chest made entirely of Amber: It is something like a Temple or building of that kind: The Front and sides, are ornamented with different sorts of Pillars, some twisted and some plain; between them are pieces of Basso relievos of Ivory. A door opens in the front and you see in the inside a little altar. It is very nicely worked, and the amber of a fine Colour and Polish, and altogether is a very Curious Chest. We were next shewn the Medals, of which here are between eight and ten thousand. They have no gold ones, but we may hope to see them at Florence, as they were sold and sent there. There is a very good suit of consular ones, in Silver, as well as of the Emperors &c in Copper: But I think the Greek Medals are the most perfect and beautiful I have ever seen. There are none at all relateing to Towns or Colonies. We saw a very uncommon Medallion, which we did not understand, neither did those with us. On one side are the heads of Antoninus Aurelius, and Verus, wth. this inscription: Antonin. Cos.III. Verus. Cos. II. On the Reverse, a Triumphal Chariot, and over: Imp: II. Cos. II. Under German. victis. There are many very rare and curious pieces in this Collection. After the Medals we were shewn a very great number of engraved Stones: rare, not only for the nature of the Stones, but for the manner of their being engraved: Many of them are fine Antiques; and others, 'tho modern equally well done. There is besides in this Cabinet a great number of Prints and drawings, which we had not time to see, except some designs of Raphaels, which seemed to be very unfinished sketches: Here are also many natural curiosities, extraordinary pieces of workmanship of different sorts, and other things proper for a Cabinet of that sort.

Palace, and Pictures. We went from hence to the Palace to take a Second view of the Pictures, amongst which the following were those that pleased me the most. 1st: A S^t. Francois, by Guido Reni. There is a great deal of expression in this. One sees the S^t. is praying wth. fervor: the Colours are not very bright, but natural. 2nd: A Young Woman, by S^r. Peter Leli: The goodness of this, exclusive of its being done by a Countryman, would induce me to mark it. The figure is natural, and elegant: the Colours, lively, soft, and delicate. It appears to me a little in the manner of Rubens. 3rd. A Roman Charity, by And. Sacchi: This is an admirable picture: The beauty of the Colours, and the force of Expression is very great. 4th. Our Saviour bound between two Men: a fine piece by, Michael Angelo de Caravaggio. 5. A dead Christ, the Virgin on one side weeping; very well done, by Guercino. 6th. The Prodigal Son, returned to his Father: 7th.. Susanna and the Elders; both excellent pictures; by Spada. 8th. S^t. Rock, by Guido Reni. This is a Capital painting.

You see S{.superscript} Rock as big as life, inclineing a little to one side; over him, an Angel in the Air; very large; & just before the Saint; a Dog, likewise very large. It is one of the finest pictures I have yet seen; Nothing can be better proportioned, bolder, and more strikeing than the Saint, nothing more pleasing and expressive than the Angel, or more easy and natural than the Dog. The Colouring is of a kind of Grey: The shadeing strong, but just and natural. In short, it seems to be a Chef d'oeuvre. 9{.superscript}th{.superscript}. and 10{.superscript}th{.superscript}. Two Pictures by Titien. One represents the Woman taken in Adultery, and the other the Virgin, our Saviour an Infant, and S{.superscript}t. John, and a man; The first is said to be done in his first manner of painting, the other in his last manner. They are both extreamly beautiful, and much too well done, for me to decide w{.superscript}ch. is the best. In the first there are a great many Figures, the Heads of which are in general very fine; Some parts of the <u>Adulteress herself</u> seem to me raither clumsy, and the Colour of the flesh too yellow, w{.superscript}ch. may possibly be owing to time. The Colouring of this, is darkish, inclineing to a kind of red; That of the other, is more lively, & to me, more pleasing. They are both so well done, it is difficult to know which to prefer. 11{.superscript}th{.superscript}. A most beautiful Madonna, by Louis Caracci. 12{.superscript}th{.superscript}. The four Seasons by Annib: Caracci, represented by four figures. Galathea in a Sea shell, for the water. Pluto, for Fire; Venus, a Cupid, and two Doves, for the Air; and Juno, or some woman, for the Earth: I don't understand y{.superscript}e. last. They are all seen en raccourcis, and very well executed. Here are many more certainly worth observation; Several heads by Titien; some pictures by Tintoretto, particularly four small ones, placed in the cieling of y{.superscript}e. 2{.superscript}nd{.superscript} or 3{.superscript}rd{.superscript}: Room: In the Chapel a Copy of y{.superscript}e. famous Night of Coreggio &c. &c.

After dinner we went to the Cathedral, where we saw an admirable Picture, done by Guido Reni. You see S{.superscript}t. Simeon holding our Saviour in his arms; The Virgin kneeling, before an Altar; a little Girl holding two Pigeons, on one side; on the other a little boy, playing w{.superscript}th. two more, upon a kind of Table; Besides these there are several other figures. One perceives in the look of the virgin, an air of simplicity and nobleness, accompanied w{.superscript}th. a great deal of respect and devotion: Most of the other figures are equally natural & well done. The Colouring is a little dark. We went to see several other Churches, but did not find them remarkable, either for the Architecture, or for Paintings.

State of Modena. The Revenues of the Duke of Modena, are estimated at about a hundred, and fifty thousand pounds pr:ann: – He keeps six thousand men, which is thought too many in proportion to his Income, as he is obliged to tax his subjects pretty high. They reckon in all his Dominions fall four

hundred thousand Souls. The Hereditary Prince has only one Daughter; &
in case he has no Son, the Dutchy of Modena, falls to the Empress.

Nothing remaining for us to see at Modena, we left it this Evening,
and went as far as Boulogna, three posts farther. The road continues very
good; the Country, flat but very fruitful, and well cultivated. We took leave
this Evening of M[rs]. Mercin & Raimond, who accompanied us f[m]. Parma.

Tuesday 19th June – From Boulogna to Florence

Road to Florence. Being told by ev'ry one that Boulogna would require at least
three weeks for to see it well, and being very sensible we should have both more
advantage, and pleasure in seeing it, when we understood a little more Italian,
we resolved not to loose our time here now, but to make the best of our way
to Florence, and to stop here in our return. We therefore set out between 3
& 4 this Morning, and did not reach Florence before 9 in the Evening. The
distance from Boulogna, is nine Posts: the road is very well made, many parts
of it paved, but the Country is very uneaven, and Hilly. At the first Post from
Boulogna we were obliged to take six horses to go up a hill pretty steep, and
which brought us amongst the Mountains, or raither Hills, for they are not
very high. These hills continue more or less quite to Florence, which makes
the road disagreable. One passes through no very considerable place & many
of the post houses are quite alone: The Country is mostly uncultivated and
uninhabited. As soon as we came to Florence, we went to Mr Charles Atkin's[1],
an Englishman who has kept a house for strangers for above........... The
price of living at this house we found to be, six Pauls (a) a head for eating, and
five for an apartment, the Servants Room included: We indeed were obliged
to pay six pauls a day for our apartement, as it was very large, and towards
the River. We lay to night in a ground apartment in another house he has,
the opposite side of the Street: In the two houses he can lodge above twenty
people; Most of the apartments very good & pretty cool in Summer.

(a) pr: day.

Wednesday 20th June – Florence

Arrival Florence. Not being fixt in our rooms, this day has passed raither
disagreeably, as commonly happens at first comeing into a strange Town: In
the Evening, made our visit to S[r]. Horace Mann[2] Resident from England.

1   In Gibbon's diary, this person is referred to as Charles Hatfield, in fact Charles Hadfield. His hotel
     'became celebrated among English travellers in the later eighteenth century' – Ingamells. He
     features, holding a punch bowl, in a caricature painting by Thomas Patch
2   Sir Horace Mann, 1706-86. First cousin once removed to Guise. A very significant figure in

Thursday 21ˢᵗ June – Florence

To day has passed in the same uninteresting manner as yesterday; only Sʳ. Hor: Mann; Mʳˢ. Ponsonby,[1] & Swinborne,[2] and Capt. Hatsel[3] came to see us.

Friday 22ⁿᵈ June – Florence

Abbey Pillory. I took my first Lesson of Italien this Morning from the Abbey Pillory,[4] who is much recommended by all who have learned of him: He understands English very well, as they say, but he certainly pronounces it very ill. He has translated several English Plays into Italien. We went this morning to see Sʳ. Hor: Mann, who with the usual politeness, that he shews alwais to his Countrymen, desired we would look upon his Box in the Theatre as our own: We accepted his Offer, and accordingly went to the Opera this Evening. The House is not very large; we heard the Comic Opera of La Contadina Bizarre; not a very good Piece; the Singers very indifferent:

Saturday 23ʳᵈ June – Florence

My Lesson of Italien employed me 'till nine o'clock; I after wrote to my Sister;[5] and we then returned a visit we had received yesterday from Ld. Fordwick:[6] He has been at Florence near five years, unable to draw himself from the Charms of La Marchi: de Corci; It may be hoped he will leave her soon as they say, he does not like her much at present.

Sunday 24ᵗʰ June – Florence

All the English except Lᵈ. Fordwick dined at Sʳ. Hor: Manns; Mʳ. and Mʳˢ. Dick:[7] He is Consul at Leghorn, come to meet the Duke of York, who is expected here. Mʳ. Littleton,[8] son of Lᵈ. Lyttleton; He seems to be a young

Florence and to all British Grand Tourists. He was also distantly related to Horace Walpole, with whom he corresponded over many years.

1   William Brabazon Ponsonby, 1744-1806, later 1ˢᵗ Baron Ponsonby. Aged 19. Became a major player in British/Irish politics

2   Henry Swinburne, 1743-1803. Aged 21. Fourth son of Sir John Swinburne of Capheaton Hall, Northumberland. Travelled extensively in Europe and wrote up many of his travels in well regarded books, including *Travels in the Two Sicilies 1777-1780*.

3   William Hatsel. Commissioned Ensign in 19ᵗʰ Foot in 1755, Captain in 1762.

4   Abate Antonio Pillori

5   Jane Guise, 1734 – 1807. Single in 1764. Married Shute Barrington, who became Bishop of Durham, in 1770.

6   George Nassau Clavering-Cowper, 1738-1789, aged 26, known in 1764 as Lord Fordwich. Succeeded to the title (3ʳᵈ) Earl Cowper later in the year. Lived permanently in Italy and became a prominent art collector and patron. He married Hannah Gore in 1775.

7   John Dick, 1721-1804. Aged 43. British Consul at Leghorn (Livorno) 1754-1776.

8   Thomas Lyttelton, 1744-79. Aged 20. Succeeded to his father's titles (as 2ⁿᵈ Baron Lyttelton and 6ᵗʰ baronet of Frankley) in 1773.

man of parts, but very particular: He has lost a great deal of money in Italy; and one hears of many ridiculous things he has done on this side the Alps. Cap[n]: Perry of Kingsleys Regiment: He was shot through the Head and Body, at the battel of Minden. Coll: Mills; a man who I beleive has almost ruined himself by projects and schemes, and is now in the Austrian Service. Mr Swinborne understands Italien and french very well; does not appear over bashful, & might be taken to be of y[e]. Coxcomb family. We went from hence to y[e]. play, where we ended the Day.

Fig 8   British Gentlemen at Sir Horace Mann's, 1763-65

Monday and Tuesday 25th & 26th June – Florence

These two days have passed in a very uninteresting way in respect to my Journal. I have commonly begun these, as well as most lately, with the Abbey Pillory, continued them by reading some of Bentivoglio's[1] letters in Italien and M[r]. Phelibien[2] in french; and ended them, either at the Opera, or by walking on the Bridge, w[ch]. is much the Fashion at Florence. About 11 or 12 o'clock the Gentlemen go out in their night-Gowns, and a large Straw hat, and either go to the Bridge, or to the houses of their Mistresses, and walk on the bridge,

1   Guido Bentivoglio 1579-1644, Italian Cardinal, diplomat and historian
2   Andre Félibien, 1619-95, French historian

or by the river till 2, 3 or 4 o'clock in the Morning. The Heats indeed make it almost impossible to stir out by Day. Monday I began to learn of M[r]. Dothel,[1] an excellent player on the German Flute.

Wednesday 27th June – Florence

We spent this Morning in a most agreable manner by takeing a walk through the Gallery, not with a design of examineing its contents, but only to satisfy a little our Curiosity, and to fix with the people belonging to it, when we should begin seeing it thoroughly. Ev'ry thing equalled if not exceeded my expectations, but my seeing so little of them now, and my intentions of seeing them again soon, are sufficient reasons for passing by in Silence the contents of that valuable Collection. Our pleasure indeed was some-what alloyed, by hearing that some very valuable things belonging to this Gallery had been destroy'd a few years since by a fire occasioned by the negligence of M[r]. Bianchi, who has the Charge of the whole. M[r]. Bianchi tho he had received orders to the contrary, built a Chimmeney to a room adjoining to the Gallery.

Fire in y[e] Gallery. He afterwards promised not to make use of it, but a fire which began there, and communicated itself to the Gallery, soon discover'd how ill he had observed his promise. By this fire the much celebrated Wild Boar of white marble, was broke to pieces: We were shewn the remains of it which are collected with intent to endeavour to restore this valuable piece; I much fear they will find that many parts are lost. One Antique, and two Modern Statues were destroyed at the same time.

M[r]. Bianchi behaved afterwards very ill, by endeavouring to accuse other people of begining the fire, and indeed by not discovering it so soon as he might: He was turned out of his place for about two years, and then restored by the Interest of Marase Botta. One would think he could have been hardly severely enough punished for it. The Selfishness of the people shew'd itself on this occasion. It was by force only that they could be made to assist at stopping & extinguishing the fire, & the only reason they gave, was that the Gallery was of no service to them; in which too they were mistaken, as it is the cause of much money being spent at Florence, which should not otherwise.

Thursday 28th June – Florence

Learning Italian has been my chief employment all to day. Great preparations have been makeing here for the reception and entertainment of the Duke of York, who had signified his Intentions of comeing here for the Feasts of S[t]. John, but to night at the hour he was expected, S[r]. Horace Mann received a

---

1   Niccolò Dôthel, 1721-1810, French-Italian flautist and composer

letter express from Col: S^t. John, to let him know, that his Royal Highness, <u>had changed his Mind</u> and was going to Genoa to be present at the Marriage of Mad^l: Durazzo and Mon^r. Spinola. This has much disapointed not only the Regency who intended shewing him great honors, but many of the nobility who had began to prepare great entertainments for him.

Friday 29th June – Florence.

Ceremony of Homages. This Morning began the Ceremonials, and Feasts annually observed here upon S^t. John's Day, who is Tutelary Saint of Florence. They have been obliged to be defer'd this year 'till S^t. Peter's day, on account of the processions wch. are usually made on S^t. Peter's day, being made on S^t. John's. These Feasts &c were instituted formerly in y^e. time of the Republick, and have been constantly continued, neither would the people be by any means pleased, were they to be abolished: They hold three days: The first, very early in the morning, is the Ceremony of all the Places and people any ways subject or dependent on the Government, sending or comeing to offer their homage, and pay an acknowledgement of their subjection. The Evening of this day, there is a race of Barbes, in the Street called Strada del' Curso. The Second day is a chariot race; and the third day, another Course des Barbes.

About seven o'clock this Morning we went to La place du Grand Duc, where we found all the troops at present in Florence drawn up round the Square, except on one side, on which were the Dragoons, who alwais come to Florence on this occasion. On one side the Square is built up a kind of Throne, for the Grand Duc, but as he was not here, a chair was left for him, and on one side was a Chair for the Regent, who soon came, preceeded by a Company of Grenadiers, and took his Seat. Soon after began the Procession. First came the Servants of the Princes, Duke's, Counts, Marquis's, and nobility, two by two on horse back, each carrying a banner, with their Arms, worked upon it; next came an Inferior rank of Gentry and others, who have a kind of Silver plate, fixed upon their left arm; thirdly, four wooden Towers drawn by Oxen, these are meant to represent four Castles or old Fortified places; fourthly, the representatives of the Town of Sienna; their chief, makes a Short speach to the Grand Duke or Regent as he passes by; fifthly, a very high wooden Towr. with S^t. John upon the top of it, and many other Saints fixed in different parts of the sides; is drawn by Six Oxen: Sixthly, all the horses intended to run that day, march one, by one, preseded by the Prize to be run for by them; Seventhly, all the Infantry march by, and lastly The Dragoons. On each side the Square, are built Gallery's for the people, the windows, and even tops of houses are filled, and all ornamented, with pieces of Silk, and Tapestry.

   This Shew is not near so fine as it might be, or as it was formerly; Instead of sending their Servants, the Nobility rode themselves; instead of dirty old pieces of Silk or Velvet, they used to have fine pieces with their Arms richly embroider'd, and instead of very little bad hacks, they were mounted on fine shew'y horses. The Towers used to be much more ornamented than at present, and the rest of the Shew more brilliant. The Towers each pay two Sequins; The Nobility considerably more and other people in proportion. These Tributes, belong to the Grand Duke, but they are, & have alwais been given to the Church of S[t]. John. As each of these orders pass by the Regent, an Officer seting in the front, reads a Charge, or declaration to them. I was too far off to be able to hear wh[t]. he said. The Novellty of the sight was pleasing, otherwise I can not say it was much amusement to me, as the shew was far from being magnificent: It lasted about an hour & a half, after which each was glad to get home out of the heat.

Course des Barbes. After dinner, we went to S[r]. Horace Mann's, who had offer'd to present us to the Regency, from whose Gallery we might see the horse race. We accompanied him first to the Street where the horses run, called Strada del' Curso. Before the race begins the coaches parade up and down this Street for some time: Here was indeed a very fine appearance; the Carriages were many of them very handsome, most of the Company finely, and many indeed richly dressed, and the windows of the Street hung with Silks, and filled with people: At the top, the Street opens into a large kind of Square, through which on each side they have built Gallerys so as to Continue the Street, only something wider. The length of the Course, which is continued through several Streets, is about two miles, all cover'd with sand. After having drove about for some time, the Company quited their Coaches, and went to their respective windows, or places for seeing from: We followed S[r]. Horace Mann to the Regency's Gallery, which is built on one side, so near the end, as to be able to see where the horses start, and perhaps near half a mile of runing. We were presented to one of the Regents, Prince Nery, who as well as many other Gentlemen very politely put us forward so as to see very well. There was a guard of Soldiers placed before our Gallery, and many dispersed up and down the Street so as to prevent the Mob, from runing into them: By this means, as soon as the Coaches were drove off, the Streets were soon cleared, and not a person to be seen standing in them, from top to bottom. It was between seven & eight in the Evening, when the horses came up the Street, to go to the place of starting; There were 14 in all, two of w[ch]. belonged to the Emperor: One of the others was an English horse called Il Grand Diavolo, the property of Mons. Alessandre. This horse is now 23 or 24 yrs: old; was bought by a Coll: Mills, out of Mr Taffs coach at

Paris, when old; and has won almost ev'ry thing he has ran for since his being in Italy. As soon as the horses come to the place of starting, a cord is stretched across before them; to this cord are fixed weights so as to make it fall as quick as possible; as soon as each horse is properly placed, the cord is let fall and the horses part together. I little expected to see them run with that eagerness, and regularity, with wch. they passed by us. Had they been mounted by English Jockeys, they would have hardly run better, than they did at present: Indeed some part of their runing may be dangerous for the horses, as they often kick, & bite one another: The Expectation of the people to know the wining horse is very great, and cannot be known at this end of the Street, 'till declared by the Gr^d: Duke or Regent: The Manner of his knowing it, is by powder fired a fixed number of times from the top of the Churches: Each horse has a fixed number of fires, and the Regent only knows those numbers: The peoples, as well as our own patience, was a little tryed on this occasion, as the number of fires happened to be 13, and they went off very slowly: The great silence of Mr. Mills has told me since, that he never belonged to Taff, but that he bought him of the Prince de Conti, who had the horse from England where he had run a Kings' Plate.

The people during this Interval, surprised me very much, not the least noise could be heard, tho there were some thousands of people, 'till Prince Nery, declared the wining horse. The Shouts of the people was then very great, and so much the more, as the Conqueror was a horse belonging to Monsr. Alessandre, who alwais gives a great deal of Money amongst them: The people always wish for Il Grand Diavolo, but he only came second this time, yet so near, that it might have been disputed, if both horses had not belonged to the same person: The Prize for the first Day is alwais given by the Convent of S^t. Gemminiano, which is in a little Town a considerable distance from Florence: The Prize consists of a large piece of velvet, and Silks to the value of about a hundred and fifty pounds. I forgot to mention before, the manner of stoping the horses, and of urging them forward. For to make them go faster, they fasten lines across different parts of their body, to which lines are fixed 5, 7 or 9 little kind of Cushions in which are a number of little spikes, which by the motion of the horse jump up and down, and I suppose would make him run till he droped down, if he was not stoped by the people who run before and frighten him back. I have really been seldom better amused than for the two hours this has lasted, the fine Shew of Carriges & dresses, the novelty and singularity of seeing so many horses run w^th.out riders, with the great order, yet eagerness of such a Multitude of people was extraordinary, & entertaining.

Saturday 30ᵗʰ June – Florence

Chariots race. The Morning of this day has been taken up like most lately, in learning Italien, or reading some French. In the Evening we accompanied Sʳ. Hor. Mann to a very large opening or Square (a) round which the Chariots were to run: Sʳ. Horace introduced us again to the Regent, who had a Gallery raised on one side; All round the Square, Gallerys were built for the people, which being thus all in view, made in that particular a finer shew than yesterday, tho otherwise it was much inferior, as the Company did not make use of their best Carriages or Dresses: After the Coaches had drove round for about an hour, the Company went to their places for seeing the race, and the Carriages all withdrew; The Soldiers who were placed all round the Square, kept the common people back, and the Place remained quite clear; At a certain distance from each side of the Square are two Stone Obelisks: A Cord is stretched between them, and the Chariots that run go round them: They go round three times; that, that comes first the third time, wining. The chariots that run are made much like a four-wheel'd open Chaise, with a Box to it, only both the body and box are very low, and the Carriage very long: The people that drive them are only common Coachmen, and the horses all belonged to the Post. There were four of them to run, but in the first going round, in turning round the Obelisk one of them fastend his wheel, in the wheel of another, broke the Carriage, lamed the horses, and stop'd either from going on. Of the two others, one was much superior to the other, and won very easily: This did not entertain us much, as I never saw much uglier Chariots, worse horses, or so bad conducted. The Prize was a piece of velvet, not worth much. Thus ended this famous Chariot race, much inferior to yesterday's in ev'ry respect.

(a) Sᵃ: Mᵃ: Novella

Sunday 1ˢᵗ July – Florence

Course des Barbes. Messˢ: Ponsonby and Swinburne, Capˢ: Perry, and Hatzfell, dined with us to day: In the Evening we went to La Strada del Curso, to see the conclusion of La Course des <u>Barbes</u>. We first drove up and down the Street, where there was a great shew of Carriages; but not in Gala, only what the Italians call Mezza Gala: We went after to the Gallery of the Regent; In respect to the race it was much the same as that, the day before yesterday: There were the same horses, but the Course was something shorter and ye. Prize, smaller. The Emperor's horse won, and Il Grand Diavolo very near falling in setting out, came third. The acclamations of the people were not near so great for the Emperor, as they had been for, Alessandre.

Abuse of Military power. I had here an opportunity of seeing to what a degree, Absolute and Military Power, are established and carried on here, and what an effect they have upon the people. A well dress'd man, that had the appearance of a Bourgeois, happening to stand in the way of a Lieutenant who commanded the Guard before Prince Nery's Gallery, the Officer not content with pushing him aside, gave him seven or eight blows wth. his Cane, with all his force: The poor man knowing by the Experience of his fellow citizens how much in vain it would be to resist or complain, took ye. blows quietly and walked off: Soon after a Serjeant encouraged by the example of his Officer, seeing a poor fellow raither too forward in the Crowd, beat him until he had almost killed him: The people saw it seemingly unconcerned, and the Serjeant, was never questioned about it. Mentioning this to the Abbey Pillory, he gave raither a stronger instance of the Tyranny of the Austrian troops; A poor fellow who was takeing down a lamp, fm. the Side of a house after some rejoycings, happen'd to let fall some oyl on the Coat of an Officer standing under: The man fearing the resentment of the Officer, was afraid to come down, upon w[ch]. the Officer told a Soldier to shoot him; raither than that the man came down, tho he might as well have been shot, as he dyed in a few days after of the Bastinado he received for greasing the Officer's Coat.

Monday 2nd July – Florence

Before Breakfast I took my lesson of Italien; After I continued my Journal. After Dinner I wrote to my Father, giving him some account of the Expences of travelling, and my living here; which I wish he knew raither better than he does, as we should be both much happier, and contented with one another. In the Evening to hear the new Opera of Il Mercato di Marmantile:[1] A very pretty Barletta: La Clementina sings sweetly: she had the part of Lana, Contadina.

Tuesday 3rd July – Florence

Earthquake. 'Tho I have neither read, or seen any thing very remarkable to day, I shall not pass it over, in Silence: About one o'clock in the Afternoon, as I was leaning, and writeing upon a Table, I perceived the Table and the Chair I sat in move very sensibly, two or three times; at the same time I heard other things in the Chamber move; There being a great deal of very loud Thunder at the same time, and the wind blowing hard, I did not take much notice of it, tho I thought at the time the motion seemed very particular; and it made me think of an earthquake. I thought no more of it for some time, till I was asked if I had felt, an Earth-quake that had been perceived all over the Town at the time

---

1   Il Mercato di Malmantile by Domenico Fischietti.

I mentioned above, wch. I certainly did very plainly, tho I was not certain of it at the time it happen'd. The weather has been very hot here for some time, and to day particularly gloomy, and close; tho I can not say it has been as yet so hot as I expected it would be; I have felt it as hot in England, tho not to continue so many days together.

Wednesday 4th July – Florence

Gallery. We began seeing the Gallery: It is just beyond, La Piazza del Grand Duca, and is the uppermost part of the building called Fabrica degli Uffici, or Ufizzi.

Chambres des Peintres. We began by seeing the Cabinets, as they call them. The first we went into is a pretty large Room, round which are hung the Pictures of most of the most celebrated Painters, all done by themselves; There are in all two hundred and twenty five. They are all about the same Size, and take in the hand: They are in Gilt frames, and the names all wrote over them. One side of the Room contains those of the Schools of Boulogna and Venice, The Roman, and Florentine take another side, and The Flemish cover chiefly a third; amongst these latter are some English: In the first side there is an excellent hand of Dominichino: the coulours are lively, vigorous, and fresh; the face bold, and very expressive. There are the Pictures of five Caracci's; of which Hanibal's is much the Best. The head of Titien may be reckoned too, amongst the best. That of Tintoretto is rekoned a good one, tho it did not please me much; One sees on one side a full length of his Daughter, by herself: On the next side are the pictures of Raphael, Giulio Romano, Leonardo da Vinci, Luca da Cortona. That of Raphael is a very indifferent piece, the coulours are dead, and the look of the face very unmeaning. It appears to have been done w^n. he was young, nevertheless one would have hardly expected to have found anything of his doing so very indifferent: That of Leo: da Vinci, is really a very good picture; as is that of Giulio Romana: On the third side, are the Pictures of Rubens, two of them; very good: of Rembrandt, of Van Dick, of Vanderwerf; this last has represented himself painting a woman in Miniature, and has shewd in it to w^t. exactness he finished his works. Here are likewise S^r. P^r: Lely, S^r. Godfrey Kneller: Holben of Basle in Swiss: Leotard of Geneva, and some english and scotch, little known I beleive. There is the head of Alba Durer a German, famous both for painting, and engraving. Likewise of Rosealba Carrera, and several other women: But several of the most famous painters are likewise wanting here; such as Michel Angelo, Caravaggio, Corregio, Sacchi, Spada, Claudlaurane, Poussin; and many other good ones. This collection was began by Leopold de Medici: (a). He bought many of them at Rome, that were sold from the Luques Academy: Many of the painters after, were desired to send their Pictures, and others sent them out of vanity. The manner of Painting will discover many of them to be done by the hand of the person they represent.

(a) He was Cardinal: There is in the same Room, a large Statute of him in white Marble; by Jiovanbu Foggini.

Chambre des Porcelaines. Out of this, we went into another pretty large Room, wch. is filled with a great quantity of China. It chiefly consists of very large vases of Blue and white, wch. they told us were very valuable, but not understanding or loving Porcelain very much, we did not examine them. In the middle of this Room there was a Table which drew our attention something more: It is what they call the Florentine work, which is the makeing, Figures, flowers and other things, out of Marbles, and precious Stones, of different Colours, so as to appear like a painting: On this Table are represented, Birds, flowers, fruits, made out of Lapis Lazuli, Jaspers, Emeralds, Agates, and many other stones, so nicely joined, polished, and varied in the shadeing, that many of the parts appear as natural as if they had been done by the hand of a painter. Without including the Materials, we were told it cost 15,000 Sequins; and that above twenty Men, were imployed for Ten years in makeing it (a).

(a)I beleive this Table may be about 5 F^t. long, & above two & half wide.

Cabinet des Idols. Out of this Room we went into another, which they call the Cabinet des Idols: In the middle of this Room is another of those tables of Florentine work, not so large but the design of the work much prettier. Here are several paintings by Bassano: The Rich man at Dinner, Lazarus laying on the ground near &c: In another part of ye. Picture a kitchen, & Larder: The Colouring in some parts are good; but the design in General is very confused, as they often are in the works of this Painter: The other Picture is the Deluge: Three good Landskips by Salvator Rosa: The Family of Paul Verones, almost spoiled. Under it a picture by Titien, I beleive not extraordinary; A young man Setting, a woman standing, with a dart in her hand, the figures small, a very good painting by Guido; But one of the pictures the most curious is the Bust of Cardinal Bembo, in mosaik work. Tho one cannot compare it to a painting, yet the shadeing is far from bad, and the parts are all very distinct. Here are likewise in this Cabinet a great number of antique figures, Lamps &c. I took particular notice of those described by M^r. Addison, which as he has given an exact account of, I shall say no more about them. There is a Sistrum, made the same, but much larger than th^t. I saw at Modena; a Tripod like that at Turin, only here is a large deep dish upon it; A mural crown; appears to me of Iron: A wooden tessera: It is about 5 In: long, & one broad, and has the answer of an oracle in Latin wrote upon it. Jubeo. si is ei fecerit. Gaudebit semper. There is another in Iron: Two or three Pateras, or dishes on which they made offerings. A Tuscan Soldier: He is in armour, has an Iron Club on his left shoulder, on which hangs a buckler resting on his back: He has two long kind of horns rising from the Top of his head out of a small sort of Helmet; and rests upon a stick in his right hand. Several Gods & Goddesses with radial Crowns on their heads: they had all eight spikes wch. appear to come out of the head: An Infinity of Lamps of different shapes and sizes: I remarked two in particular, a Heathen one; In the back part are the figures of Diana, and Apollo, under a kind of Arch or Circle that goes near round, on each side the figures of two Tritons blowing their horns; one of these is broke off. In the middle between the figures are holes for the oyl, in number three; The other is a Christian lamp; It is in the Shape of a Ship; on one end is S^t. Peter who steers it, on the other end S^t. Paul; the places for the Oyl come of the Side; It has a Chain to hang it up by: They are both of Oyl. But I have not yet mentioned one of the most valuable things perhaps in the Room, which is a Pillar of Oriental Alabaster: It is twisted from top to bottom; the heigth of it is six feet, nine or ten Inches, and Circumference two f^t: 8 In^s: It is of a beautiful Clear white, and well polished: The Base and Piedestal, are of different colours, and not belonging to it originally: This valuable piece was found at the palace of Hadrian.

Thursday 5th July – Florence

Chambre des Arts. We took a second veiw this Morning of the things I have been spakeing of, and went next into La Chambre des Arts. Here are some very antient paintings; almost the first that were done: Two by Johanni Angelico [Fra Angelico], who lived about the latter end of the fourteenth Century. One represents the marriage of the Virgin: There are, S^t. Joseph, a Priest, & ye. Virgin and several more men, one of whom has broke his rod, because it did not grow; and he whose rod sprang was to marry the Virgin, wch. happen'd to S^t. Joseph; as they told us the Story. 'Tho these pictures have certainly little of the Merit of those done fifty or a hundred years later, yet one sees by those that the painter that did them was by no means ignorant in his business: The figures are certainly a little stiff, and the Drapery raither formal, but the faces are far from being void of expression, and 'tho the Colours are not very strong and bright, they are far from being bad. Another picture done by one Phill^o: Lepi [Filippo Lippi] about the year 1400 is considerably better: There are two pieces by And: Montegna, one of Corregios Masters: A Picture of Pope Julio the Second by Raphael: very well done. Two old Men, playing at Cards, by Espagnioletto [Lo Spagnoletto, José de Ribera]: much damaged. In this Room there are many peices of very curious Wax work, and Ivory carved and turned. Amongst the former, the progress of Corruption in a body after death, is so naturally done as to make the sight very disagreeable: It is represented in five different states: first just dead; the least bloody matter about the Mouth; in the second the body, is swelled and turned of a livid blue; in the third you see it burst and the Bowells comeing partly out, and many other parts beginning to putrify; in the fourth the body is in the highest state of putrefaction; and lastly it is reduced to a skeleton. It is a pitty so good a workman, had not employed his skill on more agreable subjects. Nothing I think can come nearer to the reality, in ev'ry respect: To render more natural he has added different, worms and flies crawling in and about the wounds, and other animals that attend those things. On one side is the Figure of time, wth. a Scythe in his hand, and several other emblems, belonging to him.

Amongst the Turned Ivory's are several large Globes, with a great number of small ones within them, very artificially done. A horse with a man on him; the hind legs only, rest on a kind of Rock, as if he was takeing a leap, which I suppose is ye. reason Mr. Keysler, says it represents Curtius, as there can be no other, I think: A round box made by Peter the great, its only merit I beleive, is being made by him: There are many more very curious pieces. Here are also in this Room severall small Casettes made of Amber, much in the same manner of that we saw at Modena.

Chambre des Tableaux Flamands. Out of that Room, we went into another, known under the name of Chambre des Tableaux Flamands: In the middle of this Room stands a very large, and curious, Ebony Cabinet, much ornamented, with different sorts of stones. Quite at the Top is a Clock: under an Organ, and about the middle a door opens on one side, when you see within a smaller square cabinet, which turns round: The four sides are very curiously ornamented in different manners: On one side are several birds and flowers made of different coloured stones, Inlaid: On the Second side the Apostles, in Amber; on a third a Crucifixion, I think of the same, and on the fourth a descent from the Cross I beleive in Ivory; which they told us was done by Michel Angelo: Many parts of this Cabinet, are ornamented with paintings upon Stones. Upon a Table in this Room is the Anatomy of a human Head, done in wax, wth. the greatest exactness, & resemblance to nature. Here are likewise many good paintings in this chamber: Two by Rubens, the composition and execution of both which, are excellent. One of these represents Venus, and Adonis: you see the three

Graces pulling the Robe of Venus off of her; a Cupid holding Adonis by the thigh: and Envy pulling him back by his Robe: In another part of the Picture, are several Dogs, and Children playing with them. This is certainly a good Picture, tho in my opinion not equal to the other which represents Hercules between Virtue and Vice. The Coulours in this are more natural, and the Shades more varied; Virtue under the figure of Minerva has hold of one of his hands; and a Venus pulls him by the other arm: There are many other figures in this Piece. A very beautiful little Picture by Necker: a woman kneeling at an Altar, and makeing an offering to a Statue of Venus: The figure of the woman is Elegant, the Colouring excellent and the Drapery of Sattin, finished with the greatest exactness. Two pictures by Vandenwerf, the greatest of both, is the great nicity of the finishing, in which this as well as most of the Flemish painters excel much more than in either the Manner or Composition. Fruits, flowers, and a Birds nest by Rachel Ruisch, very natural, and well done: A woman sleeping by Mieris: I never saw any thing hardly so natural, and nicely finished: Her Head falls backwards, and her arms hang down, in the most easy, but expressive manner. Two very pretty Landskips by Jean Brill: Two more, by Breughills.

Friday 6th July – Florence
We returned this morning to the Flemish painters, not hav'ing had time to examine them all yesterday: There is beautiful little piece of Flowers; by Vanendele: I never saw any so natural; Two very good Landskips, by Vandermeer. An English woman, full length, by S[r]. Peter Lely. A most excellent full length of Pimontel a Spaniard, by Vandick. I think this is one of the best I have seen of his doing since I left England. There are several more by Van dick, by Vanderwerf; some by Ghirandaio, Albert durer, & others of which as they did not please me much, I think it better to say nothing. – From the Flemish painters we went into the Chambre des Mathematiques, which is a large Room but ill filled. The Room is hung round with large Plans of Tuscany: There are two very large Globes; a large Magnet, which will hold up about forty pounds: Models in Brass of the Farnese Hercules; of the Apollo of Belvidere, Antinous, and some others. But one of the most curious things, is a picture on which are several Heads, trophies and other things, which by the help of a Glass full of angles, plac'd at a certain distance, reduce them all to one head, w[ch]. was the likeness of one of the Great Dukes. In the Middle of the Picture is a large Trophi, of Arms, Colours &c: on each side a Smaller one; over the Middle one a head, on each side ye. head, two more, under the Middle Trophy two more heads: A Tube wth. the Angular Glass is placed at a certain distance; and by

applying your Eye to a very small hole at the end of the Tube, you see one Head composed out of all those upon the Picture; and by covering any one of them, you find one part of that Head is also cover'd. –

Chambre de L'Hermaphrodite. We passed from this Room into the Chambre del' Hermaphrodite. Here we saw the Statues of the Hermaphrodite; of Jupiter; of Pan; of a Satyr; of Caligula and his Sister: a young person, with the Bulla; and some others, of all which I shall speak when we come to the part of the Gallery, where the Statues are. Amongst the Pictures: there is a last Supper, by Barocchio: good piece. A Ganymede, with the Eagle, both very large. They are well done by Gambiani. A great many designs by Michel Ange, Raphael and other masters: A last judgment by the latter, admirably done in a kind of Indian Ink.

Behind the door stands an immense Priapus, the form of it is exactly that of a Penis, supported by the hind legs of a Lion: It is near three feet in length and of a bigness proportionable:. Upon the very end is an excressence, of wch. I don't understand the design: Round the Pryapus are carved several figures of birds, and other animals, all which have one of their ends in the shape of a pryapus.

Saturday 7th July – Florence

Haveing been three days together to the Gallery, we thought it better to stay at home this morning, partly to continue our Journals wch. began to be a little behind hand, and partly to read some account of the Statues before we saw them. For this purpose we borrowed of the Abbey Pillori one of the volumes of the Museum Florentinum wrote, by Ant: Francese: Gorry,[1] professor of History. This work altogether consists of ten volumes in large Folio. Four of these are not quite so curious, and useful as the rest, as they only contain an account of those pictures which the painters have done of themselves, with some account of the lives, and works of the Authors: Another volume contains the Prints of all the Statues, with a short dissertation on each: The prints are not very well engraved, but the account of them is well wrote; Two volumes more give an account of the Medals, and Intaglios; and the Inscriptions &c are in a separate one: The two others I beleive contain the Busts, Best paintings, and many other things contained in this valuable collection: The original price for the ten volumes was, Forty Sequins, but they are at present much cheaper, and I know these six last volumes, which are the most material, may be bought for twenty one. It is wrote in very good Latin, printed in a very

---

1 Antonio Francesco Gori (1691-1757). Published his '*Museum Florentinum*' in 12 volumes between
   1731 – 1766.

large, fine caracter, and the work in general is reckoned a very good one. Any of the volumes may be bought separately: That of the Statues, I think is valued at six Sequins. Was I not stopt by Æconomical reason, I should certainly buy six vols:. immediately.

Sunday 8th July – Florence

The Corp of English dined to day at Sr. Horace Mann's. We met several new Comers; Two Countrymen, Mr. Ellison[1] and Mr. Blanchard[2] just come from Rome. They are neither very young, but the former I take to be more than thirty. The two other strangers, were Venitiens; one of them talks english pretty well. From hence we went to Porta St. Gallo, where the Company goes ev'ry Evening.

They commonly drive round about a quarter of a mile, and then come and stop by the Gate: From hence just before the Gate shuts, they go to the Piazza del duomo, where they stay 'till the Opera begins: This is just the tiresome round we made this Evening, and many others, for want of having a better place to go to, and to do like other people.

Monday 9th July – Florence

This morning we returned to the Gallery, and continued examineing La Chambre de l'Hermaphrodite: We saw a great number of small figures &c in bronze, some antique, some modern. What pleased us the most, was a young Hercules, strangling the two Serpents: This is very natural, and well done:. He has hold of the Serpents just below the head; one in each hand. He appears as if seting on the ground, by the position of his Legs: – A Fawn, very well done by Michel Ange. – A Neptune with a Trident in his hand, going to kill a sea monster he is standing over; – The monster is very particular: The Head has the face of a Man, only frightfully ugly, the body and tail, mostly like a fish, only very ugly also. A Cock, very well done in marble: This is not only valuable from its being very well Carved, but from the uncommonness of finding any antique figures of Birds. In this Room is a great collection of Miniature Pictures, that were mostly collected by the Cardinal Leopold, and which he alwais took with him when he travelled, to hang up in his Inns, and Lodgings: They are kept in an upright stand, in which are Sixty draws, each of which contain 9 Pictures. The Bottom of most of ye. drawers are cover'd with black velvet, and the Pictures have a narrow frame of Silver: In the middle of each drawer, is one picture larger than the others those round being commonly

1   Henry Ellison (1734-95)
2   Wilkinson Blanshard (1734-70)

of an equal size. We could not learn whom they represented, 'tho it appears by numbers, and letters on the back of them, that there has been a Catalogue of them: They are well, tho not remarkably finely done: The dresses of many are very particular. –

Camera dell'Arsenale. Hav'ing pretty well examined this room, we went into, La Camera dell' Arsenale: A great part of this chamber was destroyed by the Fire I mentioned before, caused by the negligence of M^r. Bianchi, for which reason most of the things, were removed to two other Rooms, 'till the other is rebuilt, which it will be very soon; the greatest part indeed being finished already.

In this Room are kept a great very many curious things, as well as many that have no merit at all: It seems to be a kind of store room, for receiving all sorts of things, good, bad, and indifferent. You see a great quantity of bronze figures, antique and Modern, Antient utensils &c, Inscriptions, and a great collection of designs, done by the most antient, as well as more modern, painters. Amongst the modern Figures in Bronze, there are the Venus of Medicis, the Wrestlers, the Fawn, and the Explorator, made from those kept in the Tribuna: They are the work of one Messimiliano Soldani, a Florentine, and seemed to me to be well executed. Here are a great many vases made of earth. Some of them are very large, and of an elegant form, and turn. They are light, and seem to be made of a fine earth, and well baked; they are most of them varnished with a reddish varnish on which are painted in black, figures of people, and flowers: They have most of them two handles, pretty near the top; one or two small ones, and were more like what we call, Pichers, had three small handles; one behind, and one on each side. I was surprised to find them so light, and perfectly well worked. They are all antient, Etruscan Vases, and have mostly been found near Volatera: Many of them were broke, and are joined together by pieces of wire.......

Here is a very curious small silver vase, cover'd over with a thin coat of Gold: Nothing can be put on with more art or exactness; Round it, are very nicely engraved a great number of Figures, intended to represent a Sacrifice: It was found at the same time and place with those I have mentioned before. – Another curious piece is a Roman Modus, made of Iron: There is no fixing the exact dimensions of it, as the bottom, and some of the lower part is lost; and the upper part is much eat in holes by rust: Upon it is engraved the following inscription.

[*translated*] "Measurements as an example of those which are on the Capitol, by the most holy authority of the most noble Augustus Caesar N---------, officially sent throughout the regions by the City Prefect and Curator of the Roads D[ecimus] Sumonius Julianus".

In the vacant space was undoubtedly a name but the modus is broke in that place.

We went in the evening to see a Mr. and Mrs. Hays[1], and their Son, who are lately come from Rome: We saw the Father and Son only. The former appears much too old to improve by travelling, if that was his Intent: There might be room for it, but I fancy its too late.

Tuesday 10th July – Florence
We returned this Morning to La Camera del Arsenale, where we examined and copied some antient Missions, and another inscription. They are well engraved on copper plates, and are very legible at this time. They are as follows:

[*translated*] Ser[vius] Galba Emperor Caesar Augustus Chief Priest Tribune of the People Consul Desinate for the second time gave legal discharge and citizenship to the veterans who served in *Legio I Adjutrix* whose names have been written below, together with their children and their descendants and (also gave them) the right to marry with the wives which they had the time when the citizenship was granted to them or, if anyone is a bachelor, with those (wives) whom they marry later, no more than one each.

On the other side of the plate the following names:

Ti. Julius	Randala Sard
C. Juli. Char	Mi. Sardian
Ti. Claudi	qui Tichini Maosium
C. Juli. C of Col	Liben Sard
Ti. Fontius	Carialis Sard
P. Gralli. P.	dem provinciae ipexius
M. Arrufi	Sardian

Continued from the same place

[*translated*] 21st December
in the consulship of G. Bellicus Natalis
and P. Cornelius Scipio

1   Mentioned also by Gibbon but otherwise unidentified.

by Diomedes, son of Artemon, of Phrygia
it was transcribed and authorised from the bronze tablet which was posted on
the Capitol in Rome on the altar of the Julian clan

The following is copied from a separate plate by Mr Guibon[1]

[*translated*] In the consulship of L. Arruntius Stella
and L. Julius Marnius
19 October
M(anius) Acilius Placidus and L. Ptronius Fronto, of the Board of Four Law
Makers were parties to the drawing up of the senatorial decree in the council
of Ferentinum in the Temple of Marcury. Q. Sergianus Maecianus and T.
Munnius Nomantinus were present to take the minutes.

Since it was the opinion of everyone: T. Pomponius Bassus, most
distinguished man, was performing with the utmost liberality the office
assigned to him by the most gracious emperor Caesar Nerva Trajanus Augustus
Germanicus which aims at the preservation of Italy for all generations to
come, in such a way that every age group must justifiably give thanks for his
supervision and that in the future a man of such great virtue may help our
municipality: when the question was asked as to what was to be done about
this matter, they decreed the following; the councillors decided that envoys
should be sent from the council to T. Pomponius Bassus, most distinguished
man, to request from him that our municipality be considered worthy to be
received in clientship in his most distinguished household, and that he allow
himself to be chosen as our patron with a tablet of hospitality inscribed with
this decree placed in his house: they decreed this; the envoys, A. Caecilius A.
f. Quirinalis and Quirinalis (. . .), carried it out.

Another mission copied by Mr. Gibbon.

[*translated*]   Emperor Caesar Domitianus, son of the divine Vespasianus,
Augustus Germanicus, Chief Priest, Tribune of the People for the 12th time,
hailed "General" 22 times, Consul for the 16th time, Censor for life.

Gave citizenship and a legal discharge to the infantrymen and cavalrymen
who served in the 3rd cohort of Alpine men and the 8th cohort of Roman
citizen volunteers who had been proved of foreign status and were under
Q. Pomponius Rufus in Dalmatia and who served for 25 years or more and
were honourably discharged by him, whose names have been inscribed below,

---

1   This however did not make it into Gibbon's Journal

together with their children and their descendants; he also gave them the right to marry the wives which they had at the time when the citizenship was granted and, if anyone were a bachelor, the wives which they married afterwards, no more than one each.

In the consulship of M. Lollius Paulinus Valerius Asiaticus Saturninusand C. Annius Julius Quadratus

This was transcribed and authorised by the 3rd cohort of Alpine men, under the command of C. Vibius Maximus, by the infantryman Venetus Daversus, son of Ditis, and Madena his wife, daughter of Piarens, from the bronze tablet which was posted on the wall behind the temple of Divine Augustus, near to the temple of Minerva.

Here are several small scales and weights: The Scales formed much in the same manner as those we use; except that upon some of them the weight is fixed to one side. Several small Ballasts, just like those we call the Roman Stillard. A great many kind of Pans and kettles, of Iron. Many Lamps – old Poignards – Keys – Rings – Instruments, and other things very indifferently formed, and worked: A horse shoe used by the Antients: It is made so as to cover the Hoof entirely.

Wednesday 11th July – Florence

We did not go to the Gallery to-day. I was employed till nine o'clock in the Evening between the Abbey Pillory, writing my Journal, takeing my lesson of Dothell, and reading the Museum Florentinum: At nine I went to the Opera, and afterwards supped with Messrs. Ponsonby, Perry, & Hatsel, who left Florence to night in order to go to Rome.

Thursday 12th July – Florence

Camera del Ciborio. This is the sixth time of our going to the Gallery. We began by a Room they call La Camera del Ciborio. In this place is the Altar Piece designed, when finished, for the Chapel of St. Lorenzo. It will be large, and wide, but at present only the lower part, and middle: It is designed to represent a Temple, but the plan of it is not very elegant, or well imagined. The work, and Stones of which it is formed are very astonishing. It is composed entirely of various sorts of presious Stones – such as Lapis Lazuli, Jaspers of several sorts, Amathystes, Agates, Chalcedons of different colours, and the Pillars are many of them Chrystal: With these different stones they have made many pictures representing parts of the old and new Testament: In many of them the People, the Architecture, and Landskip part, are very natural.

Some of the small figures intended to adorn this Altar, are very beautiful: Two in particular are remarkable for the fineness of the Stones of which they are composed, as well the art of placeing them. One is that of Saint Paul: The whole head and beard is of a Chalcedone, found near Volatera; the upper part of the face, of a Flesh Coulour, and the beard, white: His upper Garment, is of Jasper, they call, bloody; the under one of red Jasper of Cyprus; and a Girdle of Lapis-Lazuli. The other figure is of S^t. Peter; His head is of white Chalcedone, a loose Cloak, of Sicilian Jasper, white and red; and a Close Robe of Amatheste of Spain. – Their are more of these figures formed of those, and other Stones, in the most curious, and exact manner: – What is already done of this Altar piece, they told us had been above a hundred and twenty years in doing, and at present is far from finished. It was began by one of the Medici Family, but as their are at present none of them to pay the expence, they do not work at it any longer.

We went from hence to La Camera dell Arsenale, where we began to examine some of the Designs of the painters, which are kept in this Chamber: There are above a hundred and twenty volumes, containing the designs, and drawings of the most famous Painters, as well indeed as those that never excelled much. In the first volume, were about six small pieces by Giovanni Cimabue, one of the most antient of whom any paintings remain: He came to Italy about the year 1240. The pieces that are kept here, are small and seemed designed for Books. They represent figures of Saints, which are very ill formed, and composed of two or three Colours, without any shadeing. They are some more, by Giotto, one of his desiples, which are very little better: Those of Leo^n. Vinci, are some of them well done, but they are in General, nothing more than, very rough sketches, and meer outlines, done seemingly in the greatest haste, and without much Care; This is likewise the Case of most of those of Raphael, of whose doing their are a considerable number. Their are several sketches of Pictures, that are at Rome, and other parts, of Italy; and likewise the rough drafts of the Cartons, at Hampton Court.

We left the Gallery early, and went to see the Library of Prince Riccardi, at his Palace; We found here Doctor L'ami,[1] to whom we were recommended by M^r. Bartoli, at Turin: D: L'ami is a man of much learning, and great parts; He is very old, and by great stinginess, or covetousness, has a very shabby appearance, and makes himself often very ridiculous: The Doctor came to see us one morning, when his figure was so particular y^t. I cant help mentioning it: His hair is long, and quite white, his face old, and wrinkled, he is thin and stoops, he had on a very dirty black Coat, a Green Waistcoat of Damask,

---

1   Giovanni Lami (1697-1770), scholar and theologian, librarian at the Palazzo Riccardi.

very long and dirty, Brown cloth britches, red worsted stockings, and brown chamy old shoes, with an old Fan made of blue paper in his hand: 'Tho his appearance is such, his conversation is lively and entertaining, 'tho we could not profit of it so much as we wished as he talks little French, & we little Italien as yet. – He has the Care of the Riccardi Library, and has made a Catalogue of its contents: – It is chiefly composed of Manuscripts, many of which are very rare, and valuable: There are in all about 12 or 1300: We were shewn a very antient Manuscript of Pliny, of the ninth Century: – It is reckoned one of the most antient, extant: It is wrote in a good & clear character but it appears to have been a little incorrect, as there are many interliniations, that appear to be by a different hand, 'tho the Doctor thought them done at the same time, with the book. It is a little deficient, at the very beginning: – Here is a very old Man[r]: Bible, and a Virgil about 300 years old, very well wrote, and at the bottom of each Page, the Story it contains, painted, and adorned with a great deal of Gilding, upon vellum: We saw one or two more I don't recollect at present: There was this evening a horse Race, up the Via Maggio, and over Pont. S[ta]. Trinita: The carriges paraded it as usual some time before the Race: I contented myself with seeing it from my window, as it was not worth much pains.

Friday 13th July – Florence

We paid our seventh visit to the Gallery this Morning, and continued our examination of the Drawings, &c. There is one volume said to contain the designs done by Titian, but I beleive it is very doubtful if there is more than one, by him; which is the Figure of a woman, a Saint, I believe; which is really very well done: The rest are so indifferent, that I should not think they could do anyone, much Credit: In a volume containing the drawings of Julio Romano, there are many pretty good. In another where are those of Annib: Caracci, there are some good Sketches, in particular of Landskips: In another a great many by Polido[a]: De Caravagio, pretty well done. The volume containing the drawings of Tintoretto, does not furnish wherewithal to detain one long.

Vestibule. Haveing passed over the drawings of the best painters wth. some attention, and found neither much entertainment nor profit, we did not think it worth our while to spend any more time, upon the numberless others, that remained, which are mostly done by Florentines, and as we were told, very indifferently, and not worth our attention: We therefore quitted them, and went to the Vestibule, where are, an infinite number of Basso relievos, Inscriptions, Sarcophagi, Statues, and other things. Just before the Door looking into the Garden is a very extraordinary figure of Isis, that was found at Leghorn, not a great while since. She is seting, with her thighs bent close up against her body, and with her arms and hands, resting upon her Knees, & laid quite streight, and flat, so as the hands, cross each other. The legs are entirely cover'd with a kind of Apron, on which are engraved, a great many caracters, and small figures of Animals: All of the Hair seems to be cut off her head, except on the right side, where there is one lock only, which hangs over her Ear: Seeing this Statue before, or behind, it appears like a block of Marble, with a head & neck placed upon it, but on the sides are marked out the body, and the bending of the thighs, and Legs: Down the middle of the back are several Caracters &c. The face is small, and flat: The Nose is mostly broke off: The Mouth is large: The Caracters were taken off, and sent to M[r]. Needham.

On one side of the vestibule is a pretty large opening, or inlet, the right hand wall of which we began examineing; in one corner stands a Marble urn, on which is the following inscription.

[*translated*] Philaetius, son-in-law, and Duseris, step-mother, being of one soul while alive (though that's hard to believe) now dead rest harmoniously in the same urn.

On the opposite side stands another urn of much the same size & shape with this Inscription:

[*translated*] To the gods of the Underworld: the ashes of
Philonicus, son-in-law, and Drysheria, step
Mother, retaining still their old hatred, refuse to be
Mixed together

They told us that these Urns are really antique, but we think that they may be much doubted, not only from the Appearance of the writing upon them, but from the particularity of finding two Inscriptions so opposite to each other: The particularity of them however induced me to Copy them. – Upon the Ground under the wall are three Sarcophagy – In the Middle is a very long one, on which are represented in high relief, a great number of figures of men and beasts, which seemed to have little relation to one another, or to the nature of ye. Stone: Such as, Apollo, Bachus, a Centaur, Lions, & other Creatures. On a small Sarcophagus on one side, is the figure of a young man laying dead, and several Cupids, or Angels, weeping over him: Upon another on the other side, are shewn the Races, and Games of the Circus. –

About three feet from the Ground, are two marble slabs, not very large, on which are cut the two following Inscriptions:

[*translated*] Appius Claudius,
Son of C., Caecus
Censor, Consul twice, Interrex three times
Praetor twice, Curule Aedile twice, Quaestor, Military Tribune three times captured several Samnite towns; he destroyed the Sabine and Etruscan armies; he stopped peace from being made with King Pyrrhus; during his time as Censor he laid down the Appian Way and brought it to the city; he built the Temple of Bellona.

The other Inscription is as follows.

[*translated*] Q. Fabius Maximus, Dictator twice, Consul five times, Censor, Interrex twice, Curule Aedile, Quaestor twice, Military Tribune twice, Priest, Augur: in his first consulship he subjugated the Ligurians and triumphed over them; in his third and fourth consulships he restrained Hannibal, unbridled after several victories, by pursuing him closely. As Dictator he offered decisive help to the Master of the Horse Minucius, whose authority the people had made equal to that of the Dictator, and to his beaten army, and as a consequence he was called "Father" by Minucius' army. When he was consul; for the fifth time he captured Tarentum and triumphed over it. He was considered the most cautious and the most able military leader for his time. He was twice elected Leader of the Senate for periods of five years.

These two valuable inscriptions which were erected in honor of Q: Fabius Maximus, and Apius Claudus; and which give an account of their actions, and of the honors they received for them; are spoke of by M^r. Addison, and have been copied and printed, by other people; but as mistakes are often made either by the Copier, or printer, I thought it well worth the pains, to take them myself.

In the Middle of this Wall is a large Basso-relievo, representing the figure of a man, near as big as life: He is holding a horse by the bridle; and the head, and part of the neck of the horse, appear on the right side of the man, as well as part of the breast and one leg. – Gorii, in his discription of this Figure in his Museum Florentinum, says, –

[*translated*] On display is a Roman Cavalryman (to describe the sculpture) which is impressive in its physique and drapery and outstanding in its beauty. He stands upright and holds a lain spear in his left hand; in his right he is controlling a lively horse by a rein. From his right shoulder hangs a military cloak which is fastened with a brooch. His body is dressed in a belted tunic.

He says afterwards:

[*translated*] Up to this point we have noted several visible aspects which we think ought to be considered when describing the sculpture. What remains is to note that the Roman Cavalryman leading a horse is called in the oldest dictionary of antiquity *transvectio* or "Parade-Crossing"; this took place in public during a Censorship or in later Imperial times while an inspection was taking place. This is not only an outstanding illustration of Roman history but in addition up to this time has never been published as such. It was the custom that cavalrymen who had been awarded a horse at public expense and had received the cost of the horse's upkeep (which was not a minor honour) came to the Censor's tribunal, each leading his own horse; if the Censors conducting the *transvectio* review allowed these men to keep their horses, they let them depart; but if not, they took the horse from them and ordered it to be sold. Livy writes that this *transvectio*, whether inspecting cavlarymen or horses, was founded by Q. Fabius Rullianus (cf also Valerius Maximus and others).

The work of this Piece seems to have been done by the hand of a Skilful master: – Under this, is an inscription, not at all relateing to the bas-relief. On each Corner over, is a small Bust.

On each side this great piece, are two small basso-relievo's, pretty done, and preserved: – One of these is supposed to be M: Antony, shewing to the people the robe, Cæsar had on when he was stabed; the other they say is, the reading or publishing his will. In the first there are five or six people only, two of whom, are holding open a large Robe, which might have been bloody, but however there appear no holes, as if any one had been stabed through it. – In the other there are several more figures one of which is opening a kind of Book. – but as the same buildings are represented in each of them, that seems another objection, as I beleive, the will was read in a private house, and Cæsars robe exposed to the people in an open place. – On another of these pieces is represented Ulyses tyed to the mast of a Ship, and three Syrens on one Side playing on different instruments. What is intended by the fourth piece is very uncertain. There are many figures, one of the principal is a woman on her knees, a man standing behind her, appearing to be pulling out her Eyes. On both sides of these Basso-relievos are several Inscriptions. One I took notice of, we imagined to be a list of horses, amongst which were many names such as we give to horses at present: There are numbers, and Letters opposite each name: Over all these, are several small bas reliefs; and four small Sarcophagy of earth, that have been found in Tuscany. The Sides are ornamented; with various Figures &c. These are most of the things worth notice on this wall.

Saturday 14th July – Florence

We returned this Morning to the Vestibule, but were prevented seeing it, as the person who used to shew us about, was engaged in shewing the Gallery to Cardinal Ste-rt,[1] who came here last night. We stoped there however a quarter of an hour, partly out of Curiosity to see his Emynence, and partly to take off the two inscriptions of Maximus, & Appius. I cannot say I had a very near view of the Cardinal, as it was only as he passed along the Gallery, at some distance from us; however I could see very plainly he looked very thin, unhealthy, and decay'd. – I thought too his looks answer'd in some measure to his character, of a very Silly Ignorant Man. Evr'y one says he is a very great Bigot: His only business here they say so is to say Mass. He is lodged just opposite us at the Corsini Palace. – The rest of the day has not been productive of any-thing worth notice.

Sunday 15th July – Florence

I did nothing before breakfast: Afterwards I wrote to Holroyd,[2] continued my Journal, and read some Italian. In the Evening we went to see M[r]. Dick, Consul at Leghorn, at a house he has taken just out of Florence; from thence we went to Port S[t]. Gallo, from thence, all Duomo, and next to the Opera, which was acted to night for the last time. It is the same Opera, of Il Mercato di Malmantile. It is much the prettiest Burletta I remember to have heard: The Musick is throughout very good, and many of the Songs very pretty. La Sig: Clementina Baglioni, who acted Lena, in it, has an exceeding good voice, and sings delightfully: she also acts her parts very well; and is very handsome at present.

---

1   Henry Benedict Stuart, Cardinal Duke of York (1725-1807), brother of Charles Edward Stuart, the 'Young Pretender'. It is obvious that Guise is does not wish to portray him in any favourable light.
2   John Baker Holroyd, first earl of Sheffield, 1735-1821. He was a friend of Gibbon and Guise from Lausanne and became Gibbon's literary executor. Gibbon was buried in Fletching church near Sheffield Park in Sussex.

Monday 16th July – Florence

On the left hand side of the Opening, or Alcove in the Vestibule, are many Basso-relievos, inscriptions &c, as on the opposite side, 'tho not near so curious. – Upon the Ground are several Sarcophogy much adorned with Bas-reliefs, which consist of many Figures, that seem to have very little connection to the thing they are upon; – On the Middle one which is very large, there stands a very curious urn. – In respect to its shape, and the work upon it, it is very much the most elegant I have yet seen; It is entirely cover'd over with carving in a sort of Flowers, and other ornaments, which are cut deep in the Marble: The handles are not very large; and resemble a little, ram's horns.

In the Middle of the Wall is a very large Bas-relief. There are several different figures upon it. In one is a Woman setting I beleive upon a little hill: There are two little Boys standing by her, one of them is holding out an apple to her: Just under her, one sees a Cow; and a Sheep feeding; and corn growing in several places: On one side of this woman, you see the figure of another, not quite so large: She is seting upon a Bird, which appears to me much more like a Swan, than any other Bird: Only half the body of the woman is cover'd, and with a Robe which seems to come from under her she has formed a kind of arch, which she holds over her head: Her hair is wound round her head. At her feet, is a Jar, laying on one side, and water runing out of it. – On the other side of the largest figure, is another woman seting on a Dolphin or some Sea monster: She is much the same size of that last described: Half her body is cloathed and she is holding in one hand a Robe, which forms an arch over her head, and in the other hand a kind of crown made of herbs. – The Principal of these figures is supposed to represent the Earth; the two others; Air, and water, as necessary to make her fruitful: – I should think that if that is the meaning of it, they should have likewise added, the fourth element, Fire, as without some heat the Earth would not produce many things, and what it did produce, would seldom come to perfection. – Whatever these figures are intended for, they are very well done, & the bas-relief altogether is much the Best I have yet seen. On the rest of this wall are many small bas-reliefs, heads, and inscriptions: These last are most of them sepulchral, and not particularly curious. – In the other parts of the vestibule you see a great number of Inscriptions, but none I beleive very remarkable: Near the top of the walls are placed round several Busts, not much worth observation either for the people they represent, or for the workmanship: There are besides a Statue or two, which I shall speak of after:

Gallery. Over the door going into the Gallery is a very fine vase, the sides of which are pretty flat, and on that towards one, you see a head of an Emperor.

Haveing pretty well examined the Vestibule, we next enter'd the Gallery, and began by the Busts, separately, thinking it better to leave the Statues 'till after: We began quite at the farther end of the East Side, of the Building. – The Busts and Statues stand together in the same Row, but alwais a Bust opposite another Bust, and the same wth. the Statues: I shall observe that order in seting them down, as near as possible.

Busts. The first Bust that presents itself is that of J: Cæsar, the head in Bronze, the rest marble. – The head altogether appears very small; the features of the face are pretty strong, and give him an old, worn out look. – His hair is cut short all over y^e. head, and one can perceave no baldness, except that his hair grows very back over his Temples. I do not find much expression in this Bust, or think it answers in any respect to the Idea one naturally forms of the look of that great man. – Opposite to this, stands an Excellent Bust of M:T: Cicero, of white marble, 'tho at present very yellow: There is a great deal of expression in his look, so that without knowing who he was, one should conclude him to have been a sensible man: Upon his left cheak, not much above the lip, is a white spot, which serves to prove that it is certainly the Bust of Cicero; He has raither an old look: – The whole of this, which comprehends, the Shoulders, and part of the breast, is antique except the nose, which like that of all the others have been broke off, and restored.

The third is that of Augustus: A pretty good one: Opposite is, Sappho: A small head, and the features of the face small; and raither pretty: It appears to me a good Bust.

The 5th. is a very good one of Agryppa: His Eyes are sunk remarkably deep in his head, and give him a very stern look: I think there is more life in his Countenance, than in any hitherto.

6th. Bust of Sophocles; pretty good. – Head only Antique.

7th. Tiberias: did not please me at all. – Ditto.

8th. Aristippus; much like the last. – Ditto

9th. Caligula. A good bust, in which one fancy's to see expres'd the caracter of a wicked man – the same.

10th. Agrippina: a good Bust.

11th. Claudius: a Middling Bust.

12th. Antonia. Not much better.

13th. A good Bust of Nero.

14th. Poppaea: does not by any means answer to the accounts of her beauty.

15th. Galba. Very expressive. The hair is something longer than of those before, but still short: it is well done.

16th. An exceedingly good Bust of Seneca: Old age is well expressed: He stoops forward much, and his mouth is partly open, as if going to speak, yet as if he was wanted force.

17th. This looks like Otho: Chiefly remarkable from its raryty.

18th. Carneades. Pretty good.

19th. Vitellius: Much the same: has the look of a Glutton.

20th. Xenocrate: I did not like it.

21st. Vespasianus. A very lively, expressive Countenance: it appears to me an excellent Bust.

22nd. Basenice: pretty good. (a)

(a) Her hair is very particularly dressed; in small curls hanging all down the side of her face, which appear almost like Snakes. There are two curls, the heigth of her Ear, two more f[m]. her temples, others to the top of her forehead.

Tuesday 17th July – Florence

M[r] Gibbon not being very well, we did not go to the Gallery this Morning. – I employed it in writeing a Letter to my Sister, and continuing my Journal. – Cardinal Steuart left Florence, this Morning: His chief employment here, was saying Mass, and looking at the body's of saints: buried in the Churches here. – M[r] Lyttleton dined with us.

Wednesday 18th July – Florence

We continued to day our Survey of the Busts.

The 23[d]. Bust is of, Titus, not remarkably good.

24th. Julia: Dau: of Titus; I beleive a good one. (a)

(a) Her hair is curled in small Curls, extremely high over her forehead, so as to come to a point at the top; and behind it is wound round in a double ring

25th. A middling one of Domitianus.

26th. Domitia: pretty good: Her hair is very particular; It is divided in the middle of her head: one half is combed forward, and is curled very high over her forehead, in very small curls; and indeed has much the appearance of a sponge, as M[r] Cochin rightly observes.

26th. A very bad Bust of Nerva.

27th. Mathidia. Indifferent.

28th. A pretty good Bust of Trajan.

29th. A good one of, Plotina.

30th. Adrian. This is an admirable Bust. He is the first of the Emperors that has got a Beard, and his hair pretty long: both of them are well done in this Bust.

31st. Another very good bust of Adrian; something younger.

32: A large and excellent Bust of Antinous: a great deal of boldness and expression in this piece: The Shoulders, and Breast, are Antique. This is the first Bust in which one sees the Eyesight marked, and in this but very slightly.

33d: A vestal, well done; she has a veil over her head.

34th. A very good Bust of Alius Cæsar. The Eye sight is more marked in this.

35: An Indifferent Bust of Faustina the Mother: Her hair is wound round and fasten'd at the top of her head.

36th. An exceeding good Bust of Antoninus Pius.

37th: A very middling Bust of Faustina the Mother.

38th: A good Bust of Marcus Aurelius, or Antoninus: His beard is very long and thick, and not very well executed.

39: A pretty good Bust of Faustina, the Daughter: Her hair is tyed in a sort of knot, upon her neck, but not low.

40: A good Bust of M. Aurelius, but he appears younger than in the last.

41. A very indifferent Buste of the same Person.

42. L: Verus, did not please me much.

43: Nor that of Lucilla.

44. A very large Bust of Sabina: very indifferent.

45. Brutus, by Michel Ange: This Bust does not appear near finished, nevertheless it is impossible not to discover the greatest expression and life, in the face of Brutus: He has a very determined, bold look.

46. The Bust of a Woman well done, by Bernini.

47. Just by the door going into La Chambre de Idols, is an excellent Bust of Annius Verus, when quite a Boy. I never saw any-thing done with more delicacy, or a more pleasing countenance; and so much sweetness expressed, as one could not expect I think in marble.

48. A Bust of Pan: Indifferent.

49: A middling Bust: person unknown.

50th. A very indifferent Buste of Adrian.

51st. A most excellent head of Alexander, larger than life. He is looking upwards, and appears to be in great torment; and it would be difficult to express distress more plainly, than what it appears to be in the face of Alexander, in this Bust.

52: A very large Bust of a woman, & very indifferent.

53ᵈ. A good Bust of Commodus.

54. A very pleasing one of Crispina.

55: Another of Portinax: The Beard & hair too stiff & formal.

56: An indifferent one of Didia Clara.

57: A much better of Didius Julianius.

58: An indifferent Bust of Maxilla.

59: That of Albinus appears to me pretty well done, It is made of Alabaster; the only one of that sort in the Gallery.

60ᵗʰ. Julia Severa, but indifferent.

61. A good Bust of Septimus Severus.

62. Julia Severa, far from good.

63: A good Bust of Caracalla.

64: A pretty good one of Plautilla.

65: An indifferent Bust of Geta when a young man.

66: A very good Bust of Geta when a Boy; there is something extreamly natural in this, and it is finished with great ease, and pleasingness: There is not the least resemblance between this, and the last mentioned.

67. An indifferent Bust of Diddumenianus.

68: One of Plautilla much the same.

69: A bust of Eliagabalus, done in a bold manner, and with judgment.

70ᵗʰ. A very unfinished, and indifferent Bust of J. Ap. Severa.

71. A bust of Alex. Severus. Bad I think.

72. One of Julia Masmica, little better.

73. Gordianus Africanus Senex. Very bad.

74. Julia Macsa, much the same.

75. Papianus – little better.

76. Antiochus Eugetes.   A very bad Bust.

77. Much such another of Philippus.

78. A pretty good Bust of Galienas.

In looking over these busts, which are many of them very valuable either for the workmanship, or because they are very scarce, one is very sorry to see how ill they have been treated, and how ill they have been repaired. I did not see one, but what has had the nose entirely lost, and those that have been supplied are commonly very indifferently fixed to the rest of the face. There are not above ten (a) that the whole bust is Antique. And the busts that have been added, are commonly composed of Marbles of different Colours, whereas, by those Antique that remain, one sees they were entirely composed of the same Marble. There were about fifteen more Busts, most of which were entirely destroyed by the fire that happened in the Gallery by the fault of Mr. Bianchi, however they hope some of them may be restored. Having examined the Busts, we turned back to the same place from whence we began them, in order to begin the Statues.

(a) I recollect that of Cicero, of Seneca, Antinous, Sept. Severus, Caracalla, Adrianus, Geta when a boy, Faustina the Mother, and Albinus, which last is of Alabaster

Statues. The first piece of Sculpture to be taken notice of, is a Group at the upper end of the East Side of the Gallery. It represents Hercules endeavoring to throw down the Centaur Nessus. One of the fore feet of the Centaur is bent under him, the other is thrust out, owing to the force of Hercules, who has hold of the Centaur's Head, pressing hard upon him and endeavoring to pull him over. – Many parts of both these figures are modern: – A great part of the Hercules, and in particular, I know, the Head of the Centaur, to be so. Strength, and force are well expressed in ev'ry part of the Hercules: His limbs are full of Nerves and Muscles; and his position is natural. – The Centaur is reckon'd equally well done.

2^d. On the right hand side of this Group, is a woman seting in a Chair. It is supposed to be Agrippina minore, Mother of Nero. The Chair which is of Stone, is made pretty long, so that a person may almost lie down in it; It has a close Back, and arms (a). Agrippina sets very low in the Chair, her left Arm over one arm of the Chair, and one leg a little crossed over the other. Nothing can be placed, with greater ease, or more naturally: The bending of her body is perfectly well expressed; and the drapery is excellent: Her left arm has been restored.

(a) There is a Cushion in it.

3^d. On the opposite side to this, is another woman, seting likewise in a Chair made much the same as the last: Tho this I beleive is well done, it appears to me much inferior to the last mentioned, in ev'ry respect . Her body is stiff, and the drapery very formal.

4th. Vir Consularis: He has his right hand stretched out, as if he was spakeing, and holds a Role in the left. He is cloathed in the Toga, which is made very large, and full of folds, by which it is imagined to be done for the latter end of the Republick, as before the Robes were much closer. – I cannot say that I think the Sculptor has shewn much skill, in any part of this Statue:

The arms restored:

5ᵗʰ. The Statue of a woman in Black Marble; very heavy, coarse, and ill executed, in ev'ry respect.

6ᵗʰ. A woman holding a Bird, something like a Swan in her right hand about the heigth of her waist, against her; with the other hand she hold up a Robe, which covers the left side, and below the waist; the right is naked; It is supposed to be a Leda: The drapery is pretty well done, and the body is easy, and natural.

7ᵗʰ. The figure of a young man, almost naked, only a loose Robe hanging from his neck, over his left arm. In his left hand he holds an apple, and a kind of Truncheon in the right. Some people say it is a Globe, instead of an apple, and that it represents M. Aurelius: Others think it, Paris: It is but an indifferent piece: Great part restored. –

We went no farther than this today: – We afterwards dined at Sʳ. Horace Manns, with Mʳ. and Mʳˢ. Hays & Son; Mˢˢ. Ellison, and Lytleton: – Mʳ. Hays, seems very stupid, his wife raither vulgar. The Son is much better than either (a).

(a) Sʳ. Horace made us laugh to a great excess, by a Story he told us a Florentine, who being ill at Vienna, told the Emperor one day; He did not like the German Phisicians; but yᵗ. he wanted to be treated in his old Florentine way, shewing him at the same time how he meant, say'd Sʳ. Horace, with his finger, and pointing to the part ailing, now the Emperor took it in another sense, and burst out laughing; – The presence of Mʳˢ. Hays did not restrain us from doing yᵉ. same thing.

Thursday 19ᵗʰ July – Florence

Continuation of the Gallery.

8ᵗʰ. Is the Statue of a young mann nake'd, holding a vase in his left hand: It is supposed to be for a wrestler: and what is antique of it, is well done.

9ᵗʰ. A very pretty figure of a Bacchante: Her left hand is upon the head of a Tyger, and she point up in the air, with the left; she bend raither forwards, one leg just before the other, and her right foot half on, & half off the Ground, as if she was running: There is great elegance in the figure, and she almost appears to move.

10ᵗʰ. A pretty good Statue of a Vestal; She has a veil over her head, but one plainly sees she had her hair long, and it is here combed back in a kind of Role over her forehead. On one side of her is a little Altar, from whence comes a flame over which she is holding her right hand; in her left she has the Patera. – Arms restored: bad.

11th. A Mercury standing, with one leg, across the other, and leaning on a trunk of a Tree: The body, and thighs, which is the only part, Antique, pretty good.

12: The Statue of a Drunken Bachus, done by Michel Ange. For all the faults that are found in this by M^r. Cochin, & other Criticks, I cannot help thinking it well executed, the Attitude very natural, and the face certainly very expressive of a drunken Man.

13. A Pomona: very indifferent in my Opinion: She holds apples, and other fruit in her lap, and has a kind of Garland of Berry &c round her head.

14. A woman larger than nature holding fruit in her hand. but indifferent: Drapery pretty good.

15. The Statue of a young man nakeed, supposed to be for Endymeon: He rest upon his right leg, bend very much forward, and turns himself backwards, holding up his right hand, and looking upwards, with his left he holds a dog, which is almost between his legs, he seems to be listnening. It is not very well done, and a great part restored.

16th. The Statue of a Man naked, but who having nothing in his hands or about him, remains unknown.

17. A Copy of the Venus de Medicis: Not bad.

18. A Mars in Black Marble: Very indifferent: not much antique.

19: A young man nake'd, seting on a kind of Rock, his right foot pressing a Tortoise, and holding something round in each hand. Only the body of this is antique, and that is very well executed. The Arms, legs and the Tortoise, have been added by some modern Sculptor, so that M^r. Gorii in his Museum, might very well have spared himself the pains of writeing so long a dissertation, by way of proveing it to be the Statue of Apollo, and that the Testiado, is a certain proof of his being the Inventor of Musick, & many other instruments.

20. Young man naked, leaning upon a trunk of a tree and holding a torch, in one hand; with the other he points upwards: M^r. Gorii has wrote a great deal, to prove it to be, Apollo Caelispex, others with more reason think it Prometheus, but it must certainly be very ridiculous to say absolutely that it is more one, than another, as only the body is antique; the rest may be attributed to the invention of a modern workman, who had a mind to puzzle those who were blind enough, not to discover the difference in the Skill of the Sculptors. The body is good.

21st. Vir Consularis: He is cloathed much like the first I spoke of: as a Role of paper in one hand, and a pen in the other; just behind him stands a round stone, supposed to represent a Case in which the Consuls kept their writeings: The hands and arms are restored: The drapery pretty good.

22^d. A Bacchus, not large, and a little Boy standings by him, altogether pretty good, but the body of the Bacchus, which is the only part certainly antique, is excellent.

23^d. Mars and Venus: Quite devoyd of ev'ry beauty.

24. Bacchus, and a Fawn; great part of this is modern, but what remains of Antique is well executed.

25th. An Antique Statue in Bronze, very valuable from its antientness, but not much so for the form, or work. – It is the figure of a Man of a moderate size, holding out his right hand, which is uncover'd, the rest of his body is cloathed in a loose robe, over a close one. Tunica lata & amplissima amictus est: quee etiamsi manicis careta: &c. Supra tunicam Pallio ampliore, sui tunica indutus cernitur; The under robe appears to me to be close, 'tho M^r. Gorii thinks it otherwise. His legs are cover'd near half way, and what he has on, is bound round, and over the feet in several places: Shoes with which the Etruscan Soothsayer is adorned are most distinctive; they cover the feet and about half of the lower leg, with very attractively arranged bindings. He has a ring upon the second finger of his left hand: Annulum gestat laeva manu in digito qui minimo Proximus est quo in more. Ut in ceteris, Romani Etruscus imitate sunt. Upon the bottom of his Robe near his feet are three lines of Tuscan caracters: No one has yet been able to tell the meaning of these no more than any other Tuscan caracters. His hair is cut very short, and he has no beard. M^r. Gorri calls this Statue, Haraspex Etruscus, and says,

[translated] A truly exceptional monument which I brought to light among the Doric inscriptions from the Museo Victorio in Rome; in my opinion it is so brilliant that I think that it may represent the prophet or soothsayer Tages, who was famous among the Etruscans at Perugia. It was found in the neighbourhood of Perugia, which I beleive at present in the Popes Dominions.

26th. But an indifferent Statue of Urania; she has a Globe in one hand, and a pair of compasses in the other. The Drapery over her breast is good.

27. A bad Statue of Clio: she leans upon a kind of Harp.

28. A small figure of Leda and the Swan, far from good.

29. Venus seting upon the trunk of tree, her left leg rested upon her right knee, and appearing to pull a thorn out of her foot: she is naked down to the waist, & a robe hangs loose over the rest of her body & lymbs. The whole of this figure is elegant, and natural, and y^e. drapery executed with judgment.

30th. The Chimera of bronze found near Arezzo. – Its head and forepart are like a Lion, and indeed the whole body, except that in the middle of the back, there grows out the head and neck of a kind of Goat: the tail which is broke off, is supposed to have resembled a Dragon. Prima Leo, postrema Draco, media ipsa Chimera, says Lucretius. Upon one of his forelegs, one plainly discovers, some Tuscan Letters. He is standing in a posture as if just ready to attack something: His mouth is open, and he appears enraged. there are no teeth in his Mouth. The body is not ill executed.

31. I think I cannot do better than transcribe Mr. Goriis description of this Beautiful representation of Cupid and Psyche.

> *[translated].*   Everyone who enjoys studying and researching ancient art considers this a most remarkable and admirable work: the most outstanding group sculpture of Amor and Psyche. It stands out as the unparalleled and exceptional work of a Greek sculptor of preeminent standing, who is to be honoured with the utmost praise; his great genius is evident in that he has devised something which is very difficult to manage; he has done so with great daring and has achieved a most delightful result. For while Amor and Psyche squeeze each other in a mutual embrace and kiss, their faces have been sculpted with such glorious skill and the most perfect success with the knife, since he has placed a very, no the smallest gap between the two. Actually their eyes are looking at each other and their mouths are open in such a way that they seem to be speaking, to be expressing their mutual love and desire, with the posture and the movement as evidence of the pleasure they are taking in their kisses – all in hard marble. He imitates nature with such skill. Psyche represents the soul and so has been portrayed with butterfly wings; her usual name is Ψυχη, meaning "soul" and "butterfly". Her top half is naked; her bottom half is draped, as befits her heavenly and divine origin. Amor or Cupid has a body which, fashioned from the soul, is held tight in Psyche's arms and touches her face with his hand, lovingly embracing her with his other arm.

Certainly nothing can be done with more elegance, than these two little figures; nothing can be more natural than the folding of their arms over each other. The wings of Psyche have been restored, they are otherwise mostly antique, 'tho I cannot help beleiving that the Heads are modern, as they fall far short of the other parts in beauty, and expression.

32^d. The Statue of a young man holding a bird up in his right hand, and on one side of him stands an Eagle; I beleive that only the body is antique, and it is very good.

33. A Woman, distinguished by M^r. Gorii under the name of Musa, and Euterpe. In her hair at the top of her forehead are two feathers, which they say

the Muses pulled out of the Syrens wings, when they attempted to sing with them. She has a role in her left hand, and with her right she holds up her robe which hangs loose over her. There is no great merit in it.

34. An indifferent Statue of a man, they call it Apollo.

35. A Bronze Statue of a young man, a very elegant Figure, and exceedingly well executed in evr'ry respect: – It is believed to be an Apollo, but as he has no particular attributes, it is difficult to say absolutely who it was designed for. – It stands upon a brass pedestal, which is much ornamented with very good bas reliefs.

36. Marsias, stretched out at full length, and bound with his hands over his head, to a tree. His skin is striped off. The body which is the only part Antique is pretty good.

37. A bad Statue of a Consul; has a pen in one hand, a Role in the other, and a kind of round Case to hold writeings in standing by him.

38. Aesculapius: A very indifferent Statue. In one hand he has a bunch of herbs, with the other he holds, or raither leans upon a Stick round which there is a Serpent twining up. Ferunt Asculapium coactum sanare Glaucum revisit, ut docet Hygisius – Gorii.

39. Venus Genetica: indifferent. In her right hand she has a kind of bow, which she appears to hold back, from a Cupid that is seting upon her left knee. She is naked down to the waist.

40. Another Consular statue, much like the last.

41. Rex Phrygius: Very indifferent: the dress is particular. It is a kind of Shirt fasten'd upon the Breast, and open down to the waist: His breaches are fasten'd in three or four places down each thigh, and open between y^e. fastenings. His legs are cover'd half way.

42. Narcissus kneeling, with one hand behind him, and the other held up in the Air; He leans a little forward, and looks down, and may certainly be supposed to be looking at himself in the water. -The body which is antique is finished with great art, and beauty.

43: A Statue, Mr Gorii calls, Apollo Pythius: He is setting naked upon a rock, with a Serpent at his feet, and playing upon a kind of harp, but as only the body is antique it is useless to give any farther description, or conjectures about it.

44. A Roman Soldier; or Miles Veles. He is kneeling on one knee, his right hand is stretched out as if he had just thrown a dart (which the Velites alwais made us of) and on his left arm he has a Shield, which is particular, being Square and hollowed in kind of folds, or as Gorii expresses it, – ad modum impricis excavatum est, et formae quadrata: Indifferent.

45. A Victory: She has a Palm branch in her left hand, & a Crown of Laurel in the other: Not far from bad.

46. Hygeia: She has a Serpent in one hand, which appears, to be trying to get at a dish she holds in the other hand.

47. A Jupiter. Near half his body is naked, the rest cover'd with a loose robe which hangs from his left shoulder: He has nothing on his feet; in his left hand he holds a thunderbolt pointed downwards: It is but a very indifferent Statue in any respect. -

There are several more Statues in the Coridore's but as they are neither remarkable for the goodness of the Sculpture, or in any other respect, it would be waisting both time, and pains to mention them any farther. The fine Copy of the Laocoon in the Belvidere at Rome, was one of those better pieces that was entirely ruined by the fire in the Gallery: Some part indeed do still remain, tho hardly enough to restore it in any perfection.

Friday 20th July – Florence

We did not go to the Gallery this Morning, and as the day has been very free from events worth rememb'ring, I will take this opportunity to speak of the Statues, I omitted describing, when we were in the Chambre de l'Hermaphrodite. *Statues in La Camera dei l'Hermaphrodite.*

[*translated*] A statue of Hermaphroditus, made from the most sparkling Parian marble, not damaged or restored, but complete with the bed itself whole and intact; it contains all the pleasures and enjoyments of art. For its individual parts and outstanding craftsmanship it is considered to be very beautiful, complete and authentic. It has to be said that it cannot be praised or admired enough.

This begins M^r. Gorii's description of this beautiful Statue. I agree entirely with him, as to the excellence of the workmanship; Nothing can be expressed I beleive more naturally, or finished with greater art; but was a person to rely on Mr Goriis account he would generally be much deceived; This as well as most of the Statues has been very much repaired; It is true that the whole body & bed are compleat at present, but it is very evident that, the Statue was broke across, slanting through part of one hip, and so down the thighs; which parts, with part of the bed, have been restored, and indeed pretty well.

In this sculpture he has been depicted enjoying sleep, with a lion skin thrown on the ground and which he is sleeping, and above the hide on a piece of cloth which hangs most elegantly from his left arm; the rest of his body is stretched out exposed to view. This same Hermaphroditus is also known by the ancients as Androgynus and Breasty, with an obviously ambiguously body-type, described in the following way by Ausonius: "Mercury was his father and Cithera his mother; his name, like his body is mixed, Hermaphroditus, a compound in sex but complete in neither, so of uncertain gender and able to enjoy neither passion."

This figure is about the Size of raither a little woman, and has all the distinctions of the female sex, except the most material one, which either never was made, or by the breaking of the Statue, has been destroyed. The male attributes are very perfect.

I shall next quote part of Mr Goriis description of a very remarkable Statue of Pan.

> *[translated]*. This most elegant sculpture of the god Pan, guardian of Arcadia whom we call Faunus is very similar to a statue of Mercury in the lower part of the trunk. It is famous for the value and antiquity of the work. In size it is roughly equal to four Roman feet, and so, since it can easily be carried by anyone, we believe that in antiquity it used to be transported from one place to another by shepherds and country folk, either for sacrifices or for the protection of the fields, the stables, and the sheep folds which he was thought to protect. In his right hand he carries a milking-pail, in his left he lowers a she-goat to the ground. His head is covered by a broad-rimmed hat which is associated with shepherds and goatherds, as well as fishermen, to ward off the dangers of winds, heat and cold, to be seen in other ancient sculptures. His chlamys lies on the ground with a knotted cloth bound across his chest and his clothes are sheepskins.

The whole of this figure except the Head, and arms, is a pedestal; He has a very long beard, and kind of asses Ears.

A Satyr: he is represented with a kind of horn in his right hand, which he holds up above his head as if he had been drinking out of the horn; in his left hand, he has a bunch of Grapes: It is common to see them in this manner, as they are supposed to be attendants & Servants of Bacchus.

A statue of a boy wearing a bulla: the ornament of the bulla was initiated by Tarquinius Priscus who first of all rewarded his son with a golden bulla because he had killed an enemy while he was still young enough to wear the toga praetexta and he wanted men of patrician rank to use it. The Romans, as we deduce from some very old monuments, took this from the

Etruscans; they often decorated the statues of gods and goddesses with a bulla. The same honour was later transferred to noble women as well. The Statue in question is no ways remarkable for the work, but from the rarity of its having the Bulla: The boy seems to be about 16 years old: He has on the Pretexta, a loose robe, which comes quite to the feet, but upon the Arms, only down to the elbow.

Valerius Maximus (III.1.1) says this about a statue of M(arcus) Aemilius Lepidus: that he, while still a boy, advanced into battle, killed an enemy and saved a fellow-citizen. There is a memorial of this remarkable deed on the Capitol: a statue of a boy wearing a bulla and a toga praetexta, commissioned by the senate. Gorii, Mus: Flor[m]:

A Group: a woman pulling a Man, and appearing to endeavour to stop him from going somewhere: Some people think it Caius Cæsar or Caligula, wth. his Sister Drusilla.

Fig 9 The Tribune of the Uffizi, 1772-78

Saturday 21st July – Florence

We have as yet been obliged to see a great many very indifferent things, to be able to find out something worth notice; This Morning we were more than made amends for the bad things we had seen in the Corridore's, by the many very valuable, and indeed inestimable things, we found in the La Camera detta La Tribuna.

La Tribuna. This room is of an Octagon form; the light comes in by a Cupola in the Top, and several small windows round the sides. In the middle of the Room stands an Octagon Table of Florentine work; at some distance from the Table, are six large Statues. Behind them against the wall several smaller ones: upon a Shelf about 6 feet from the Groins a great many small pieces of Antiquity, and Busts, and round the wall above this a great many valuable Pictures: There is a kind of Alcove filled with different pieces of work in precious stones, and on each side of this is a kind of Closet filled with valuable things of various sorts. – In speaking of these things I shall content myself to mention only those that are most remarkable or, at least pleased me the most. – *Venus de Medicis.* At entering the Octagon, the first thing that must strike the Eye, and draw the attention of ev'ry one, is that master piece of Sculpture, the Venus de Medicis. I am afraid to attempt giving any description of her, as I am very well convinced, how impossible it must be not only for me, but for any one, to confer a tolerable Idea of the Beauties and Perfections of this Statue. Venus is here represented with her head inclineing towards her left Shoulder: Her Right hand is placed before her breast, and her left over a part, which her modesty bids her conceal: Her body somewhat bent, and leaning forward, seems expressive of a kind of shame, of her being naked; and her right knee being a little bent, which obliges her to bear lightly upon her toes, all contribute to increase the Idea of Modesty, and decency. – Her hair is of a yellowish Brown, caused as is beleived, by their hav'ing been formerly gilt: Her Ears are bore'd; and it is well known that the antients used often to give her ear-rings of precious Stones. Her head is certainly very small, and 'tho at present very pleasing, might perhaps be more proportioned to her body if it was somewhat larger: 'Tho it would be difficult to find fault with any feature of her face, and 'tho undoubtedly some parts are done with the greatest skill, and delicacy, I cannot myself help thinking she has an unmeaning, unexpressive countenance. Her neck is truely beautiful: Long, finely turned, less'ning properly towards her head, and swelling at the bottom: Her breast is perhaps still more compleatly finished; In some parts so free and natural, at the same time that one sees the greatest effort of art, assisted by the most perfect imagination, exerting itself, and happily producing more attracting beauties, which we imagine in a Venus such as we see in this, 'tho seldom I beleive are found in the real works of nature to the same degree: – The lower parts of the body are equally beautiful; What can be better executed than the fleshy parts, which appear so beautifully plump and delicate, that upon touching it, one is surprized not to find them yeald to the pressure: How beautiful are the Shoulders and lower parts of her back; neither does the partition in her back, wch. M^r. Kesler thinks too deep, appear so to me. The Sculptor has shewed his skill greatly in more trifling parts; what can be more delicate, & perfect than her knees and the parts joining both above & below: Her very feet don't fail to have an equal share of beauty. – I think it impossible to examine her thoroughly, and not be convinced that the arm, and hands (which partake but little of the beauty, of the rest) are by the hand of some inferior workman. They have surely very little of that round, full, fleshy look which distinguishes the other parts: One sees in them a disagreable stiffness & dryness: and particularly in the left hand: The Head may very probably have belonged to some other Venus, not quite so large as this, and which if one may judge by the work of the Head was little inferior to this: – But how much in vain is it to attempt a description of her: Mr Gorii very rightly says:

[*translated*] Without doubt no words, by their power, skill or colourful rhetorical flourishes, can adequately express the quality or quantity of its beauty, craftsmanship and refinement.

She stands upon a Pedestal about 3 feet high: On the other Stone to which the Statue is fixed is the following Inscription

[*translated*] Kleomenes, the son of Apollodorus, of Athens made this

There are many reasons for thinking that Cleomenis was not the author of this Statue; First, that, 'tho he is known to have been a great Sculptor, and many Antient Authors mention his works, no one ever mentions his makeing a Venus; Secondly, the badness of the greek, wch. instead of ΕΠΩΕΣΕΝ should be ΕΠΟΙΕΙ: and thirdly nothing can be more evident or plain, than that all the fore part of the Stone, did not belong originally to the Statue, but has been joined since. M^r. Gorii says of it

[*translated*] It is the opinion of many men that its creator was either Pheidias or Praxiteles or Scopas whose "naked Venus", standing near the Circus Flaminius, surpassed the "Venus of Cnidus" of Praxiteles, according to Pliny. But this is still a matter of opinion.

There is a Dolphin against her left foot, and two little Cupids setting upon him – The Sculptor seems to have given all his attention to the Venus, and to have taken little or no pains about the Dolphin & Cupids which are very indifferently executed.

This Statue which was brought from the Medici Palace at Rome by order of Cosmo the third, suffer'd much by Carriage; It was broke across the legs, thighs, and arms: They have been pretty well restored, tho the cement wth. wch. they have been joined is of a very different colour from the marble, which was of a fine white, 'tho it is at present turned a little yellow: It still retains a beautiful Polish in many parts.

Venus Calestis. To the left hand of this Venus stands another, called by M^r. Gorii Venus Calestis: She is raither smaller than the Venus de Medicis; is very beautiful tho will by no means bare being compared with her: She is naked down to the waiste, which is one of the reasons for calling her, Calestis, she has a kind of Diadem round her head: Her right hand is bent up to her head, and appears to be doing something to her hair; With her left hand she holds up some loose robes that cover her from the waiste to the knees. We employed about two hours in examineing these two Statues, and found that in respect to the former of them, one might employ as much more time without being tired, and might still discover new beauties.

S^r. Horace Man introduced us this Evening to Count Lorenzo, Minister or raither, charge d'affaires from France. Madame de Lorenzo had a small conversattione where we staid about an hour: – She talks french very well.

Sunday 22nd July – Florence

We went this afternoon to Le Marquis Guadagni, at the Piazza del Duomo, to see a horse race, which was very bad: In the Eveng: we returned to an assembly in the same house. There was a great deal of Company; most of them engaged in Games I understood nothing of. This is a very large, handsome house: there were many rooms lighted up, but most of the Company set in a kind of Court, w^ch., as the weather was very hot, was cover'd over with Cloths on purpose, & was very pleasant.

Monday 23rd July – Florence

Faunus. We returned this morning to La Tribuna. The next Statue after the Venus Calestis is Faunus.

[*translated*] An outstanding Greek sculptor, who has obviously sculpted this statue with exceptional skill, created Faunus, celebrating the rites of his father Liber in a way that has been recorded by the ancients. For with his body bent, with his head lifted up a little, with stretched arms and hands and with his whole body he has been portrayed in such a way that he seems to be dancing. In his hands he holds cymbals which would have been made of bronze, as if he is about to crash them together at that very moment. His face is difficult to see, but his eyes have been sculpted very skilfully. With his right foot he presses on a crupetium.

Ev'ry part of this Statue is executed with the greatest skill, and in the most natural manner: M[r]. Gorii from whom I took the above description, attributes it to Praxitiles: The Head, and arms, which were broke off, were restored by Michel Ange, and in the opinion of most people they are equal to the rest of the Statue. It is impossible for a face to be more expressive of that wild Joy, and Gayity, which one should expect to see in the Countenance of a danc'ing Faunus. – His tail is broke.

Explorator. The fourth Statue is the Explorator, or Arrotino: It is the figure of a man kneeling upon his right knee, his body bent forward, his head thrown a little back, – holding a knife, against a Stone upon the ground, with his right hand, and pressing it close to the Stone with two or three fingers of his left hand: – Various are the opinions, whom this figure is meant to represent; It is a Common opinion that it is intended for some Country fellow, who happening to over hear some of Catalines Conspiraters, went and discover'd them: M[r]. Gorii thinks it may be one Milichium, wheting a Poignard given him by Flavius Scevinus (a), who was the chief author of the Conspiracy against Nero, who afterwards had this Statue made of him for discovering his danger to him. Ev'ry part of this Statue is finished with great truth, and exactness, but the Head and neck seem superior to many other parts. – He has a cloth hanging loose over his Shoulders.

(a) Qui Pisoniana conginationis adversos Nerorem Cesarem praecipius acutus fecit Tacitus

Pancratiastæ. The fifth Piece, is a most admirable Group of two wrestlers, or the Pancratiastæ. One of them has thrown down his adversary, and lays upon him. His left thigh comes over the Hip of the other, and that leg is under the others left leg, so as to bear up the foot from the Ground. He thrust his left shoulder hard upon the right shoulder of the other, and at the same time, with his left hand forces back the right hand and arm of the other, so as to give himself an opportunity to give the other a blow upon his Head; in order to do which you see his right arm and hand, with his fist clinched, drawn behind him. The other which is undermost sustains the whole weight with his left hand and arm, and one sees plainly attempts to over throw the man that is upon him. One can not be otherwise than surprized to see with what truth and exactness, ev'ry muscle that ought to appear, are here expressed; How exactly the Sculptor has given to ev'ry part the quantity of force it ought to act with, by the effect that that force must have upon the part, acting or acted upon. The Heads are well done, 'tho much the inferior part of the work, especially of the uppermost man: The great difference there is in the manner of working that head, from the rest of the figure, give great room to suppose, it did not belong to it originally. I could not find out wh^t. M^r. Kesler meant by the broken arm: They appear all of them to me very entire, except the right hand of the man who is uppermost, which has been broke in the Statue, but could not have been in the real person, as it must have naturally fell down, and been incapable of strikeing in the manners you see him prepared to do: – I suppose the most skilful Anatomist would have great difficulty to find fault with the formation of ev'ry limb & part, or placeing ev'ry nerve and Muscle, and I beleive the best Sculptor would have equall difficulty to find fault with the execution of any part of it.

The Sixth and last large Statue is that of Venus Victix; It is of almost a Colossal size; She has an Apple in her right hand; As she is naked her Modesty, directs her where to place the other. Many parts of her are not antique. She is not void of Beauty, but it is almost eclypsed by the Superior charms of her neighbour, the Venus Anadyomene, or Medicis, as she is commonly called. – - – -

Small statues &c. Behind these six large Statues are placed several small ones close against the wall: The following ones appeared to me the most remarkable, or best. A little Morpheus; he has wings upon his head, and a Bunch of Poppy's in one hand, wch. rests upon the ground on one side of him; There is also another figure of Morpheus, much the same size, but it has no wings on the head; but a kind of Moth just by. They are both very well executed. In speaking of the Statues in the Gallerie I forgot to mention a Morpheus I saw there, and which is of Black Marble; I think they call'd it touch-stone. M^r. Addison observes upon seeing it, that he has never seen a Morpheus that was not Black, which he says has some relation to night, the proper season for Sleep; – The two Morpheus's I saw in the Tribune are both of white marble, which is raither unfortunate for M^r. Addisons ingenious remark: but one must imagine that they were not there when M^r. Addison travell'd, for they are certainly in ev'ry respect much better worth his observation. These are certainly antique, the other is not.

The figure of a boy in Marble of a dull blackish colour: I beleive it is Ethiopian, and they call it Basalt: It was intended to represent Britanicus:

'Tho it seems very evident that the Head and body were never designed for each other, as the body is cloathed with the Toga Virilis, which does not agree with the Head, wch. is plainly that of a boy not more than nine or ten years old: And besides Britanicus was killed before he was old enough to put on the Toga Virilis. The Head is pretty good. – There is a Silenus and two or three more such figures, I think not worth mentioning. After these follow the Antiquities upon the Shelf; The most remarkable are the following. – First the Diana Ephesia: It is about a foot high, & chiefly remarkable for the simbols, and allegorical figures with which it is ornamented: I shall take some extracts from Mr Gorii's description of them.

> [*translated*] I shall briefly deal with several aspects. The first thing to notice is the crenellated crown which is associated with her, not only to increase the majesty and dignity of her head, following the example of the Egyptian gods, but also to show both her power over all the peoples and cities under the moon and the virtue and kindness of her nature as the protector of all.

He here quotes some authors, who call her,

> [*translated*] Queen Diana, exercising power far and wide, and the unconquered protector hav'ing power over countrys, & being the Protectress of Towns & Cities,

&c. &c.

> [*translated*] Diana is shown clothed, in my opinion, so that everyone may more freely venerate her, conspicuous in her more heavenly appearance. The neck and chest of this goddess have been much less decorated than we see in other statues: however, from a stylish collar between her breasts hangs a crescent from a small branch which carries a palm arranged with a circle of leaves. The palm is sacred to this goddess, commemorating her birth from Latona; Apuleius tells us that the palm is sacred to Iris as well as Diana.

The rest of the body of this same Diana is decorated in four sections, in each one small images have been sculpted in relief.

In the first section portrait bust are shown: on the right is Diana or Luna, on the left is Apollo or Sol. Behind the shoulders appear a discus or a sphere or a crescent moon in other statues like this one of this same goddess, as Menetrius has published. However, here wings of birds flying up high like this seem to have been shown but the head of Apollo radiates light, decorated in a circle like a discus or a spherical cloud.

In the second section have been sculpted the three sisters, the Graces, whom the Greeks call the Charites; they are naked and have their arms around each other. People in antiquity made these goddesses the protectors of beauty of appearance, and they are the companions of all the gods. This remarkable statue clearly shows them to be additional companions of Diana as well. On both sides one can see two cornucopias, full of fruits and flowers, of which one is carved in the upper portion and given to Sol, the other to Luna; this is to show, as the Mythwriters believed, their generosity on the earth and their oversight of all matters relating to fertility.

In the third section a sea nymph has been sculpted, sitting on a goat and carried across the sea with a sail filled with breezes and accompanied by a dolphin; an ancient poet says that Apollo travelled across the sea in a four-horsed chariot and that Diana also was carried across the deep on a two-horse chariot, and that she sank into the Ocean and from there they say she rose again.

In the last section have been shown three *Genii* companions or attendants of Diana: the middle one holds a bow, the one on the right a spear, the one on the left a quiver. Finally, Diana of Ephesus is shown with open hands and outstretched arms in a gesture used by the those making prayers and sacrifices; this is how she reveals herself to her devotees, listening to their supplications and prayers.

The second piece we observed was that of Hercules choacking the Nemean lion: The Lion is represented with his Head under the arm of Hercules, with one foreleg round his thigh, and the other upon his arm. It is but small, I beleive about 14 Inches high: It seems well executed.
Thirdly, a very elegant figure of Juno Regina: In her right hand she has a Paterra. In her left hand which is held up, she has a kind of Truncheon, or what in latin, is called Sceptrum, sine hastum, tho it resembles much more a truncheon, than a spear.

Fourthly, a very pretty Cupid; he has neither bow, nor arrow.

Fifthly, and Sixthly, two beautiful heads of two Boys; One of them is Marc⁵: Aurelius; and the other a Nero: They are both valuable pieces of Antiquity. Seventhly, a very good head of Tiberius in Blue, Turkey Stone. 8ˡʸ: A very good head of Nerva, when young. Ninethly, a Canopus, made of Chalcedoniy. Just by the Door is a very curious picture in Mosaic work done in the year 1615. An owl, a Gold finch and many more birds are represented in the most natural manner.

We went this Evening to an assembly at the Marquis de Caponi: This is one of the most antient and ritch families in Florence. They have a very fine house, and the gardens for this place are pretty: There was but little company this Evening, and it was altogether very dull, & stupid. La Marquise is raither pretty than not. They tell some ridiculous story's of her great delicacy, and [*space left at end of line*].

Tuesday 24th July – Florence

Pictures. This Morning we were employed in the examination of the Pictures in the Tribune, or Octogon: We began by those below the Shelf, which runs all round, & on wch. are placed the Bronzes, &c: – The Head of Swiss Paisainne, by Holben. She has only a plain white Cap upon her head, wch. comes far over her face, and gives her quite the appearance of an honest, plain country-woman, which Holben too has most admirably expressed by the unaffectedness and simplicity of her Countenance. I think it an exceedingly good head. – Not far from this is the Head of S^r. Rich^d: Southwell, and another of Luther, by the same hand – they are both well done. – An exceeding pretty picture by Titian of the Virgin, and our Saviour. – A most beautiful Picture of the Virgin by Annibal Caracci. An Adoration of the Shepherds, by Vanderwerf. It is impossible to imagine any thing to be finished with greater exactness, or to a greater degree, than this little piece: The Flemish Painters distinguish themselves, much more by the great delicacy of Colouring, and the Labour they bestow upon the most minute parts, than by good drawing, or by their Imagination, for which reason one is more surprized than pleased by seeing these laborious performances: There is a Picture by Gherar-Daw, very well done, and much in the same manner of the last, only not quite so exactly finished. S^t. Joseph, a man at work, the Virgin and our Saviour very young, and behind them an old woman, by Rambrant: It is a very good Picture; the Shades strong, and have a fine effect: The Colours are fine, tho perhaps raither too strong. A good Picture of Raphael by Leonar: de Vinci. The first Picture over the Shelf, and next the door, to the left, as one comes in, is a very beautiful one, done by Corregio: He has represented the Virgin Standing up, and looking at our Saviour, who lays upon the ground before her. The Colouring of this Piece is very fine; The Head of the Virgin is very pleasing, whether it be too big for her body or not, as M^r. Cochin remarks it is: He is certainly very right in saying that the Child is too small; and I think there is no doubt but his head is too large; there is certainly too something very disagreable in the bend of the left hand, & arm, of the Virgin.

A large Picture of a Cardinal by Titian, which is very well done.

A very beautiful Picture by Hannibal Caracci. He has here represented a naked woman laying with her back towards you: A Satyre presenting a basket of Flowers to her: and two young Children. Ev'ry one of these figures are drawn in the most natural manner. The woman supports herself on her left arm, wch. is thrown behind her. The shadeing of the back is perfectly well done, except that towards the bottom it seems too dark. The Colour of the Satyr too, is remarkably dark: – This Picture however is esteemed one of the master pieces of, Annibal Caracci.

Three Pictures by Raphael, each done in a different manner; The Subjects of two of them, finished in his first, and second manner, are the same; The Virgin our Saviour, and S^t. John; the third Picture done in his last manner, is the figure of S^t. John, when a large Boy... – The two first, 'tho better, are much in the stile of his master, P: Perugino: There is a hardness, and dryness, in the Colouring, and a formality in, the figure, which one does not see in his last works; In the S^t. John the Colours are much more soft and beautiful, and the figure drawn with more ease and freedom: The head is finely finished, and full of expression: – But tho this piece is much better than the two others, I think it much inferior, to many others I have seen of this masters. The proportions seem to me very ill observed: the left leg in particular seems much too long & large.

Two Pictures by Guido; one a Virgin, in his last manner; the other a Cleopatra, in his first manner; – The Virgin has a veil over her head, with her Eyes cast upwards. The Colours in this piece are bright, and Clear, and certainly soft, and beautiful; nevertheless I cannot say that they please me so much as the darker, grey kind of Colours, which one sees in the Cleopatra; done in his first manner.

We left the remainder of the Pictures for another day.

M^ess. Lyttleton, Ellison, Gibbon, and myself dined to day at M^r. Dicks, a little way out of Florence.

Wednesday 25th July – Florence

L^d. Palmerston[1] came here to day. – We dined with him at S^r. Horace Manns. – There was a Race between three Boats upon the Arno this Eveng: just before our windows: The boats were ugly, the men Rowed ill, and fortunately it was all over in about ten minutes. The Crowd of People and Coaches, was the

---

1   Henry Temple, 2nd Viscount Palmerston, 1739 – 1802, aged therefore 25. He was the MP for East Looe at the time. Guise and Gibbon had met with him previously in Lausanne. He was on his way to Rome, where he bought several pictures and antiquities. His son was Prime Minister of the United Kingdom in the mid nineteenth century.

same as if it had been worth seeing. – We went afterwards to La Comtesse de Acchiolis, where there was a pretty large Assembly – The Countesses vanity and passions seem to increase, with her age and ugliness, which are already pretty well advanced.

Thursday 26ᵗʰ July – Florence

Naked Venus of Titian. We went this Morning to see the remainder of the Pictures in the Tribune. – The first object of our admiration was the beautiful, Venus of Titian: – It is as difficult to give a good Idea of this incomparable piece, as it was of the Venus of Medicis, Painting in this is carried to as great perfection as Sculptor is in the other: Titian has here given to our view all the Charms of a most beautiful female figure, laying quite naked at full length upon a white Bed. – She is raither turned upon her right side, her head, and the uper part of her body, raither higher than the lower, and supported by her right arm, which is bent, and in her right hand she holds some flowers. Her left arm is brought over her body, and with her left hand she prevents the modest Eye from being offended; and her left leg is lay'd over the right: Her hair which is of a bright chestnut colour, is part plated over the top of her head, and part falls in flowing curls upon her right shoulder. – As one of the perfections of painting, seems to me to be, that of makeing the thing painted agree in ev'ry respect with, what is intended to be represented, and to convey to the Spectator, the idea of the Painter; if that is an excellence, this Venus I should imagine must be perfect. The roundness of the limbs, the delicate plumpness of the body, the fine carnation blush which glows through a tender, delicate skin, gives you the Idea of a young Venus, and the features of her face convince of you of her youth: – Nothing can be more happily executed than ev'ry part of this master piece of Titians. -Upon the bed just by the feet of the woman lays a little, yellow and white Dog, sleeping; and very well done: In the back ground of the Picture is a woman kneeling down to take some cloathes out of Chest, which is held open by another woman standing by. These figures seem raither too small in proportion to the rest, and for the distance; This half of the Picture has a light coloured ground; the other half, for the Upper part of the Venus, is of a Dark Colour: Some painters think the ground ill chosen. –

Over this is another Venus, by the same hand. She is leaning on her left arm: There is a Cupid hanging, and looking over her Shoulder; In her hand she holds a bunch of Flowers: At her feet there is a little dog: and just above a bird. This Venus appears in ev'ry respect older than the other. It is certainly a fine piece of painting, but appears to great disadvantage, and looses much by being hung, so near the other.

'Tho there are undoubtedly many other good and valuable paintings in this Room, as they are most, or all of them, mentioned by Cochin, and I have already given an account of those y[t]. pleased me the most, I don't think it worth while to take any more notice of the others.

Cabinets. In one side of the Room is a kind of Alcove, or Cabinet, which is ornamented, with pillars of Lapis Lazuli (the Capitals of which are of Gold,) with Bas-reliefs in Gold, and all the sides coverd with different precious Stones, most of them very large; In the Top is a remarkably large Pearl, and a Topaz of an extraordinary bigness. – The two Cabinets on each side are filled with vases made of Lapis Lazuli, Cristal, Jasper, Granate and various other stones: These are all of them remarkable either for the largness of the Stones, or for the workmanship.

In the middle of the Room stands a large Octagon Table of the florentine work: – Like those I have already mentioned, it is chiefly remarkable for its being composed entirely of precious Stones, worked with great art and exactness: – We were told it cost above forty thousand Sequins.

We dined to day with Lord Palmerston; Mess: Lyttleton, Ellison, Blanchard, Abbey Pillory, & Doctor Cochin were of the Company. – I have not time to say any more at present: – In the Evening we went to Consul Dicks, where we found, Mesdames Accioli & Minorbetty.

Friday 27th and Saturday 28th July – Florence

Hav'ing finished seeing the Gallery we thought it better to rest two or three days before we went to any new place, especially as we were both far behind with our Journals, and had a great deal to write; so that we employed our Mornings, instead of going out, in writing; and we had no other engagement for the Evening than takeing a sober walk with L[d]. Palmerston, or hearing M[r]. Lyttleton's extravagancies.

Sunday 29th July – Florence

Dined to day in a very numerous Company at S[r]. Horace Manns. Mesdames Accioli; Minerbetty, & Dick, L[d]. Palmerston, Mess Littleton, Ellison, Blanchard, Wolfe & Moula (who I forgot to mention, came here Friday) Dick, an Italian, Guibon & myself, I think were all the Company: – In the Evening we went to a horse race; If I describe it, it would be only a repetition of what we saw S[r]. Johns day; the same horses, in the same place; Indeed we had the additional pleasure of seeing the Grand Diavolo, win; He has won twice at Pistoia, since he run here last; and I am told that Alessandre has been offer'd 1000 Sequins for him, although he is twenty-two or three years old. – We went after this to see some dancers upon the tight Rope; There was a German that danced remarkably well with the Pole; very little without.

Monday 30ᵗʰ & Tuesday 31ˢᵗ July – Florence

Doctor Cocchi being engaged both these days, we could not see the Medals as we intended, and therefor employed our Mornings, as usual when we staid at home. Monday, we dined with Mʳ. Ellison, and Mʳ. Blanchard, and in the Evening went with them and Lᵈ. Palmerston to sup at a Country house, Charles has about a mile out of Florence; Tuesday Lᵈ. Palmerston, and Lyttleton dined with us, and we walked upon the Bridge, or near it till 11 o'clock.

August: Florence 1764.
Wednesday 1ˢᵗ August – Florence

Palazzo Pitty. We went this Morning to see Palazzo de Pitty, where the great Dukes commonly reside; – I beleive it is not near finished; but the front of it, in its present state, seems to be very far from handsome; It is a Rustic building, very low, and of a vast length, and gives one more the Idea of a Fortress, than a Palace. – There is a Court in the middle of the Palace that is really handsome, and compleat. Tho I cannot help thinking myself, it is too small for its heigh. It is entirely rustic, and consists of three orders. The first Story, Doric Pillars; second Ionic, & third Corinthian. The rustic seems to me to have a bad effect in Pillars, especially in the manner one sees it in the Ionic Pillars here, which are composed of great square, unhewn stones. In the other Pillars they are round.

      The Staircase of the Pala is very spacious, and handsome. There is a very numerous and handsome Suit of Rooms, in the front next the Town: It is altogether a very large building and contains as the servant told us ...... rooms. – They are at present fitting it up in a very handsome manner for the reception of the Great Duke; which is raither unfortunate for us, as we are prevented thereby seeing a great many valuable pictures which they have been obliged to take down, least they should be hurt by the work, and workmen. This however has not deprived us of the sight of a few of the most valuable, which still remain in their proper places. – The first paintings we were shewn, were the Ceilings in the long Apartment looking over the Town. – In a pretty large room that lays to the right hand at Comeing in, is a cieling painted by Pietro da Cortona: It represents a Man who appears to be trying to persuade a young man, to quit the Arms of a woman who holds him back: It is well done, but the colours seem to me very weak, and in ev'ry respect much inferior to some paintings one sees just below the Cieling in the side of the room. They are all in the shape of the picture part of a Fan, and relate to some historical Story. The following pleased me the most: Seleucus, K^g: of Syria, giving up his wife Stratonice to his son Antiochus. – You see Antiochus who appears weak and ill, laying upon a bed, and a Phisician standing by and feeling his Pulse; before the bed stands Seleucus holding his wife with one hand, and moveing the other as if to signifie the intention of giveing up his wife. Each of the figures in this Piece are expressive of its particular character, and the Colours are lively and vigorous.

In another is represented the Story of Scipio Africanus, restoreing a Beautiful young woman, his prisoner, to the Celtibarien to whom she was engaged. – In one part of the picture is Scipio setting down, and pointing to a man who stands, by a woman, who is likewise standing before Scipio. This is well done tho I think hardly so well done as the last.

Another very good piece is Alexander after haveing made prisoners the family of Darius. The tent is not there, as it usually is; but you see a Queen kneeling down, and several other woman kneeling just by.
There are five more all relateing either to profane or sacred history. They are most of them well done.

In another Room farther on, is a cieling done by the same hand; In the middle are painted the Arms of Medicis (a): On one side a naval combat; on another side, a woman (the emblem I suppose of Tuscany or some Town) seting down, and a great many figures of Men and women, some of them in Chains, and kneeling down, others standing near her. – The Coulours of this piece are bright and strong, the figures well designed, and the heads of the women in general full of Grace: The whole is highly finished.

(a) The arms of the Medici, are, Six Balls; in the middle of one of them are three Fleurs de lys, given to

We went through four or five more Rooms on this side of the house, the Cielings of which were painted either by Pietro da Cortona, or Ciro Ferri. There is one Chambre the side walls of which were painted by one Nasini of Siena. On one side is represented, Death; on a second side, the last Judgment; on a third Heaven; and on the fourth; Hell; I cannot say that I think either the Subject well treated or the painting well executed. – These Rooms are all very richly ornamented with Gilding, and appear as if they would be very handsome when finished.

We were led through several rooms in which there are a great number of indifferent Pictures; but at last our attention was fixed by a most beautiful & perfect performance of Raphaels. It is a round picture, and commonly distinguished by the name of, La Madonna della Sedia. – You see the Virgin setting in a Chair, and holding the Infant Jesus in her Lap; the little S^r. John is standing by. This picture is filled with all the expression, sweetness, and delicacy imaginable. The Head of the Virgin is beautiful; I think I never saw any face so expressive of innocent satisfaction, and great good nature, and mildness of disposition; The Head of our Saviour is incomparably done; and the little S^r. John 'tho I think something inferior to the others, is nevertheless, worthy of admiration; The Colouring is very good; – One never seems satisfied wth. looking at it.

M^r. Ellison, and M^r. Blanchard dined with us to day – They left Florence this Evening – The former we are told is a relation of Lord Ravensworth – He looks near 30 yrs: old; and his behaviour agrees very much with that account: He seems sensible, and not to want knowledge: M^r. Blanchard, they say, was bred a Phisician, is something younger, and I have no reason not to say as much of him as the other, only that I don't know so much of him. Nothing more worth writeing today.

Thursday 2nd August – Florence

We returned this Morning to Le palais Pitty. – In a large room we passed through, we found a great number of large Pictures placed one upon another in a manner that we could not see them, at that time, and were told we could not at all, without a particular permission, which we intend having, if worth the pains: – In the next room we went into, we saw an excellent picture, by André del Sarte. On one side is S^t. John, on the other S^t. François, and between them the Virgin, and the Infant Jesus; – The Colouring is certainly bright, strong, and soft; the figures easy and natural, nevertheless the picture seems to me much less pleasing than some others less talked of, and praised. The face of the Virgin is very unmeaning, and all the figures have something very uninteresting.

A very particular Annunciation, said to be done by Paul Veronese. The Virgin is quite at one end of the Picture, and an Angel at the other end: Between them you see a building upon Pillars and quite in the Middle you discover through the Building a distant view of Trees, and Landskip; – It is esteemed as a good Picture, but at present, it appears to me damaged, and to have no great remains of beauty.

An exceeding good Picture of Cardinal Bentivoglio, by Van Dyck. – One finds no one that has succeeded better than him, in painting the Pictures of real People.

We came next to a most beautiful Allegorical Picture by Rubens; – He has expressed in this piece more fire, and livelyness of Imagination, that I remember to have seen in any Picture before. The Subject of it appears Poetical. In the Middle of the Picture is a Man in Armour, drawn forward by a Fury with a Torch in his hand, at the same time that a beautiful woman endeavors to hold him back; Another woman follows, seemingly in the greatest despair: — It is impossible for figures to be more expressive than those four: — In the Man in Armour you see the most determined resolution; In the Fury a most horrible wildness, and kind of Madness; in the first woman a melancholy sadness: and in the other that seems to be runing after, with her head thrown back, and arms extended, you see the greatest degree of Mad despair: In another part of the Picture is the Temple of Janus, with the door open; and several figures, intended to represent different, arts and sciences, all thrown down, and in disorder. -

We saw several more pictures this Morning, but in ev'ry respect so much inferior to those already mentioned, that I think it would be waisting both my time, and Paper to take any more notice of them.

In the Evening we took a walk in the Gardens belonging to the Palace; They are called Giardino di Boboli, and seem prettily planted, and disposed in walks, and open Groves; There is a piece of water in one part, with an Island in the Middle, which is entirely planted, with Orange Trees, Lemons, and other things of that sort: — Opposite the inward Court of the House is Built an open Amphitheatre, in the middle of which is a open space I suppose for combats of wild beasts.

M^r. Lyttleton, Lord Palmerston, M^r. Gibbon, and myself walked here 'till nine o'clock, and then for want of a better employment, went to the Theatre to see the Rope Dancers.

Friday 3rd August – Florence

After the usual employment of takeing my lesson of Italien, we went to the Gallery: Came home early; continued my Journal: It is very difficult to keep up a Journal, when one has so many things to see, and other occupations beside. – Lord Palmerston, Mess^s. Lyttleton, Loups a Duchman, Gibbon, and myself dined with Baron Wolfe. The Baron appears more simple, ev'ry time one sees him.

In the Evening we accompanied S^r. Horace Man to an assembly at La Comtesse de Guicchardini's: She is of the same family with the Author of y^e. History.

Saturday 4th August – Florence

Staid at home this Morning. All the same company that dined yesterday with

Baron Wolfe (except the Duchman) dined to day with Lord Palmerston. – In the Evening we went to a very handsome and numerous Assembly at S^r. Horace Manns. His Garden was illuminated, and ev'ry thing done in a very elegant manner, and different from any, we have yet seen at Florence.

Sunday 5th August – Florence

Bⁿ: Wolfe and M^r. Moula dined with us; In the Eveng: we went to Consul Dicks: where we found a Mrs Franks, her Daughter <u>Polly</u>, a Clergyman, and some more from Leghorn: – I know nothing good, or ill, of either.

Monday 6th August – Florence

Lord Palmerston, myself and Gibbon dined with Lyttleton: In the Eveng: went to La Comtesse dell Ricco.

Tuesday 7th August – Florence

We were shewn the Medals this Morning, by Doctor Cocchi, who has the care of them. They are now kept in a large Chambre by the Gallery. The whole number of Medals amount to about 29,000: They consist of great Bronze, small Ditto, Gold, and many in silver. There seem to be but very few, of the very first Emperors: The great bronze I beleive are pretty compleat, and very well preserved. The others may be equally, but we did not examine them so much. There are a great many relateing to Colonies; – The time given for examining so great a Collection, is very unequal to what they require, more particularly for one who is so little conversant in this Study as myself, and as there are some very uncommon medals that require a particular attention.

Upon the reverses of the Medals representing Men, or women that were deified, you often see some bird flying up to heaven with their Soul: An Eagle commonly carries the Male Soul, and a Peacock the Female: We were much surprised for that reason to see an <u>Eagle</u> flying off with that of Faustina. We saw here the pound Sterling in Silver; cast in the time of Charles the First. You see upon it, Charles on horse back; the date, 1643 and motto: Exsurgat Deus, et dissipentur inimici ejus. –

Wednesday 8th August – Florence.

Lord Palmerston, M^{ess}. Lyttleton, Hay (lately come here; not known to any of us), Wolfe, Moula, Coll: Mills, Gibbon, myself and some others dined with S^r. Horace Mann to day. Lord Palmerston left us this Evening, and went I beleive to Lucca: Intends going soon to Parma by Genoa, into the South of France, to Paris, and I beleive home the begining of the winter: – We have reason to regret his being gone; – He is reserved 'till he is pretty well aquainted with his Company; afterwards not too much so: He does not appear to have very quick parts, or very lively imagination, but has certainly a very good memory, a great deal of knowledge, – and an exceeding good Sense, and Judgment: He travells more to inform, than to amuse himself, and few people take more pains to a better purpose. We supped this Evening at Consul Dicks.

Thursday 9ᵗʰ August – Florence

Employed this Morning in reading and writeing. Mʳ. Lyttleton left us this Morning: He is gone to make a little tour of Leghorn, Sienna, &c; pour chasser l'ennui, which he complained much of here. – I beleive few People wish his return. – I never knew any one succeed so well in makeing himself generally disliked; and entirely by his own fault, as he does not want for parts, or knowledge that might make his company more desired, if he knew how to use them.

He has a very lively imagination, very quick parts, and a great memory; seems to have read many books, but studyed none; Has a great stock of vanity, which makes him think himself superior to most people, in Family, talents, and knowledge, by which means he often affronts those that have the advantage of him in both. – He would appear very ambitious, and flatters himself with ideas of makeing a great figure in publick life, and being a Man of Consequence, in which it is impossible he can ever succeed, if he does not act with a little more modesty, to make himself better liked, and with a little more Judgment and steadiness, to be more depended upon: – His chief design in travelling in Italy seems to be, to amuse himself.

Sʳ. Horace Mann, took us this Evening to three Assembly's. First to La Comtesse de Galli, where there was a small assembly of old women; for which reason we went to La Marquises de Garini's, where there was a much better assembly, in a better house. This is not an ancient but a ritch family, for which they are obliged to a handsome young Fellow of this family, who was a great favorite of one of the Medici's: – Not being able either to talk Italien or Play at Cards, we were not sorry to leave this house early, and go to Prince Strozzi's, where there were some people that talked french.

Friday 10ᵗʰ August – Florence

Palais Riccardi. We went this Morning to see the Palais Riccardi: like most of the houses here, it is very large, and contains two parts of the same family: The Greatest part of this house was built by Cosmo de Medicis about yᵉ. year 1430, and enlarged by the Marquis de Rivalti (of the Riccardi family) and who bought it of Ferdinand the Second. –

After going up one pair of Stairs, you come into a very handsome Gallery, very well proportioned as to heigth, breadth, and length; It is ritchly ornamented with gilding, and Glasses; The Cieling from one end to the other is painted by Luca Giordano, in a very bold, and beautiful manner: The figures, of which there are many, are Graceful, and natural, and the Colouring is bright, and strong, without being tawdry, or Course. It is the most pleasing Gallery I have yet seen: In one Side of the Room are several little Cabinets -with wire before them, where are first against a red velvet a great number of Cammeo's, and Intaglios, which may be very valuable, without our being able to know it by seeing them in that manner. -

We went from the Gallery into several good Rooms, and in which there are a considerable number of Pictures, most of them of a middling rank; – The two best I remember to have seen on this floor, were a S^t. John, and a S^t. Matthew, both painted by, Carlo Dulci. These are very expressive, and natural, and 'tho finished to a great degree, are not so exact or delicate as to loose their force.

We went up another pair of Stairs, into the smaller Rooms and which serve for the winter habitation: – We soon felt that the Italiens act very sensibly in respect to avoiding the Heats and Cold: In the Summer they alwais inhabit the Ground floors, in Spring and Autumn, the Second floor, and in Winter they avoid the Cold by makeing use of the Third Storey. – It was there that at the expence of being a little roasted, we saw two, or three good pictures. One of them most admirably done by Rembrandt: The subject is particular, as his often, are, and I think it is painted strongly after his manner, by which, it seems to me, not difficult to know his works. The Chief object in this Picture is an old woman picking a fowl; On both sides of her you see Copper pots, kettles, and rush baskets. The shadeing of the woman's face is remarkably dark, but you see an extraordinary expression, and truth in the drawing. The Kettles &c: are done very naturally, and highly finished. – In the same Room is a Picture of our Saviour and S^t. John when very young, most admirably done, by Rubens. -

In the next Room are several pretty good ones done by Flemish painters. Over the Chimney is a picture done by Pompeio Battoni, now liv'ing at Rome: – It represents an Alliance between Painting, Poetry, Sculpture, and Architecture: – All the flesh Colours are natural; the others are bright, but appear to me very faint, and as if they would not be durable. The Picture altogether is pleasing.

There are two very valuable Librarys in this Place, one in a large Room, upon the Second floor; the other in three or four small Rooms, on the third:

– There are a great many very fine, and curious Manuscripts in both of them: One of the most uncommon in the latter is a commentary upon many antiquities of Italy but in particular, upon those of Rome, by Bernardus Oricellarius,[1] a Florentine. – It is very well preserved, and very valuable for the fineness of the Latin, for the things it treats about, and the manner of treating them, and indeed for the hand writeing itself, which is really remarkably good: – M[r]. Gibbon (thinking I beleive it may be useful to him in some future publication) has with great difficulty obtained permission of the Canon Riccardi, (to whom this Library belongs) to have it copied:[2] – In the other library there is a remarkably old, and fine Manuscript of Pliny: – We were shewn some others, which I dont recollect, very particularly, at present.

For want of a better place to go to, we went in the Evening to Consul Dicks, where we staid 'till near ten o'clock, and then came home.

Saturday 11th August – Florence

Laurentine Library. We went this Morning to see the Library of Manuscripts belonging to the Convent of S[t]. Lawrence: I say, of Manuscripts, as there are very few printed books, only a few that were some of the first printed at Florence: – The room they are ke'pt in, is of a very considerable, and handsome size ev'ry way, and the Books are very uncommonly, but conveniently placed for use; Instead of being put on Shelves, they are here all placed in Desks, with a seat (or Bench) before each Desk; A row of these Desks and Benches, run down each side of the Room: Each Book is chained to the Desk, which is necessary in a Library where people so easily get permission to make use of the Books, as may be done here. – The Abbey Bandini is Librarian; He has printed a Catalogue of the valuable collection entrusted to his care: – The following are some of the most antient, and remarkable that were shewn to us. Machiavels History of Florence, and his Prince in his own handwriteing. It is wrote in a good runing hand. The Decameron, or Dodecameron (a) of Bocace, copied from the original of Bocace, during his lifetime by one Mannelli, his particular friend: – It appears exact, and very well wrote; The best edition of Bocace, is that taken from this Manuscript. A very good Manuscript of Homer, wrote in the 13th Century. – The same printed at Florence in the 15th Century. – I never saw any Greek book, better, if so well printed: which makes it a little difficult to beleive they were come to that perfection so early. A very fine Manuscript of Virgil, wrote about the year 500. The five first Eclogues, and as far as the

1   Bernardo Ruccellai, 1448 – 1514.
2   This is not referred to in Gibbon's journal for this date, but is covered in Gibbon's entry for 30 August.

line, "Proetides inplerunt falsis mugitibus agros", have been most shamefully stolen out of it. The person who was guilty of is certainly unpardonable, as he has almost spoiled a very valuable Book, without any possibility of gaining anything by it himself, or its ever being of service to others. – Perhaps he might not have been more to blame if he stolen y^e. whole. A Tacitus written in the 10th or 11th Century; well preserved. A Livy, not remarkably antient; deficient in the same places as the printed Copies: – A very antient Bible out of which they are collating for the use of M^r. Kennicot.[1] The people employed to do it, they say seldom work at it, & proceed very slowly. – Most of these Books were collected by the Medici Family. –

> (a) A Collection of Tales. Bocace was born about the year 1319,[2] he wrote many other Books

Lorenzo Chapel. From hence we went to the Chapel, just by the Church of S^t. Lorenzo: It was began in the year 1604 by Ferdinando I^{mo}. dei Medici, after a design, and under the direction of Matteo Nigetti, a very famous Architect. This Chapel was designed for a burial place for the Grand Dukes of the Medici Family; which is raither more probable than a Story many people here believe; that Ferdinand intended getting the Holy Sepulcher, and placeing it here: – The Heigth of this Chapel, is near 100 bracchia; its diameter 48 ditto.

The form of it is Octagonal: One division intended for the Entrance; in that opposite to it, the Altar (a) is to be placed, and the other Six are to be filled with the Monuments, of so many Grand-Dukes: – 'Tho began so long ago, it is not as yet near finished, neither is it likely it ever should be, at least in the manner it was designed to be at first: – It is not very likely any future Prince, will think himself obliged to spend the sum, that would require; merely to compleating a pompous Mausoleum, for the Grandeur, and Vanity of a Family y^t. <u>formerly</u> was great.

> (a) See, some account of the Altar, page 45, under the article, Ciborio

The walls are entirely lined with the most curious, and uncommon Stones (a), and Marbles. The pilasters, and the most considerable parts between them are of Jasper di Barga, which is of a most beautiful Red, and white. It is very hard, and difficult to finish highly, but when it is well worked, (as it is here) it takes the most perfect polish.

1   Probably Benjamin Kennicott, 1718 – 1783, a Hebrew scholar
2   In fact, 1313.

(a) Such as Lapis Lazuli, Amathists, Jaspers of different sorts, agates, Chalcadoins, Porphiry, &c &c

The six Monuments, built of the designs of Michel Ange, are in a fine Style of Architecture, and executed in a noble, bold manner: Some of them are made of an Egyptian Granet, and a Green Jasper from Corsica; the others are of a whiteish oriental Granet. The Egyptian Granet, is Green and white, mixt very close, in very small spots of each colour: The Oriental is almost white, but with some Grey spots very small. Over each Monument is a Nick in which is to be placed a bronze Statue, Gilt, of the Duke that is buried under it: The arms of each are worked below in precious Stones of different Colours: In the intervals between the Monuments, you see the Arms of all the Towns belonging to the State of Tuscany: Over two of the monuments are placed Cushions of red Jasper, very much enriched with Diamonds, and other Jewels. The Capitals, of the Pillars, and many parts, such as Cornices, and Bases, But as this will cost too much, if it is ever finished, they intend it should be by painting it : – The Architecture, and form of the Chapel is pleasing, and I suppose for the value of the Stones with which it is lined, and the manner of working them, may vie with (perhaps exceeds) any thing in Europe; nevertheless from the largeness of the place, the beauty of those fine stones, is in a great measure lost, and perhaps have not so good an effect as if it had been made of more Common Marbles.

Vault. Under this Chapel is a very spacious, and good Vault intended for the <u>real</u> burying place: In this Vault are three very good Statues. The Virgin made by Michael Angelo, very fine: our Saviour on the cross by J: Boulogna [Giambologna] and a S^t. John, I beleive by a Disciple of M: Ange's. – In the Sacristy on one side the Chapel are several Monuments, by the Sides of which are some excellent Figures made by Michael Angelo: There are some that are not near finished, and others that are thought to be, by one of his Scholars.

After having passed two hours very near (not in) the Church of S^a. Croce, I went to S^r. Horace Manns, where there was an exceeding good assembly. ----

----

Sunday 12th and Monday 13th July – Florence
I employed Sunday Morning in continuing my Journal & reading Machiavel: – Dined tete a tete with Gibbon: – In the Evening we went to S^r. Horace Mann's, who took us to a small assembly's at La Comtesse del Nero's, which

for want of more acquaintance, or from the natural dullness of the place, we were soon tired of, and, therefore quited it, and after takeing a little walk by the River, each retired to his own Room.

Monday Morning was spent nearly the same as yesterdays; the Evening in driveing about in our coach and walking afterwards.

I have found a little indisposition in my stomach for a day or two past, and was surprised this Morning to find my Eyes turned yellow, and to be told by ev'ry one it was the begining of a Jaundice: It does not give me much concern, as I am very well, except my stomach feeling fuller, & more loaded than usual: Took a slight purge.

Tuesday 14th August – Florence

Palazzo Vecchio. We went this Morning to see the Palazzo Vecchio: – Neither the Building, nor what it contains, afford where with all to detain a traveller very long: – The Wardrobe caused us more astonishment than pleasure: It is a pretty large Room, the four sides of which are entirely made into Closets which are filled with Silver plate, and Silver Gilt: – This plate consists chiefly of immense Dishes, Vases, Chests, &c. imbosed, and often ornamented with Jewels. In one of the Closets there are four very large and fine Posts for a bed, and other parts necessary for it. In another, an immense quantity of plate of an extraordinary size for the compleat furnishing a side Board: Amongst these are, a very large Vase for holding water, another for catching it and washing things, several very large kind of Chests for Ice's &c, &c. But the most curious thing here is a Faceing or Front of an Altar Piece. There are four score pounds weight of Gold, and six pounds and a half of Jewels, employed about it. There are a great many very large Pearls, Topaz, Emeralds, and many other sorts, 'tho very few if any Rubies. In the middle Cosmo the Second, is represented kneeling before an Altar; both of them are made chiefly of small Jewels: The Robe of Cosmo consists entirely of small diamonds, as does the Crown laying on the Altar: Upon the Top of this fine piece are the following words, the letters of which are all composed of …… and are very near (perhaps quite) an Inch in heigth. – Cosmus II. Magna Etrurice Dux, ex Voto. We were next shewn the great hall, which is really a most noble, and well proportioned Room. The length is 96 Bracchia, and breadth 48 (a): We could not find out the heigth of it. The entrance, which is at one Corner, is certainly very ill contrived, as are the windows which are small, and very ill placed. The Cieling and walls are painted by Vasary, and I believe represent different parts of the history of this place during the Republick. – Round the hall are a great number of Statues, not very good. – We went from hence to the Fabrica degli

Uffizzi, or, the place where they work, what is called the Florentine work. The workmen employed about this occupy the second Story of this Building, or that immediately under the Gallery. They are chiefly employed in working for the Emperor: They were at this time makeing two small tables, to be sent to Vienna. From the beautifulness of the work they seem more properly pictures. One of them is a sea veiw, in which is a Ship, and several boats and many other Objects, which are all as well imat'ed by dfferent colourd precious Stones, as they could have been by the Colours of a Skillful Painter.

The other I think was a land-skip where you see men, women, sheep, Cattle &c, &c, as naturally represented as possible, and only by the natural colour of various stones, thus curiously inlaid. – We asked one of the men, how long he had been makeing the figure of a Turk which is designed for one of these pieces; He told us he began it in February last, and had worked at it constantly since, which is more than 6 Months, and it is not near finished; – There are alwais a great number of men employed. Here is a table that was above 15 year in makeing, by 20 Men.

(a)About 172 F^t. long. & 86 B^d.

Wednesday 15th August – Florence

Did not go out 'till the Evening, and then we took a solitary walk at the Cashines, a fine field under a wood about a mile, or less out of Town; When we came back, we drove about the Town to see some ridiculous ceremonies, of the ridiculous religion of these bigoted People; – I think they celebrate to day the Assumtion of the Virgin, or her flying up to heaven, body, cloaths, Soul, altogether. This is a Solemn Festival, and in the Morning they pay her all possible honors in the Churches, dressing her very fine, and entertaining her with fine Musick. In the Evening they repeat the same in the Streets: – You see her in ev'ry Street finely dressed, Illuminations round her, bands of Musick, and Crowds of people singing to her.

Thursday 16th August – Florence

Palazzo Corsini. Our employment this Morning was the Seeing, Le palais Corsini. This is one of the most magnificent palaces in Florence; It is situated between Il Ponte alla Carraia, and that of S^a. Trinita. The front is very extensive at present, and will be more so when finished; but at this time only one end is Compleat: From the middle of the Front, there is a small Court runs in, so that the Sides, almost form two wings, which are joined by a Terrace, with a Balustrade. The Stairs are very spacious, and handsome; the Approach to

them is not quite so much so, being under, and through, many arches, w^ch.
are raither obscure. From the Top of the Stairs you enter into a very large,
and handsome Salloon, which has indeed the fault of being too high for the
size of it, otherways: This Salloon may be justly critisized for the number of
windows, and Doors there are round it, and which in all amount to thirty
two. Sixteen of them are even with the floor; the Sixteen others are about half
way up the room, even with a narrow Gallery that runs all round. The house
being very large must necessaryly have a great number of Chambers, which
indeed there are, but most of them raither small. You see a great number of
Pictures in ev'ry Apartment, and many pretty good, 'tho few Capital ones. –
Here are several by S^r: Rosa, two in particular please me much; one is the view
of a rock down the precipice of which, you see a peasant leading a horse;
very well described: There are several more men, and horses. The other
is Landskip in which is a wood, some Cottages, Cattle, water, &c; all very
well disposed, and naturally imitated. Venus holding, and weeping over the
Dead body of Adonis, and a Cupid standing by, Crying also, most admirably
painted by Annibal Caracchi. Ev'ry part of this piece, is expressed with the
greatest truth and force. – The Head of a woman by C^o. Dolce. The woman
has a reath of Bay leaves round her head; she is very handsome, but one
is nevertheless more pleased by the fineness of the painting, than by her
beauty; It is an excellent Picture and finished with great nicety, but which
does not diminish the force of y^e. Colours. The Head of a dead Christ, very
well done, by Cigoli. A S^t. Sabastian, by Carlino Dolce. It is a half length,
very highly finished, & the Colours very beautiful. Two very good pictures
by Luca Giordano, one represents the Combat between Turnus & Aneas;
Turnus laying on the ground expireing; The other is Aneas having his wound
dressed, there is old man by, wth. a bunch of herbs: a Venus laying upon the
Clouds, and some other figure. – There are many pictures that they tell you
are by Guido, Titian, Raphael & others. They are really good pieces, but I
beleive not by those masters.

Caractures. We went from the Corsini Palace to see some pictures, &c at M^r.
Patch's[1] an English painters. He is at this time finishing a large Picture for the
Duke of York. The Subject of it is, the Dukes leaving Florence, in which the
Duke, and evr'y one else there represented are drawn in Caricature. In the
middle of the piece is the Duke going down the Steps from S^r. Horace Manns
house; S^r. W^m. Boothby,[2] & Coll^l. S^t.John are walking towards the Coach,
before him: – Behind the Duke is S^r.Horace Mann, L^d. Fordwich, Abbey

---

1   Thomas Patch, 1725-82, English caricaturist and painter. He painted several 'conversation pieces'
     of Grand Tourists in Florence, often at Sir Horace Mann's house.
2   Sir William Boothby, 4th baronet, 1721-87, Master of the Horse to the Duke of York

Nicolini, Pillori, Dothel; and many more I did not know: These are very like
the Originals. All round, you see a great number of the Dukes attendants,
and people whom curiosity have drawn together, but of whom the Painter
has taken some likeness. The Scene is supposed to be in La Piazza del Grand
Duca, and there is a view of Il Palazzo Vecchio. – S[r]. Horace Mann, the Abbeys
Nicolini and Pillori, are certainly very like, 'tho somewhat, outré. M[r]. Patch
has likewise just finished the Copies of two fine Paintings, by Salvator Rosa.
Lord Spencer[1] has bought the Originals of Mad: La Comtessa di Accioli, and
gives her two Copies to hang up in their place. I beleive the Originals cost near
600£: besides paying for the Copies.

Fig 10 The Cognoscenti, 1764-65

Friday 17th August – Florence

Ayant pris medecine Aujourdhui, qui m'empeche de sortir le Matin, et ne me
permet pas de rester tranquille long tems de suite, il faut que je me content
d'etre Peripataticien, ou Philosophe ambulante.

Saturday 18th August – Florence

Maliabecchi library. We went this Morning to see the Dukes Library, commonly
known by the name of the Magliabecchi Library, from his haveing collected

---

1   John, Viscount Spencer, 1734-83, later (1765) 1st Earl Spencer.

the greatest part of them, and being Librarian to the Duke. I beleive there are near 40,000 printed Books, and some manuscripts, but we could not hear of any very remarkable.

We were shewn the side of a middle sized room, that was filled entirely with the Letters he had received from his different Correspondents, of which I was told he had between three and four thousand: It is certain he had acquired such a reputation for learning in all parts of the world, that there was hardly a man of any learning, whom he did not know, more or less: But I beleive he was more remarkable for strength of memory, than Genius. The former was so remarkably great, that he never forgot anything he ever read, or heard read: Some one haveing a mind to prove it, went to him one day in great concern, and told him he had lost a very valuable manuscript that he had read to him some time before, and knowing the strength of his memory was in hopes he might recollect part of it. Maliabecchi soon surprised the Gentleman by repeating his Manuscript from beginning to end, without missing a word. *Church of S^a. Croce.* We went from hence to the Church of S^a. Croce, a very large building, but not finished of the inside. On the right hand side on comeing into the Church, is a handsome Monument erected to Michael Angelo Bunoroti, so celebrated for his skill in Sculpture, in which he excelled more than in painting, 'tho he was reckoned a good Painter. – There are several more monuments, 'tho not very remarkable in any respect. There are several pretty good paintings, and some chiefly esteemed from being the work of antient painters. Joining to this Church is a very large Convent, inhabited by over a hundred Franciscans. The inquisition was formerly in this Convent, and 'tho removed at present they have alwais great weight in it: Here is a library chiefly consisting of manuscripts, but of which the most valuable, have been carried to y^e. Lawrentine Library. S^r. Horace Manns assembly was a resource for this Evening. I forgot to mention yesterday the arrival here of two M^r. Damars,[1] Brothers; They are Sons to L^d. Milton.

Sunday 19th August – Florence

Wrote and read all the Morning – Nothing new. – The two M^r. Daymirs, the Baron, Moula, Cole. Mills, Patch, Gibbon, and myself dined at S^r. Horace Manns. I forgot to add M^r. Hay, and no great matter I beleive if one remembers him or not: He talks a great deal: so much the worse, without he talks to the purpose: Then he should hold his tongue; sans doubt. Desired by S^r. Horace to go to the La Casa Ricchi, but thinking my Face too yellow, chose

---

1   John, b 1744, George, b. 1746. Aged therefore 20 and 18. John died in 1776 and George became the 2nd Earl of Dorchester. He died, unmarried, in 1808.

not to expose it. Finding my Stomach not perfectly well, and the yellowness
continuing, resolved to consult some one to morrow.

Monday 20th August – Florence

Consulted Dr. Tocsetti who told me (what indeed I knew) that I had a slight
appearance of a Jaundice, which he beleived I might get rid of by only takeing
the next day a slight purge, drinking 6£ of water (a) the same morning, and by
takeing for seven Mornings after a little Rhubarb, and drinking petit lait after
it. Staid at home all day.

(a) Noceri

Tuesday 21st August – Florence

Kept at home this Morning, by yesterday's prescription. Employed in reading
a new work of Voltaires, Sur la Tolerance. – In the Evening took a walk; &
ended the day at home.

Wednesday 22nd August – Florence

Poggio Imperiale. Spent the Morning in my Room, 'till 12, then walked out.
In the afternoon the Abbey Pillori, Mr. Gibbon, and myself went to Poggio
Imperiale, a palace belonging to the Grand Duke. It is a short mile from the
Town, situated upon the Hill, in a direct line out of the Porta Romana. It is
one continued ascent from the town to the palace; on each side the road, is
a Row of Cypress Trees, which being pretty high, and the space between not
very wide, makes the Avenue appear much too narrow. At the Top of the
Avenue, just before the palace, is a large Circular opening surrounded with
a Cypress hedge, which being pretty high confines the view from the lower
windows. The front of the palace is as plain as possible, and indeed ugly, and
the apartments within are in no respect good enough to deserve the name of a
palace, if it did not belong to a Prince. There are three Apartments upon the
first Floor, and as many on the Second; Each of these consist of a great number
of Chambers, – most of which are small. There is a pretty large Room, with
a Cove Cieling on the first Floor, but it is very low, and ill proportioned. On
the Second is also one good Sized Room, and pretty well proportioned. The
furniture of the palace may have been very handsome, but it is at present very
old, and indifferent. Most of the Rooms are hung around with pictures, some
of which are valuable; – I recollect the following: A Saint Sebastian, very well
done, by And: del Sarto. The Virgin Our Saviour and some other figures by

the same. The Coulours are fine, and figures natural. Two heads by Titian; both worthy of that Painter. A flight into Egypt, by Luca Giordano. This is a very pleasing piece. The figures, which are raither small, are easy, natural and full of Grace; the Coulouring soft, lively, and beautiful. Several heads by Albert Durer; More valuable for being antient, than for the beauty of the painting. His figures seem to me very stiff, and disagreable, and colours dry & harsh. Adam and Eve by the same, middling. In the former there are several Animals represented – amongst other things are two Partridges, so superiorly finished in ev'ry respect, that I doubt much his doing them. There are many more, w^ch. 'tho not of the first force, are really good ones. In one of the largest rooms is a Statue of a dead Adonis, in white marble, by Michel Ange. It is an exceeding good piece of work; executed in a very bold manner, and very naturally. These are the chief things I recollect in the house. We went afterwards into the Gardens, which are small, and very ill laid out. There are some water works that are very trifling, not to say childish. We returned home, and spent the remainder of the Evening, chez nous.

Thursday 23rd August – Florence
Cathedral. We went the Morning to see some Churches, and first, S^a. Maria del Fiore, or the Cathedral. It is a very handsome building, and a very great size ev'ry way; indeed, it is said, to be considerably larger than Saint Pauls. – It was over 150 years in building, and finished under the direction of Brunaleschi in the year 1445. A great part of the inside is lined with marble, and all the outside is cover'd with it (a), except the Portal, which makes a bad appearance being so much plainer than the rest. The stile of the Architecture is Gothick, but much more simple that one commonly sees it. The Cupola which was built entirely under the direction of Brunaleschi, is a noble proof of the great skill of that architect. It is much the most beautiful I recollect to have ever seen. It is Octagonal, of a great Size, and height (b). The form is very pleasing to the Eye, and has a nobleness, yet a lightness, that is very strikeing. It was painted by Succaro, and may be well done, but the attention is so much taken up with the building itself, that the painting is hardly observed. I think this is the first time I remember to have seen the Choir placed directly under the Cupola. It is Octagonal like the Cupola, and raised three or four steps; surrounded with pillars and balustrades. At the Great altar in the Choir you see three Statues representing God, our Saviour, and an Angel, by Bandinelli: That of our Saviour is admirable well done, but he has made a sad, stiff, ugly old Figure of his Father. Round the outside of y^e. Choir are some pretty good Basso–relievos.

(a) With black & white marble, worked, and inlaid in a very expensive manner

(b) The heigth from the Ground to the Top of the Cupola is 185 Brachia

Just by the Cathedral is a Tower, the outside of which is entirely covered with black and white marble: The heigth of it we were told is 140 Brachia: We went to the Top of it, that we might have an opportunity of getting a good Idea of the form of the Town, and of the Situation of the most remarkable places, in, and near it. The Town appears nearly round, seeing it from hence: The Streets in general are very streight, & long, 'tho not very wide: There are a great many very good palaces, and some publick buildings, which make a good appearance; nevertheless I cannot say I think Florence deserves the Title of, Fiorenza la bella. Sᵃ. Maria Novella is a large, handsome Square, tho the buildings round it are not very Magnificent. Il Piazza del Grand Duca is pretty large. Il Piazza del' Sᵃ. Croce is spacious, the houses indifferent; on one side is the Church. The next largest is Piazza Sᵗ. Marco, and Piazza Vecchia. There are many more small Squares, or Places. --

We went from hence to the Church of Sᵒ. Spirito, which is large and handsome, but where I saw nothing very remarkable, except the Altar Piece composed of fine Stones and Marbles, but wᶜʰ. I should not imagine had cost near so much as Mʳ. Kesler says it did. Joining to it is a large and handsome Convent of ……. The two Mʳ. Damers dined with us to day.

Friday 24ᵗʰ August – Florence

Stai'd at home all the Morning; except makeing a visit to a German Prince who came here yesterday. His title is Shwartsenburg; whether a Sovereign Prince, or not, I cannot be informed at present. It is said that the Emperor shot his father by accident one day a-hunting, and to comfort the family made the young prince a very considerable present in Money, and alwais shews him particular favor. – We sent our names to a Mʳ. Monk,[1] just come from Sienna.

Venison. We dined to day at Consul Dicks, and were so fortunate as to have a haunch of Tuscan venison for dinner, wᶜʰ. I had a great Curiosity to taste. I was much surprized to find it little inferior to good English venison; It was fat enough, and had a very good flavour. There are great quantities of Deer, in the forests near Pisa, and they kill them without distinction of age, Sex, or season, so that it is a great chance if one meets with that wᶜʰ. is good. The Italians despise it, and commonly give it to the poor people, or Galley Slaves, &c. It all belongs to the Emperor, so that it is extreamely difficult to get any of it.

1   John Monck, 1735-1809. Master of Ceremonies in Bath. His portrait was painted in Rome both by Angelica Kauffman and Pompeo Batoni.

We went in the Evening to La Casa Nero, where there was a very good Assembly. There were two Sposa's, or young women engaged to be married. The unmarried women never appear in company 'till a little time before they are to be married, and that it is publickly known.

Saturday 25th August – Florence.

I took a ride on horseback this Morning, with the youngest Damar (George). The Environs of Florence, fruitful, and pleasant. – We dined with the Damars. – We went in the Evening to S[r]. Horace Manns assembly: Pretty numerous. Marquise of Corsi, was there: She is fat, & not very handsome. Play'd at whist wth. M[rs]. Dick, & Seg[a]. Ganni.

Sunday 26th August – Florence.

Peggi. Myself and the two M[r]. Damers, went this Morning to Peggi[1] a Palace belonging to the Duke, situated about five Miles west from Florence. Haveing heard it much talked of by the Florentines as a fine Palace, I was much disapointed to find nothing more than a tolerable good house, prettily situated; but from the building size, or furniture, no ways deserveing the name of a Palace. – We made this little excursion on horseback, and as the country is very pleasing, and road good, should have been very well satisfied with it, if it had not ended by my horses falling upon my Leg in the Street of Florence, and hurting me, more than I remember to have been by any fall. – Pull'd my Boot off wth. great pain; my whole foot so bruised, as to oblige me to keep in my Chair all day. Arquebusade my remedy.

Monday 27th July – Florence

Can't walk, but made a Shift to hop down Stairs, to dine wth. Lyttleton, who came f[m]. Lucca last night. He exposed himself very much during his stay there.

Tuesday 28th August – Florence

My Foot obliged me to stay at home all day.

Wednesday 29th August – Florence

Too Lame to go out this Morning: Mareshal Botta arrived here last night from Vienna; and all the English being desired by Sr. Horace Mann to go wth. them this Evening to visit the Mareshal, I went there, 'tho with great pain, and

---

1   Referred to by Gibbon, who did not go. Gibbon estimates that it was about 7 miles. Bonnard wonders whether 'Le Peggi' is Poggio a Caiano, although this is 10 miles distant (Bonnard p 219).

trouble. The Mareshal tho 75 yrs of age is very Stout, and came here in 10 days from Vienna. He did not spake to any, but Sr. Horace Mann.

Thursday 30th August – Florence

Not well enough to walk much. The Damers, Gibbon and myself dined with Wolfe. - Ld. Ossory arrived here to day.

Friday 31st August – Florence

Afraid to venture far, 'tho much better. Ld. Ossory, and all the English, dined at Sr. Horace Manns. Went in the Evening to La Comtse. de Lorenzo's - a very good Assembly. Play'd at whist with, Ld. Ossory, Mr. Lyttleton, and Gibbon. Lost a Sequin. Wrote to my Sister.

September Florence
Saturday 1ˢᵗ September – Florence

Baron Wolfe, Moula, Gibbon and myself dined to day at Mʳ. Dicks. – Some venison, not so good as the last. In the Evening went to Sʳ. Horace Manns assembly, which was very numerous. – Made a party at whist, with Lᵈ. Ossory, Mʳ. Lyttleton, and Mʳ. Damer. – Won two Sequins.

Sunday 2ⁿᵈ September –   Florence

Stai'd at home 'till the Evening, when we went to Porta Sᵗ. Gallo; from thence to Sʳ. Horace Manns, where we met a Mʳ. Apthorp,[1] nephew to Sʳ. Horace: And accompani'd them to the rehearsal of a new opera, at the large opera house. This Theatre is much larger than the other, but not near so convenient: The boxes are all very deep, and narrow; so that only those in the front can either see or hear.

Monday 3ʳᵈ September – Florence

Library of Palazzo Pitty. We went this Morning to see the Lybrary in the Palais Pitty. It is on third floor and occupy's two very large, and very handsome Rooms. In the first, there are eight thousand volumes, that have most of them been brought from Loraine: In the next room which is considerably larger, there are near 25 thousand. They are all placed in great order, and by the account of the Lybrarian it is a very good and compleat collection. We were not shewn any, particularly curious. – In a smaller room on one side, there are a considerable number of Manuscripts; and above 500 Oriental ones. In

---

1 John Apthorp, 1730 – 1772, aged therefore 34. His wife, Alicia, niece to Sir Horace Mann, died on her way to Italy in 1763.

this room we were shewn two very large Folio Volumes, containing the drafts and accounts of many of the most considerable Towns and palaces in England France, Germany and Holland, that Cosmo the third had taken during his travels through the above named Countries. – We looked at many of the drafts, which seem'd to be done wth. exactness, and accuracy. The Emperor allows three hundred scudi (or Crowns) pr. Ann: for buiing books for this Lybrary. – I suppose the Salary of the Lybrarian is not very considerable, since, ('tho he is considerable enough to wear the order of the Golden Spur) he did not refuse to take a few paoli of us.

Messrs: Lyttleton, Damer's, Baron Wolfe, & Moula dined with us to day. The dinner, and some time after, passed agreeably, but the Evening was spent much otherwise, owing to the Proud, obstinate, & quarrelsome, 'tho perhaps cowardly disposition of M^r. .... who hav'ing very grosely abused the rest of the Company, most gladly excused himself to all, except M^r. G..... with whom he was desirous of continuing the quarel, first hopeing he would not be disposed to fight him; and next, that if he did, thinking he should have much more the advantage of him, than of any of the others. However after hav'ing exposed himself very much, and shew'd an ungenerous, <u>mean</u>, obstinacy, he thought proper to acknowledge the spirited, steady, and generous behaviour of M^r. G. and to give him the satisfaction desired by himself, and his friends.[1]

Tuesday 4th September – Florence

The Church of the Annunciation (dell' Annunziata) is large, and well built, and 'tho handsome, does not afford any thing very remarkable either in respect to the building, or what it contains; in a Chapel behind the Choir, are some basso relievos in bronze, that were made by Giov: Bologna [Giambologna], and seemed curiously worked, but I could not get near enough to them, to see them distinctly. The most remarkable objects are the paintings in Fresco round the Cloysters of the Convent joining to the Church. They were done by several hands, of whom Andrea del Sarto, was the Principal, but they are all much damaged by time, and weather. The much celebrated piece called La Madonna del Sacco, seems to be much hurt, 'tho it undoubtedly is still very pleasing, and much superior to the rest. And: del Sarto has here, represented the Virgin, sitting wth. the infant Jesus in her Lap; S^t. Joseph at a little distance is setting on a Sack. The head of the Virgin is graceful and very pleasing; The figure of S^t. Joseph is very natural, and the drapery in general is finely executed. In another

---

1   Unfortunately Gibbon's diary stops abruptly on 2nd September for 3 weeks so there is no reference to whom this person was, but it could only have been Lyttleton.

Cloyster we saw a good bust of André del Sarté. – In a Chapel just by the Church are some pretty good Statues, said to be by Jean de Boulogne [Giambologna].

From the Annonciade we went to Sᵃ. Maria Novella, a handsome Church, without hav'ing any thing particularly worth ones attention, at least as we could see or hear of.

Mʳ. Keysler was happier than us in finding fine painting and sculpture at Santa Trinita, where we could not see either one or the other. The Church is small, and a good deal ornamented. The façade is handsome.

Sᵗ. Gaetano, another Church we have seen this Morning, does not afford any more than the last: the Chief thing I could see, worth any notice, is a Chapel belonging to the Corsini family, which makes a very handsome appearance; It is much ornamented with historical Sculpture in very large Basso-relievos against the walls.

We dined today with Lyttleton, and the Damers.

Wednesday 5ᵗʰ September – Florence

Did not go out this Morning: – In the Evening we went to see the new Opera, which did not please much. Mʳ. Woodhouse,[1] son of Sʳ. Armine Woodhouse, was brought here this Morning from Rome, in the unhappy state of Madness; He has been so about two Months: the Cause uncertain, at least to us.

Thursday 6ᵗʰ September – Florence

 Did not go out 'till the Evening, when the two Mʳ. Damers, Mʳ. Gibbon and myself, went to supp at Charles's Country home.

Friday 7ᵗʰ September – Florence

The two Damers come up to us, prevented my doing much this Morning, except takeing my Lesson of Italien and the flute. Desired by Lyttleton & the Damers to join them in dineing: began to day. – In the Evenᵍ. went to Mad: Minerbetty's: she is sister to the Countesse of Accioli: Her house is good. Play'd at Whist with Lord Ossory, Damer's, and Mʳ. Apthorp. – Won seven Sequins.

Saturday 8ᵗʰ September – Florence

The Morning employ'd entirely in my room. In the afternoon we went to a Christening at ...... It is the Custom here, as in many places in Italy, upon the birth of the first Son, to invite a great number of people to the Christening,

---

1   John Wodehouse, born 1741 and thus aged 24. Became 5ᵗʰ baronet in 1777, MP for Norfolk in 1794, created Baron Wodehouse in 1797. Died 1834 aged 93. Presumably his madness did not last.

and they all come in their finest Cloaths. Upon this occasion their was a great assembly, and very well dress'd. Ices, sweatmeats, &c, were the entertainment: The house is very large: We went about 4 and staid 'till 6. In the Evening there was a fine Assembly at S[r]. H Manns.

Sunday 9th September – Florence

I wrote to my Father by this Days Post.
At home all the Morning: Din'd together as usual. In the Evening went to the Opera.

Monday 10th September – Florence

Prato &c. I rode out on horseback this Morning wth. the Damers. We went to Prato where there is a Manufacture of China belonging to the Senator Genori: We are told they make a very considerable quantity; Indeed we saw a good deal there, and there seem'd to be many workmen employed. The China appeared to me fine, and white. They work it well, and paint it very nicely. The highest price they ever make any of, is a Sequin pr plate: They make all sorts of Figures, and ornamental China: I remember seeing the Venus of Medicis copied in China, as well as many more Statues. – In returning from hence we passed by Castello, a palace belonging to the Grand-Duke; The outside makes a very poor appearance, and the inside, they say, makes a little better, for wch. reason we did not go in (a).

In the Evening to the Italien Comedie at the little Theatre. – Sono stato da la Gattai: é Bellina.[1]

(a) We went this morning to see y[e]. Gallery leading from il Palazzo Vecchio, to Pitty: See an account of it on the 13th. Ins[t]

Tuesday 11th September – Florence

Wrote a letter this Morning, and took my lesson on the flute. From 7 'till nine, la Gattai: afterwards at Mad: Minerbetti's: a very numerous and handsome assembly for Mad: Spinola of Genoa. – M[r]. Lyttleton, and L[d]. Ossory made Banks at Pharaoh. Mess: G: Damer, Apthorp, Gibbon, & myself punted. – Lyttleton punted 50 Seq: at a time: We staid here very late; supped afterwards with L[d]. Ossory; plaid after supper. L[d]. Ossory, and Lyttleton, won 700 Sequins between them of M[r]. Apthorp. – I lost eight Sequins during the Evening, & night.

---

1   A rare use of Italian, perhaps as a code. See entry for 16 September below.

Wednesday 12th September – Florence

Palazzo Gerini. We went this Morning to see the Gerini Palace: It is very spacious and handsome: There are a great number of Pictures, some of which I beleive are very good: – Two small landskips by Salvator Rosa: a Saint Sebastian by Guido: excellent. Over this a very good Picture by Guercino: I have forgot the Subject: a holy Family by Paul Veronese; Good. Saint Andrew going to be Crusified; by Carlo Dolce. It is remarkably fresh, very highly finished, and indeed the figures of St. Andrew, and of the man that is prepareing the Cross, are expressive and well done. The Portrait of some man by Rembrandt: very good. Sr. Hor: Mann, Ld. Ossory, Apthorp, Gibbon, and myself dined to day at Mr. Dicks. – Venison, very fat, but not so fine tasted as the first time. – In the Evening, to the Opera: – Supped wth. the Damars who were to set out to night for Lucca.

Wednesday 13th September – Florence

Long Gallery. I forgot to mention on Monday, our going that Mong: to the Gallery: – We did not go, so much to see any thing there, as to see the Gallery that leads from it, to the Palais Pitty. This Cover'd way passes first over the houses by the side of the river, then over il Ponte Vecchio, and from thence is continued over a Church, and other buildings, 'till it comes out in a Court on one side of the Palais Pitty. They tell you it is an Italian mile in Length, which I think impossible tho it is of a great length. The greatest part of it, is of a very good weadth, but in some places they were obliged to make windings, and contract it, which has certainly spoiled the beauty of; It is nevertheless very handsome, and shews the magnificence and Grandeur of the Prince by whom it was built. On the walls are paintings representing historical story's of Charles the fifth; Henry ye. fourth &c.
Passed the Evening at Dicks.

Thursday 14th September – Florence

At home all the Morning: To the Opera in the Evening.

Friday 15th September – Florence

The Morning at home: – Holroyd and Major Ridley,[1] our old, Lausanne acquaintance, came here this Evening from Lucca, to our no small satisfaction. A Mr. Bolton[2] (I beleive Irish) came with them. A thin Assembly at Sr. Horace Mann's. -

      Mr. Lyttleton left Florence this Evening to the no small satisfaction of

---

1   Major Richard Ridley, 1736 -89. He was the son of Matthew Ridley MP and half brother to Sir Matthew White Ridley MP.

2   Theophilus Bolton, b c.1735, d of consumption in Genoa 1765.

most people in it, and particularly S^r. Horace Mann, to whom he has certainly been very impertinent, and troublesome. His great pride and vanity, which have made him think himself above all ranks of people, and exempted from observing the rules and Customs of places have made him universally hated, and generally dispised.

Sunday 16th September – Florence
With La Gattai this Morning: – Holroyd, Ridley and Bolton dined with us: – Afterwards saw a procession of 250 young Girls: – I don't know at present on what account: – Afterwards to the Opera: -

Monday 17th September – Florence
Spent the Morning with our old Friends: – We dined with them, L^d. Ossory, M^{rss}. Apthorp, Mills, & at Sr. Horace Manns. – L^d. Ossory seems raither of a serious disposition, sensible, not bright, and talks little: He is very fond of play, and I beleive understands most Games pretty well: He has won near 1000 Sequins of M^r. Apthorp, during his stay here. – In the Evening we went to M^r. Dicks, where we supped.

Tuesday 18th September – Florence
I took a walk about the town this Morning to look at some of the Statues &c, of which there are many very good ones at Florence. Before the old Palace is a very large handsome Fountain in the middle of which is the Statue of Hercules of a Colossal Size, and round the fountain are a great number of smaller statues in Bronze, many of which appear to me very well executed. On one side of the Fountain is a very large Equestrian Statue: It does not appear to me to be remarkably beautiful, or perfect in any respect: – Under an Arched building just by the Palace is a Group of three figures; representing the rape of a Sabine (or raither only, the carrying her off). It is very natural; done with a great deal of expression, and very well grouped. This as well as those round the fountain were the work of J: de Boulogne. Hercules killing the Centaur, by the same person, is most admirably executed.

[Half page gap in original diary]

Wednesday 19th September – Florence
Went this Morning to the Gallery with Holroyd &c; We dined together: In the Evening to the Opera.

Thursday 20th September – Florence

Much hurried this Morning in preparing for our departure: Ld: Ossory, M[r]. Apthorp, Gibbon and myself dined at S[r]. Horace Manns: Play'd 'till nine in the Evening wth. Lord Ossory &c, at Whist: Then went to hear an Italien Tragedy: found it very dull: The Italien Language seems much fitter for Musick, than Tragedy: – La Gattai.

Friday 21st September – Florence

L[d]. Mountstewart[1] came here this Morning, accompanied by Coll: Edmonston, and a M[r]. Mallet of Geneva: – Took leave of Consul Dick, from whom we have received the greatest Civilities. – L[ds]. Ossory, and Mountstewart, and all the English dined at S[r]. Horace Manns to day: – In the Evening we took leave of the Opera, and bid adieu to many of our Acquaintance whom we met there.

[Gap of few lines and then two blank pages]

Saturday 22nd September –   Fm. Florence to Lucca

We left Florence this Morning about 8 o'clock, takeing the Pistoya road to Lucca, where we arrived about six in the Evening: Our being so late was owing to being stopt for want of horses. The distance between Florence and Lucca, is six Posts, or I beleive between Forty and fifty Miles. The road as far as Pistoya is very good, and over a fine, rich plain; but immediately beyond, it runs nearer the Mountains, and becomes hilly, and pretty much confined, 'tho just before one comes to Lucca it opens again into a fine, 'tho not extensive plain, round the Town. Hearing from ev'ry one that there was little or nothing worth seeing at Pistoya, and fearing to get late to Lucca, we stop'd there no longer than to change our horses. – It was near Pistoya that Cataline was defeated, and lost his life in a battle against the Proconsul Manleus. – The nature of the Country about, and beyond this place makes it more than probable that it was the design of Cataline to retire beyond this hilly and difficult part of the Country into the plain round Lucca, where by the fruitfulness of the Country he might have maintained his army very easily, and from the difficult access to it have easily prevented the enemy from following him.

    We found the two M[r]. Damers at Lucca, whom I accompanied this Even'g: to the Opera, where I had the pleasure of hearing L'Amicis. She has

---

1   John Stuart, (1744 – 1814, aged therefore 20), Lord Mount Stuart, later 3rd Earl and 1st Marquess of Bute.

a very pleasing voice and sings so well, as to be thought little inferior to the Gabrieli.

Sunday 23ʳᵈ September – Lucca

Mʳ. Gibbon, the two Damers and myself walked this Morning round the fortifications, which are said to be about three miles in all, 'tho by the time we were in walking it, I can hardly think it more than two. The prospect from these ramparts is very pleasing. The Eye indeed is soon stoped by the Mountains which almost surround the Town, and are not very distant, but the Plain within them, in the Middle of which Lucca is situated, is very rich and well cultivated. The fortifications are not very strong. – When one considers the small extent of this State, it seems surpriseing that it should have been able to preserve its liberty so long. An entire harmony and concord amongst themselves, with the assistance, and protection of some foreign power is the only means of supporting themselves, becoming a prey to the Dukes of Tuscany; 'tho if Princes were not more governed by ambition and Covetiousness, than Justice, and Generosity; This Little Republick, might naturally hope to have a Protector, and preserver of its Liberty; raither than an Enemy to it, in so powerful a neighbour as the Grand Duke.

The Government of Lucca is much more worth the attention of a Traveller, than any thing else the Town or neighbourhood affords. Unluckily we had no letters of recommendation, so that we were obliged to leave the place without being able to inform ourselves about that principal object, in any other manner than from Kesler & Addison, but in whose accounts I beleive one may confide: – After haveing finished our walk round the ramparts we visited two or three Churches, in which we saw nothing remarkable, except two or three good Pictures. Our Savior on the Cross, Sᵗ. Catherine, & Sᵗ. Jules on each side, by Guido Reni is admirable. – We all dined together, and went in the Evening to the Opera.

Monday 24ᵗʰ September – Lucca to Pisa

We went this Morning as soon as we were up to see the Miraculous Image of the Virgin in, the Church of Sᵗ. Pietro Maggiore. As this Story is related at length in Keslers Travels, I shall say no more, than to add, one or two new circumstances, wᶜʰ. the Priest that shew'd it us, related. The Priest, and several others near, told us that they had often tryed to find the bottom of the Hole in which the Gamester was swallowed up, but alwais in vain; He added in the most Solemn Tone, and air, that some years since they had let a Dog down a very considerable depth, and that he came up dead, and very much burn't: –

The Image of the Virgin is painted in stuko against the wall: The Infant Jesus is in her left arm: On her right shoulder you see a bloody mark, which was caused by the Stone strikeing her there. We were shewn some blood in a little bottle, that the Priest said ran from that shoulder, at the time the Stone was thrown at the Virgin; and which tho so long ago, appears very fresh. We were asked to kiss it, but did not think it necessary.

Immediately after returning from the Church we got into our Chaise, and left Lucca, proceeding for Pisa, which is two Posts distant, and where we arrived about 12 o'clock: – The road between these two places is pretty good, 'tho pretty hilly. One passes chiefly between Mountains, till one comes near Pisa, where the Country open a little. In a little plain about a mile from Pisa are some hot baths, much frequented ev'ry summer: We stoped there just long enough to see them. The Baths are very neat, and I beleive well contrived for bathing. I drank some of the water which has little or no taste. There is a large house where the Company assemble, and two rows of Lodging houses. – As soon as we came to our Inn at Pisa we were visited by M[r]. Acton[1] a relation of M[r]. Gibbon; who insisted on our dineing with him; – M[r]. Acton has the Title of Commodore, and the Command of his Imperiall Majesties Fleet, which consists of three or four old Frigates.

The Chief things worth seeing at Pisa are the Cathedral; Il Campo Santo; The Babtistry, and the Leaning Tower. These lay all together, and are indeed very much worth seeing: – Haveing too little time, to enter into any detail about them, and as they are very particularly, and well described by Kesler, and other Travellers, I shall say little about them: – The Cathedral 'tho a handsome building, is not at all remarkably so: It is of marble on the outside; much ornamented, 'tho without taste, or Judgment: The two Doors that are said to have been brought from Jerusalem, are very ill worked. The others are much better. There are two pretty good pictures by A: del Sarte, Il Campo Santo, which is built in a Gothick stile of Architecture, is very particular, and may be well reckoned handsome; The Cloyster which goes all round is very wide, and has a very good appearance. The Sarcophagi, of which there are a great number all round, have no great merit; Many of them are much ornamented wth. basso relievos, which are much damaged, and otherwise, not much worth notice. The walls are much ornamented wth. paintings, whose chief Merit I beleive, is their being very antient. There are several antient Inscriptions preserved in the walls, that are very valuable.

The Babtistery is much ornamented with Pillars & Basso-Relievos. The Pulpit is remarkable, for some very Curious carving. The font in the Middle is

---

1　The relationship with Gibbon was via their two fathers, with Acton père acting as physician to Gibbon père on his Grand Tour. Acton père settled in Besancon, where Acton fils was born.

very large; and originally designed for Babtiseing by immersion.

The Leaning Tower is very remarkable for the very great inclination. It appears very plainly from the bass on one side being entirely under ground, and on the other entirely above, that the Inclineing of it, is owing to the fault of the foundation, and not to any design of the builder. Indeed it is plain he tryed to correct it towards the Top, as it does not incline all the way equally. – We went to the top of it, from whence we had a good view of the Town, which tho pretty long, does not seem to contain any great number of houses. The Arno runs through the middle of it, over wch. river there are three bridges: One appears handsome. We went to the Phisick Garden, where there is nothing remarkable: The University of Pisa is not very flourishing.

Tuesday 25th September – f^{m}. Pisa; to Leghorn

From Pisa to Leghorn are two Posts. The road is sandy, otherwise very good; A great part of the way is through a Forest, 'tho some time before one comes to Leghorn it opens into a very flat, low Country. We got to Leghorn – about 11 o'clock: M^r. Acton,[1] Nephew to the Commodore, immediately came to see us and invited us to dinner, which we accepted, and met there the Major of the Place, and one, or two more officers. After dinner we made a visit to the Governor. -In the Evening to the Comedy, which was certainly in ev'ry respect bad enough. The Opera house is large and handsome.

Wednesday 26th September – Leghorn

We took a walk this Morning to the Darsena, and Port: In a large opening before the former we saw the Statue of D: Ferdinand, and the four Black Slaves, chained to his Pedestal. They are all of a Colossal size, and indeed executed with a great deal of Judgment, and are full of expression. From hence we walked to the Port, and along the mole; These are so well and exactly described by Kesler that I shall, nor could, add much to it.

We could plainly see the Islands of Corsica and Gorgona from the Mole; the latter indeed is not above 80 miles[2] from Leghorn. The entrance into the Port is but indifferent: The water is so shallow that a 30 Gun-Ship could not come in: However they say much heavier might be brought near enough to destroy the Town with ease in a short time. At the end of the Mole there is a fort which mounts 40 pieces of Cannon, but as it is built of Stone, it would soon be beat to pieces, with great detriment to those upon it

---

1 John Francis Edward Acton, 1736 – 1811, therefore 28 in 1764, later (1791) the 6th baronet. He became commander-in-chief of the Neapolitan Navy and Army 1779 and in 1795 Prime Minister of the Kingdom of Naples.

2 He may have meant '18' miles, approximately right. It is in fact 22 miles.

from the breaking, & flying of the Stone. M[r]. Acton, the Major of the Place &c dined wth. us to day: In the Eveng: we went to see some of the Garrison exercised: They differ'd from the Austrian Troops we had seen at Milan: They were commanded by a Major Dixon,[1] an Englishman.

In the Evening we went to a very dull Assembly at La Marquise de Silva's, and f[m]. thence to the Play. M[r]. Burnaby, Chaplain to the English Factory, and M[r]. Rutherford,[2] Banker, &c came to us this Mong.

Thursday 27th September – Leghorn.

In walking round the Town this Morning we looked into the Jews Synagogue, which is a large but very plain building. – We went into a Greek Church and took notice, that there was not one Image in it, tho many paintings. – We went from hence to the Port where we took a boat, and rowed to the high tower, to the left of the Entrance; Here are alwais 40 Canon:. I went to the Top of the Tower. From hence we rowed out to see one of the Emperors largest, and best Ships: She mounts 40 guns, is as many years old, and in bad condition. He has two more, much smaller, and in a worse state: They are now building a Frigate of 20 Guns: – They are but in weak Condition to carry on a war wth. the Algerine, who has just declared war against them. The manner the Bey of Algiers declared war, was by sending for the Emperors Consul at Algiers, and giving him a Slap on the Face. – We had an opportunity here of tasteing some Corsican Oysters, w[ch]. I think were the largest, and best I ever eat. We dined to day wth. the Major of the Place, where we met the French Consul, M[r]. Acton, and several Officers.

We accompanied M[r]. Burnaby to see M[r]. Dicks house, where he shewd us a very beautiful Picture, & Bust. The Picture represents, an Angel delivering S[t]. Peter from Prison: It is admirably done by Guido.

The bust is of Seneca; I think in ev'ry respect preferable to that in the Gallery at Florence. It is much the finest bust I ever saw.

Leghorn is fortified all round: The number of Troops in it at present if Compleat, would be about 3000: – Its inhabitants are computed at above 40,000: There are about 16 English houses, in very considerable Trade, and rich. The Jews amount to 16 or 18,000: Some very rich. The Town is now very healthy, 'tho formerly so much otherwise.

Friday 28th September – Leghorn to Sienna

We left Leghorn very early this Morning, and did not get to Sienna 'till eleven at night. All the first part of the road is very good, and the last part only hilly,

1   Possibly Major Henry Dixon who later commanded in the Tuscan and Venetian armed forces.
2   Robert Rutherford (1719-94), a son of Sir John Rutherford of Teviotdale. A merchant at Leghorn, agent for the Russian fleet and for these services created a Baron of the Russian Empire in 1775.

and a little rough, otherwise good. There are eight Posts and a half between Sienna and Leghorn, but the Posts are very long. The Country a great part of the way, neither fine, nor fruitful.

Saturday 29th September – Sienna

We went this Morning to see the Cathedral which is a handsome Gothick building: The Façade of the Entrance is highly finished and much ornamented. The outside is entirely cased with black and white marble, wch. in my opinion has not a good Effect. The Columns and some other parts within are the same: But the most remarkable thing in the inside of the Church is the pavement: you see there, many parts of the Bible represented by marbles of different Colours inlaid and engraved in a very Curious manner. It is at present all cover'd with boards: We were shewn two pieces, one, the intended sacrifice of Abraham; the other Moses strikeing the rock: Some parts of them are very well executed: – Near this is a Pulpit, curious, for the bass-relief, shewing, the history of our Saviour from his birth. In a Chapel, w[ch]. is called the Lybrary, are some pretty good paintings, said to be done by Raphael: Their chief beauty is the freshness, and beauty of the Colours: Some heads are pretty good: but if they were done by Raphael, it must be w[n]. he was very young.

In the Middle of the rooms you see a very pretty Group of antient Sculptures, representing the three Graces: They have certainly a great deal of Merit: It is a great pity they are so much damaged: One of them has lost a head an arm, and, I think, both Legs; The others are likewise much maimed. We saw nothing besides that was very remarkable. The Town of Sienna is far from handsome: It is built on very uneaven ground, which makes the streets appear very indifferent: Baron Schlabrenders (a) and his Governor, whom we had already known at Florence, M[r]. Gibbon and myself dined together, and very great reason we had to be discontented with our dinner, 'tho at the best inn, in Sienna.

L[d]. Mountsteuart, and M[r]. Mallett,[1] called upon us after dinner: Le Marquis Borghese conducted us to an assembly in the Evening, which did not give us any great Idea of the brilliancy of y[e]. Sienna assemblies. Convinceing proofs of the ignorance of the Italiens in general, offer'd themselves here. We supped this Evening wth. Lord Mountsteuart, Mallett, Author of the History of Denmark: – a sensible man.

1   Paul Henri Mallett, 1730 -1807. Born in Geneva, became a professor in Copenhagen where he wrote his history of Denmark. Returned to Geneva as a professor and then was employed by Lord Mount Stuart as his tutor. On their return to London, Mallett was commissioned to write a history of the House of Brunswick.

(a) A Prussien

Sunday 30th September – fm Sienna to Rome

We took leave of Sienna this Morning, and proceeded as far as Radocofani, which is just six posts from Sienna. The road is in general very good, but the Country very hilly, uncultivated, and barren: – Radicofani, where we lay, is a small village, very near on the frontier of the great Dukes Territorys. About 20 Miles to the left of it lies Montepulciano, famous for its wines. Better here than at Sienna.

Monday 1st October – Road to Rome

We went five Posts and a half more to day, which brought us to Viterbo. One passes through, Aquapendente, Bolsena, and Montefiascony. At the distance of about a post f^m. Radicafoni one comes into the Eclesiastical State. The road passes very near the Lake of Bolsena, or Lacus Vulsinus. Montefiascony famous for Muscadel wines. The road to day has been mostly, very hilly, rough, and bad; Some parts bad pitching, and all full of large, loose stones. We were dreadfully shook. The Country very different from that yesterday, being flatter, more fruitful, & better Cultivated.

Tuesday 2nd October – From Viterbo to Rome[1]

We left Viterbo very early this Morning, in order to reach Rome early in the afternoon, having five posts and a half to go. The weather was so bad that we could not see much of the Country we passed through, and the road so exceedingly rough and disagreable, that it took our attention off from ev'ry thing else. The weather, and road became much better for the last post, and gave us, an opportunity of seeing a fruitful, and pleasant Country. At a short mile from Rome, the road crosses the Tyber, over the Bridge, Milvius, at present called, Ponte Mole, famous for the defeat of Maxenteus, by Constantine in 312. At a little distance from hence, the road becomes quite straight, and continues so between walls, and houses quite to Il Porto dell Popolo, by wch. one enters Rome. Just within the Gate, it opens into a very extensive Square, in the middle of which is a fine Egyptian Obelsik (a); Opposite the Gate, two handsome Churches, and three handsome Streets, branching off different ways. We were stoped at the Gate, and told that our Chaise, and ev'ry thing in, & about it must go down to y^e. Custom house: We sent our Chaise there, & walked to our Lodging.

---

1 Gibbon's daily Journal stops here. It picks up again in December, but only dealing with specific areas such as 'Peinture & Sculpture' and 'Antiquitès et Architecture'. Despite the French titling, the entries are written in English.

(a) This was brought by order of Augustus.

Fig 11 View of the Piazza del Popolo, *c.*1750

Wednesday 3rd October – Rome

Wrote to my Sister this Morning: – Ev'ry thing much dearer than at Florence: – Received the visits of Mess[rs]. Ponsonby, Martin,[1] Baron Wolfe, &c: Supped wth. the latter. M[r]. Martin has made the Tour of Sicily.

Thursday 4th October – Rome

Went to see some new Lodgings: Took 2 apartments over the Baron. Returned our Visits. &c &c &c.

Friday 5th October – Rome

M[r]. Byers,[2] a young Scochman, being much recommended to us, as an Antiquarian, we spoke to him to day, and agreed to begin our View of y[e]. Antiquities to-morrow, at the same hour as M[r]. Ponsonby, he hav'ing already engaged him, and began. – We took a short view of S[t]. Peters, which really exceeded my expectations, in magnificence, & grandeur.

1   James Martin (1738-1810). He came from a rich banking family and in London lived in Downing Street next to Pitt the younger. He was elected MP for Tewkesbury in 1776.
2   James Byres, 1733-1817, aged therefore 31 in 1764. He was a Scottish painter/architect, antiquarian and dealer and, as implied above, a celebrated cicerone.

Fig 12 View of the Roman Forum from the Capitoline Hill, 1748

Saturday 6th October – Rome

I shall not attempt writeing so particular an account of what I shall see at Rome, as I have hitherto done, of w[t]. I have seen in other places, as the number of things one sees each day, wth. any discription of them, or Conjectures about them, would employ ones whole time, and prevent the reading many things necessary to be read for the thorough understanding, w[t]. one sees. – I shall therefore only mention most things in the order we see them, and be more particular about those y[t]. please me particularly.

At ten o'clock this Morning, M[r]. Gibbon, M[r]. Ponsonby, and myself, attended by our Antiquarian, M[r]. Byers, set out together, to see, and examine the remains of the noble works, of the inhabitants of this once Capital of the World. As M[r]. Ponsonby had already began we, raither continued wth. him, than began in the usual manner, or place.

We began at the Tri[l]: Arch of Septim: Severus, & turning to the left, saw the remains of the Temple of Concord, and of Jup[t]: Titans; behind this last, some small remains of the Portico Publico, and from thence to where the Capitol was, but of w[ch]. there are no remains at present. There is a handsome palace built on the same spot, or thereabouts: We went to the Top of a Tower ris'ing from this Palace, fm. whence we could well see, the places where the buildings on this hill stood, or were supposed to stand. – By w^t. can be collected from the best authoritys, y^e. Temp: of Jup^t: Capitolinus stood upon y^t. same ground on wch. at present is the Church of Aracelli, and y^e. Rock or Citadel on y^e. opposite side, or on y^e. Tarpeian hill.

We next walked into the Forum Boarium, where at present is y^e. Church of George in Velabro: Area quae posito de bore nomen habet. On one side is a square building on open Arches, I beleive, a Janus, and the only one remaining: Near it, a building erected by the Goldsmiths; from hence we went down by the side of Circ: Maximus, and turning to the left, round the Palatine hill, went down the Via Nova, which brought us to Constantines Arch. ------

The Arch of Septimius Severus, standing at the bottom of the Hill, and at the begining of the present way up to the Capitol, is a great part it now under Ground: It is thought that above twenty four feet are hid by the falling down of the ground.

There are only three Pillars of the Temp: of Jupiter Tonans remaining, and they are buried except about 12 or 14 feet, but one may easily see, by w^t. what remains, that it must have been a very beautiful building: Corinthian pillars, fluted; Capitals &c, finely finished: Pillars above 50 f^t. high. The Arch of Constantine must have been a most magnificent and beautiful building: Pillars of Jal: Antique; Frise encrusted wth. Porphiry; ornamented, with the Basso relievos taken from the Arch of Trajan: One sees here plainly how much the art of Sculpture was fallen in the time of Constantine.

Sunday 7th October – Rome

Being Sunday we did not continue to day wth. our Antiquarian: We made a visit to M:Piccolomini Governor of Rome, and to ……..

Monday 8th October – Rome

M^r. Byers took us this Morning to see the Tarpeian Rock. In a Court belonging to one of the wings of the building at present upon the Capitol we saw the remains of an immense Colossal Statue. There is the Head, and feet perfect: Well proportioned, & worked. A most beautiful basso relievo of a woman, representing a Province; I beleive Bulgaria: She is leaning on her left hand, in a most pleasing, pensive posture. Her head, and one arm restored: very well. In going up the Stairs of this wing, we saw some good Basso relieves of a Triumph, Sacrifice &, of Marc: Aurelius.

After passing through some old houses we came upon y^e. Tarpeian Rock. A man might easily break his neck there at present: There is a higth of above 60 feet, perpendicular: You see on one side that it is an entire rock, of Solid Stone. From hence we went to the place where was the Circus Maximus, but which at present is only a Garden: It is easily to discern the form of the antient Circus; but the size of it is much diminished by the falling down of the Ground on the Aventine hill on one side, and by the earth, dung &c, that has been laid on the other.

After this we were struck wth. admiration, & wonder by the Colosseum, or Amphiteatre of Titus. What an Idea does the immensity, and Solidity of this noble remains of Antiquity, give one of the Magnificence, riches, and indeed greatness, of the Romans. This, as well as most of the pieces of antiquity one sees here, seem as if intended to resist the attacks of time, and in spite of the ignorance or neglect of future ages, still to immortalise the Splendor, and power of their first masters.

[gap of seven lines]

Tuesday 9th October – Rome

We began to day by examineing the Equestrian Statue of Marcus Aurelius, now standing in the Middle of the Court before the Buildings, wch. stands upon the ground formerly called y^e. Intermontium. It is without exception the most perfect piece of the kind I ever saw: the Man, and horse, seem equally well executed: If there is any fault, it seems to be in the right thigh of the man, wch. appears to me too flat: It appears plainly that it was formerly Gilt, by some parts being a little so at present.

We went from hence into the wing of this building, in which are kept the Pictures. There are two large rooms hung round, wth. pictures, many of which are certainly very good: – Those that appeared particularly so to me were the following.

1st. A Sybbel by Guercino. She is setting in a very thoughtful manner, with a pen in her hand, and a book before her. She has a kind of Turban on her head, and a loose robe hanging from her shoulder. There is more expression of Sense, and thought, in her look, than I almost ever saw: and indeed much more than that painter commonly gives to his figures. – M^r. Strange[1] I am told has engraved it.

2^d. A S^t. Sebastien, by Guido.

3^d. The same, by Anibal Caracci: These are both excellent, and 'tho, very different, we were all in doubt which to prefer, the Master, or the Scholar.

---

1   Sir Robert Strange, 1721 – 1792, aged therefore 43.   Spent four years in Rome in the 1760s. Knighted by George III in 1787 after he engraved West's picture of The Apotheosis of the Royal Children.

The first has most softness; and the latter most expression.

4th. A sketch of an Angel by, Guido. Admirable.

5 and 6th. Two small pictures by Annib: Caracci.

7th. Fortune flying over the Globe holding a Crown in her right hand wch. is extended, and a palm branch in the left hand. This is I think one of the most elegant and pleasing figures I ever saw. The Colouring is in his last manner, and done in the softest, and most natural manner. There is a Cupid endeavouring to hold her. This is likewise very well done.

8th. One of Alexander's Battles supposed to be done, by Julio Romano, but since entirely painted over by Pietro da Cortona; It is full of life, and expression. There are several more excellent sketches by Guido, and a great many other pictures very good, 'tho inferior to those I have mentioned.
This afternoon went to S^{t}. Peters, and examined some of the Mosaick Pictures (a).

(a) Second view. – an excellent picture by Guercino representing, Cleopatra kneeling down before Augustus – a good Sybbyl by Dominichino: – several good Guercinos

Wednesday 10th October – Rome

We saw this Morning the Prison made use of by the Romans; Extent of the Capitol Hill; Arch of Titus; Temples of Sun and Moon; and the Temple of peace. The Prison was on one side of the Capitol Hill, and is at present under the Church of S^{t}. Jioseppe de Falegniani, or otherwise called S^{t}. Pietro in Carcere, from a tradition that S^{t}. Peter was confined there. There were three Prisons one under another; There were no doors into the two under ones, but the Criminals were let down through holes in the Ceiling. It was in the lower one of these in which Jugurtha was confined. He was let down naked, and it is said he lived four days. The lowermost may be near 40 feet under ground, and it is about ten feet square. – There is at present a Spring of water in the Second. The Arch of Titus is pretty entire; It is much ornamented, and the work very good. The sides of the inside of the arch, are two basso relievos representing Titus's triumphal entry, and the carrying before him the Candle stick with the table of the shew bread, y^{e}. two silver trumpets &c, belonging to the Temple of Jerusalem. This Arch w^{n}. entire, consisted of one great arch, and a square door or way, on each side.

The Temple of the Sun and Moon stood on the Side of the Esquiline hill, near the Via Sacra, and now in the Garden of S^{a}. Maria Nuova. They joined each other, one facing the East the other the west. There still remains enough, to make them out easily. The Cieling of the Tribunes, which are still remaining of both, were cemicircular, and ornamented with Rhomboids nicely done in Stuko; the sides of the eggs and anchors and the Middle a small rose. They have a very good effect.

There still remain three vast Arches, which made one side of the Temple of Peace: By what remains it is easy to see of what an amazing size this Structure must have been. Each of the remaining arches form, a Chapel, (or division) at least …. feet deep, and proportionably high, and as the opposite side was the same, of how great a heigth must the arch have been that joined them, and how amazing the Columns that supported it: They were of one entire block of white marble. Such were the works of y^e. Romans. This Temple was situated in the Campum Vaccinum (a), and near the Via Sacra (b).

(a) Is y^e. present name: On one side y^e. Via Sacra, not far fm. the arch of Titus.

(b) It was built by Vespasian about the year of Rome 823 and of Christ 70: perhaps a yr or 2 after. In it were put the things taken fm. the Temple of Jerusalem.

Thursday 11th October – Rome

We spent this Morning in seeing the Pictures, Statues, Intaglios, Cameos, &c belonging to M^r. Jenkins,[1] an English painter, who has been settled here several years, and who employs himself chiefly in buying Pictures, Antiques &c. (a) He has at present a very good Collection of each of the above, and of which I remember the following in particular. An excellent head, crowned I think wth. bay leaves, by Salvator Rosa. An old man, by An: Caracci. An <u>excellent</u> Picture, by P: Veronese, representing a Soldier embraceing a naked woman, a boy holding the woman about her knees, and a dog standing against the boy. A holy Family, thought to be by Corregio; Admirable. Two naked boys, by Guido; one in his second manner, the colouring, and shades, strong: The other in his last more faint, but I think more graceful, and pleasing. A naked Venus by Titian: She is in the same attitude as that at Florence, but only 6 or 8 inches long. It seems to me to have as much merit as possible. – A most admirable piece by Minx [Mengs]; The Colouring has all the force, and softness of the more antient paintings.

Amongst the Statues I shall only mention a Venus,[2] which M^r. Jenkins esteems equal in beauty to the Venus of Medicis. 'Tho she appears to me

---

1   Thomas Jenkins, 1722-1798, and thus 42 in 1764. Trained as a painter but was primarily occupied as a cicerone and dealer. Became very rich and influential, but, as Guise implies, not always well regarded by his British contemporaries – see Guise's footnote.

2   This is almost certainly the Barberini Venus – acquired by Gavin Hamilton, sold to Jenkins and then sold to William Weddell of Newby Hall in 1765. It was sold at Christie's in 2002 for nearly £8m.

inferior to that incomparable Statue, I think her in ev'ry respect very beautiful. Her face perhaps better, but her body and lymbs want that fleshy plumpness and softness, as well as the beautiful turn, so finely and naturally expressed in the Venus, at Florence.

Amongst his Cameo's, there is one remarkably fine, and wch. they say he values at about 500 Sequins. It is the head of Caligula in a Chalcedonian Agate. The head perfectly white, and ground a dark colour. He has a very fine Intaglio, which belongs to a gold bracelet, which is likewise very nicely worked. We were shewn two Gold Armilla, which the women wore near the top of their arms. He has many more Pictures, and other things, which we had not time to see at present.

(a) And selling them again very dear.

Friday 12 October – Rome.

We returned this Morning to the Capitol to see the Statues &c, that are kept in the Wing on the right hand. In the Court, behind a fountain is a Colossal Statue, supposed to represent the Rhine, but known by the name of Marphoreo, or Marforeo, wch. name it may be supposed he took f^m. the Forum Martis where it lay formerly. The head, and some parts of the body are good. At one end of the Cloyster round this Court, is a very large and fine Marble Sarcophagus of Alexander Severus, and his Mother Julia Mammaea, found near Frescati. On the Top, lay the Statues of Alexander, and his Mother, indifferently executed. The bass-relief on the front is very good, but it is very doubtful w^t. it represents. Most imagine it to be Tatius, and Romulus; and the Sabine women stoping the Soldiers &c by their prayers.

In a small room, in wch. are kept nothing but Egyptian figures of black Marble, all brought f^m. Adrians Villa, is a very curious double bust, being the head of Isis joined to that of a Bull. They are both well executed, and supposed to be done by some Grecian artist.

M^r. Ponsonby being obliged to leave us, we did not continue here, but went to the Temple of Antoninus and Faustina, which from the present remains, it is easy to beleive must have been one of the largest, and most magnificent in Rome. There is now no more of it remaining than y^e. six Pillars in Front, and two of each side, that formed the Portico, with their archetrive and Cornish, and a Considerable part of the side walls. These Pillars were about seventy feet high, each of one entire piece of Numidean Marble: The base; Capitals (of the Corinthian order) and archetrive were of white Marble, beautifully worked and ornamented: The numidean Marble is of a blueish

(a) and white colour, the veins runing very long, much in the same manner you see them in Deal Boards. We saw besides this some small remains of the Temple of Romulus and Remus, behind wch. is supposed to have stood the Temple of Venus, high enough to be seem over the other, into the Via Sacra, which runs before all these three Temples, wch. stand between the Arches of Titus, and Septimius Severus.

(a) Some times raither Green

Saturday 13th October – Rome

Left wing of y^f Capitol. Paid our second visit to the Statues &c kept in the right hand wing of the Capitol. In the wall of the Stair Case are fixt pieces of an ancient plan of Rome engraved upon marble, but broke in so many parts and otherwise damaged, as to be of little service towards forming one from it. Two good Bassorelievos, one representing the Apotheosis of Faustina, the other part of the Triumph of Marc: Aurelius. These two pieces belong to the Triumphal Arch of M. Aurelius of which no part is to be seen at present.

Here is an apartment of 5 or 6 Rooms, filled with Sarcophagi, Statues, Busts, Inscriptions and other pieces of antiquity. Two of the Sarcophagi are particularly fine, and the subject of the Bass-reliefs particularly well adapted to their Situation: One of them, is that of Zenobia Queen of Syria. On the Sarcophagus is represented a battle of y^e. Amazons, refering to her being so warlike and courageous a woman. I don't recollect the subject of the other. In y^e. same room wth. these, stands a most beautiful Urn, of the most elegant Form, and ornamented in the most pleasing manner. – In y^e. next Room many Statues; none remarkably fine: A Psyche and Cupid much inferior to that at Florence.

In the next room two very large and bad figures of two Popes, in Bronze. – A most beautiful Statue of Antinous in Parian Marble. Ev'ry part of this Statue are perfectly well executed, but if any odd, the head, wch. is y^e. finest I ever saw, is finished with the most art. After those in the Tribune at Florence it is the finest I have yet seen. – A dying Gladiator. This may be ranked amongst the very fine pieces of Sculpture. – A very good Statue of a Vestal. The drapery is excellent. – A Juno: The head very fine. – A Marius. A very good Statue, full of Caracter and expression. – An Isis, well executed. – In this room are two Mosaic Tables made out of a Pavement taken from y^e. Villa of Adrian. They are very beautiful, and highly finished, and well preserved. – In the next three rooms are chiefly Busts, and some particularly good, such as, those. of Alexander, Caligula, Claudius, Hadrian, Trajan, <u>Faustina,</u> Messolina, Ariadne, and a few others. (a) They are in general very well preserved, very few of them being any way broke or damaged, wch. I think is their greatest excellence, otherwise they are much inferior to those at Florence.

(a) A Commadus

Sunday 14th October – Rome
This being a day or repose for M^r. Byers, each of us employed himself in his respective chamber. I spent my Morning in continuing my Journal, and writeing some french Letters. – In the afternoon M^r. Gibbon and myself went to the Garden of the Villa Medici; just by. The Gardens are pretty large but not lay'd out in our manner. Just before the House are two immense Cisterns, each made of an entire piece of Egyptian Granet. Round the Garden are a great number of Statues, but not many I beleive very valuable. Under a very indifferent building on the farther side of the Garden, is the Celebrated Family of Niobe. Many of the figures are admirably done. They are all in different attitudes in respect of their bodys, 'tho all except two or three looking upwards, as if seeing, and trying to avoid Apollo's darts. One, lays flat on the ground as if dead, one, embraces the Mother; and another stands bent, and looking down in a Mournful Posture. We have some difficulty in accounting for the Horse wch. stands in one Corner, with both his fore feet pretty much raised from the Ground. They have been pretty well preserved, and where broke, pretty well restored: – From hence to Mr Ponsonby's.

Fig 13 the Niobe Group, Villa Medici, 2020

Monday 15th October[1] – Rome

Being wet weather this Morning, we did not continue seeing the out of door Antiquitys, but went to M^r. Jenkins to see the remains of the Pictures we had not time to see the last day. He shew'd us a great variety of Pictures, and very good ones, 'tho few by the very Capital; and chief Painters, and as there were none very remarkable, I shall only mention one by Carlo Dolce: It represents, Susannah and the Elders: Tho it has the greatest expression and life, yet it is finished with all the delicacy of a Miniature. It has the finest effect when seen at a distance, yet will bare the nearest examination.

Tuesday 16th October – Rome

Continued amongst the Antiquities. – At a place called, Il Macel de Corvi, we saw the remains of two Sepuchers, which at present only help to make the walls of two houses. They stand just at the bottom of one side of the Capitol Hill. Upon one of them is an Inscription, wch. says it had been granted by the Senate &c, as a Burial place for the Family of Caius Publicius, &c: See Nardini p: 26 & 7. –

Tem. Of Pallas. We went from hence to the Temple of Pallas, the remains of wch. stand near the Forum of Nerva. There are now standing only two or three Pillars which formed the Colonade on one Side.

It appears by this remains that the Colonade on the side was open, and over it there was an Attick, part of which you still see; In the large Pannel of the Attick is the Figure of Pallas in basso-relievo. A great part of the Pillars are buried, but it appears plainly they were of a great height: They were fluted, and of the Corinthian order: The whole entabliture is very much ornamented. On the frise several figures of Pallas.

T: of Mars Ultor. Not a great way from this in the Forum of Nerva stand the remains of a Temple, supposed to be that of Mars Ultor. There is at present part of the side Colonade consisting of three Pillars, a Pilaster, with the side wall of the Temple, and Cieling between them. These small remains shew y^e. great size and magnificence of this Temple: Above 20 feet of the Columns are at present under Ground; From the size of them it plainly appears the building was near 80 feet high. The walls were cased wth. white marble; the Cornish, and Cieling ornamented in the most beautiful manner: Pillars & Pilasters of white Marble; Corinthian order. Joining to this is a large Piece of an Antient Wall; For what this wall served is very uncertain, but it is the highest, and has the most solid appearance of any wall I remember to

---

1   15th October is the date remembered by Gibbon as when he first thought of writing a history of the decline and fall of the Roman Empire – the 'Capitoline vision'.

have yet seen: It must be above 90 f^t. high, and is composed of stones of an immense size.

There are two or three belts run along it. This wall for greatness ev'ry way, is suitable to the other works of the Romans. Just by the Temple is an arch through the wall, half of which is under Ground.

Trajans Pillar. From hence we went to the Forum of Trajan situated in a valley between the Capitol and Quirinal hills. It is in this Forum that is placed that astonishing, and noble Pillar of Trajan. The design and intention of the Pillar, the execution of it, and the reason of its being built in that place, are perhaps equally great and remarkable. What could be nobler, or more to the honor of an Emperor, than to have such a monument erected as a repository for his Ashes; on the Top of wch. his Statue was placed, and on its sides his great actions represented. The Structure of it, and the Sculpture upon it are equally worth notice. One is amazed to see the vast pieces of Marble of wch. it is formed, as well as the manner in wch. they are worked; and how beautiful are the Bass-reliefs with wch. the whole column is cover'd, representing Trajans war against the Dacians. The particular reason for placeing it there, was to shew that the Ground was equal to the Top of the Column, before Trajan had it taken away even to y^e. bottom of the Piedestal for to build the Forum, &c. This pillar is formed of about 32 pieces of Marble. The Base is of 2 Pieces; The Piedestal of 4; the Column of 25; and the Capital of one (a). The last measures 14 feet English, Square. The Stair-Case is cut out of the Solid Stones, winding up through the middle of them. They are of a very convenient heigth and weadth: I counted the Steps twice and found them to be 186 in no: The bass-reliefs, as I have said, seem very nicely executed, but from the infinite number of figures, and different things that are represented, it appears raither confused. – The heigth of this Column I beleive is a hundred & twenty feet. The Piedestal is ornamented wth. Trophies, most elegantly worked: The Torus of a most beautiful form, with leaves and kind of Acorns most delicately releaved: – a wreath on the Base equally well executed: S^t. Peter stands on the Top of this noble Monument.

(a) These don't make y^e. 32, but the others are in the piedestal for the Statue, and the Torus to y^e. Piedestal of y^e. Column: – This last is of only one Stone. – The Base of y^e. Piedestal is of 2 Stones: the Base of the Statue of 2 more

Wednesday 17th October – Rome

Palazzo Rospigliosi. It being wet this Morning, we went to the Rospigliosi Palace: – In the Palace, are very few good paintings; the principal one is, Andromeda and Perseus, by Guido, wᶜʰ. like most of his, is very beautiful: (a) The Figure of Andromeda is easy and Graceful. The twelve Apostles, said to be by Rubens, are far from haveing the merit, the works of that master commonly have. – In a Summer house in the Garden you see that admirable piece of painting, the Aurora, by Guido. It is painted in Fresco upon yᵉ. Cieling. One discovers in each of the figures of this piece, – that incomparable Grace and Elegance so peculiar to the Paintings of this Master. With how much Judgment has he placed the Aurora, and wᵗʰ. how much lightness the Hours seem to dance. How fine is the drapery, and particularly that of Aurora. The Colouring of the whole is admirable, and done with all that Glow, and Strength of Colours that caractarized his Second Manner. Guido had three different Manners of Colouring. The first very dark, indeed Blackish, and often with a Green Cast; He fortunately quited this, and made use of the most beautiful and pleasing colours such as form the Aurora: Not contented, he changed these again for the worse; and made all his Pictures of a Pale Wan Complexion.

(a) Some say it was done by Eliz: Serani, Scholar of Guido.

Thursday 18ᵗʰ October – Rome

We saw to day some few remains of the Temple of the Sun. The Statues upon Monte Cavallo. Some fine paintings by Dominichino, and an antient painting in Fresco, what is left of the above mentioned Temple is kept in the Garden of the Colonna Palace, upon the Quirinal hill: The ascent of this hill which begins from the Colonna Palace is very considerable: One goes up at present by a long flight of steps in the Garden, on the Top of which are two pieces of The Temple of the Sun, or Vicus Solis, built by ....

Temple of yᵉ Sun. They consist of a block of Marble 15 ft: by 10 that formed part of the Cornish; and of another Block 18 by 12 that made part of the Archetrive & Frese. These pieces are very well worked, and elegantly ornamented: The Temple according to the dimensions of the parts remaining must have been considerably more than a hundred feet high. We next examined the Statues on Monte Cavallo standing before the Pope's Palace. They are two Colossal Statues of two men, each standing by a horse, wᶜʰ. they appear to have been holding, 'tho at present the bridles are lost: The two men are perfectly well executed; the horses I think bad. It is uncertain for whom they are done, or by whom. The Inscriptions on them are modern.

Sᵗ. Silvestro Monte Cavallo. In the Church of Sᵗ. Silvestro Monte Cavallo, are several good Pictures, but in a side Chapel there are four admirable ones by Dominichino, done in Fresco, one at each Corner of the Cupola. One represents Queen Sheba, and Solomon, a Second David dancing before y^e. Arc, a third Esther and Ahasuerus, & the fourth Judith with the head of Holofernes.   The first and last have lost their Colours considerably by the damps of the wall; the two others are still as fresh as when first painted.

Antient painting. In the Garden of the Aldobrandini Palace is a Summer house, where they preserve a very valuable piece of antiquity.   There is fixed in the wall of the house an antient painting in Fresco, representing a wedding.   In the middle of the Picture you see a bed, on one end of which sits the Bridegroom very near undressed, with an air of impatience; at the other end of the Bed is the Bride cover'd wth. a loose robe, and an elderly woman stands by her, seemingly instructing her.   There are several more women, & I think one man, in different parts of y^e. Picture, differently employed.   M^r. Byers seem'd to agree with us in thinking, that the figures were well drawn, but that y^e. perspective had been ill observed and y^t. there is very little variety.   The Colours may have been good but y^e. picture is too much damaged for to judge of them.

Friday 19th October – Rome

Novitiate. We began this Morning by seeing the Noviciate, or S^t. Andrea de Jesuiti, built under the direction of Bernini.   It is of an oval or Eliptick form, wth. a Dome rising from the outward wall: I think it one of the most pleasing small Churches as I have yet seen: The Inside is intirely cover'd wth. very beautiful marble, and in the Chapels are some good Pictures, 'tho none very remarkable.   That over the Great Altar is by, Bourguinione.   What is most worth seeing belonging to these Jesuits, is the Statue of S^t. Stanislaus Coska, kept in the same room he formerly inhabited.   His head, hands, and feet are of white Marble and body of a very beautiful Black.   He is lying on a Bed of Yellow Marble: This is one of the finest piece of Modern Sculpture I have seen. Le Gros the author of it, has certainly shewn great skill in the execution of it: Nothing can be done more naturally; and elegantly, than both the Body, and the Drapery.

Diocletian Baths. From the Jesuits Church we went to the Baths of Dioclesian, situated between the Quirinal and viminale hills, or rather at the end of both. I was much disapointed in finding them so imperfect, for tho there are still considerable parts remaining, they appear to me very insufficient, for to make out, & distribute, the different Baths, and rooms, which are known to have been there, with any degree of certainty.   The whole circuit of these Baths, was about 1200 paces: The form of the whole a long square.   The outward wall is supposed to have been disposed as follows.   The great entrance, in one of y^e. long sides: Opposite to it, the wall was built circular (a), and had arches going from it, under wch. were seats for the people to see the foot races. In the side walls they suppose the Philosophers, &c, had places for disputeing &c. Next to these inwards they make a large opening for the races &c: and in the middle they place the great hall for exerciseing in bad weather, and round it the different Baths, sweating, swiming, dressing, and other rooms. Of all these are now standing, first, the Theatridion, or Circular wall: At each Corner of this is a Circular building, supposed to have been Temples: one of them is now the Church of S^t. Bernard, the other a Hay-loft. Secondly, some very small parts of the side walls. Thirdly, the great Hall, wch. now forms the Body of the Church of S^a. Maria degl' Angeli (b). This is of a noble size. There are still standing in it, eight columns, of Granet, 15 feet in circumference, each. There were six large arches by wch. they passed out of this into the other rooms: One of these still remain: On one side of this wall the walls of two rooms are still standing, and on the other they shew you the foundations of several Baths. These are the remains of this vast building, that are shewn at present: But by the manner it is explained, I don't comprehend, how there could be room enough for the infinite number of people of both sexes that are said to have made use of these Baths: I cannot help thinking there were more buildings, than what are laid down on y^e. modern Plans. (c)

(a) The Theatridion.

(b) This room is near 180 feet by 52 within the outward Columns: From wall to wall I beleive 190 by about 62

(c) I forgot to mention our dineing to day with a Coll: Scott;[1] and Major Abercromby,[2] lately come from Florence

Saturday 20th October – Rome

Forum of Sallust. S^a Maria della Victoria, where we began this Morning, belongs to a Convent of Carmelite nuns. This Church is most exceedingly ornamented, but I think in a bad taste. There is one very good Picture of y^e. Magdaleine by S^n. Babtiste Mercati: but there is a much better, of a Madonna, with our Saviour, & S^t. Francis, by Dominichino. The Forum of Sallust, is supposed to have stood here. We left this and went to the place where the Circus of Sallust is beleived to have been; and which is a valley between the Quirinale hill, and what was formerly called Collis Hortulorium, and is known at present by the name of Monte Pincio: On one side of the Circus is an Old wall, which supports the Earth of the Quirinale hill. In one Corner you see

1 Not identified

2 Probably Sir Ralph Abercromby, 1734-1801. Later MP for Clackmannnanshire and lieutenant general

the remains of a Temple, supposed to have been dedicated to Venus. There
are no farther remains of any thing now, and it is become a fine Vineyard, and
Garden. – Where the Gardens of Sallust stood is very uncertain; some think
joining to the Circus: Nardini says, between it, and that of Flora.

Villa Ludovisi.   From hence we went to the Villa Ludovixia, the owner of
which is Duke Sora, who is also Prince of the Isle of Elba. We saw here some
excellent Statues particularly three. First, a Mars, supposed to [be][1] tired
and resting himself, which are both perfectly well expressed. 2[dly]. Papirius
(sirnamed Pratextutus, and Descendant of Papirius Cursor) and his Mother: It
is relateing to the Story of her asking him what had passed in the Senate: Her
anxiety to know what had passed, and his trying to excuse himself from telling,
but with an air of being reddy to yield, are most admirably expresst. The
Bodys, and Lymbs of both figures are as natural as possible, and the drapery
finely executed. It is one of the finest pieces of Sculpture I have seen in Rome.
Just by this stands another very good piece of sculpture tho inferior to the last
mentioned. It represents the Story of Arria and Corinna Patus; she is dying,
and he has just stabbed himself. The figure of the Man is very well executed
(a). – Over the door in the first room, is an excellent Bass-relief representing
the Head of Pyrrhus: One of y[e]. best I have seen here.

      The Gardens of this Villa are large, and well planted. They are filled
with Statues, some of w[ch]. have merit. There is a Summer house in w[ch]. you
see an Aurora, by Guercino. Aurora here is represented seting in a Chair, &
drawn by two horses. The hours are blotting on the Stars, and at the end you
see Night under the figure of a Woman, and a Boy sleeping by her. The figure
of Night is most admirably done; I don't think the rest equal to it. – In the
room over this you see a Fame flying before two Heroines; by the same hand.
They are all painted on the Cielings. – From a Ballcony at y[e]. top of the house,
is a fine prospect of Rome.

      (a) The action of his stabing himself is awkwardly expressed: the Arria is
      natural. 2[d]. view

Sunday 21st October – Rome
Wrote a french Letter to my Sister this Morning; continued my Journal: Read
in Nardini. Dined with Baron Wolfe, with Gibbon, Coll: Scot, and Major
Abercromby. This last served all the last war in America: Coll: Scot pays his
expences. The Colonels chief passion seems to be that of Gameing, and he
seems perfectly well calculated for it. These two Gentlemen have been here

1   Rare example of a missed word

about ten days, in which time they pretend to have seen Rome very well: They may have seen it, as one sees a Country, by rideing through it full Gallop.

Monday 22nd October – Rome

Villa Albani. We went this Morning to the Villa Albany about half a mile out of Town. The house is a modern building and indeed very handsome, 'tho the Architecture is not the most chaste. The Front is raised upon a handsome Colonade (a), and the <u>Arches spring from the Pillars,</u> which are all of fine Antique Granets. The Front is much ornamented, but I think the windows which have all of them double Pediments, either Circular, or Triangular have a very indifferent effect: You descend from the house into the Garden, by a double, and very gradual Slope: On y^e. farther side of y^e. Garden, just opposite the house is a very handsome Circular Colonade upon antient Granet Pillars; and under the Colonade are a great number of Antique Busts, Statues, Sarcophagi and other things: In an opening in the middle of it, stands a very large Statue of Isis (b), entirely of Oriental Alabaster, but only half of it, is Antient; In the Middle of the Garden is a very fine Fountain: The water falls over a very large Bason of Granet, which is supported by four very large, and fine Antique Statues (c). There are two more fountains, over each of which is an antient Statue representing some River. These are the Chief things worth notice in the Garden, which is prettyly situated and has a fine prospect. At each end of the Colonade under the house, is a Bason of beautiful Granet; They are both of an immense size: – In the Middle of one is worked in Bass relief a Medusa's head, and finely executed: In the walls you see a great number of Antient Masques, and under the Colonade a great number of Statues &c. – Ev'ry Room in the house has some fine Marble in it, most of the door Cases are made of it. In an Elyptick room, at first comeing in, you see two very large Pillars of Giallo Antique (d): They are the finest I have seen, being of the most beautiful yellow, finely polished, and each of an entire piece. In a small room on one side there are a great number of very fine Porphiry Vases, all Antique except one which they say cost the Cardinal near a hundred Pounds, yet is not very large. In another room over the Chimney is the finest bass-relief I ever saw; It represents the head (e) of Antinous and nothing can be executed, wth. more life, or more naturally. After passing through several Rooms in which are some fine Marbles, and in particular two Tables of Antient Mosaick, beautifully wrought, we came into the finest, and most expensive room I have ever seen (f). It is entirely lined with the most beautiful Marbles, and wh^t. is called, the Pierre dure, the dispositions of which I don't recollect enough to describe particularly, and shall content myself with remembering;

that there are four very beautiful Pillars of Porphiry; two at each end of the Room, which support the Pediments of the doors: The door cases are I think of Gall Antique, the walls of different sorts; Several Pillasters the middle of wch. are filled up with fine Mosaick: A great Circle in the Middle of the Floor, of Sicilian Jasper, the other parts of Numidian, Carrara, and other fine Marble. Over the doors are large figures Gilt, and the Frise round the room, is all ritchly ornamented & Gilt. The cieling of this Room is painted by Minx, and in a manner that may vie wth. some of y^e. most famous of the Antients. He has there represented Apollo and the nine Muses in the most beautiful manner, and in the finest Coulours. There is a greater warmth and harmony of Colours, than is common to modern painters, and his figures may almost vie with those of Guido, for ease, & Elegance. – We are told that this Villa has cost Cardinal Albani above 120000 pounds, and y^t. it is worth much more. He has not paid for half of it, so that at his death it will be destroyed by his Creditors.

(a) It is about 50 yds long; much too high in proportion to the rest of the house over it.

(b) The second time I went it was removed under the long Colonade runing f^m. one end of y^e. house.

(c) I beleive Fawns.

(d) I beleive more than two ft: diameter

(e) It is a bust more properly as the breast & shoulders are comprehended. second view.

(f) The proportions of this room are not very exactly preserved; it is I think 50ft: by 28

Tuesday 23rd Rome – October

S^a. Pudenziana, wth. which we began this Morning, is a small Church, and I suppose would be hardly taken notice of by Strangers if it was not for a tradition of its being built on the same spot of Ground on which stood the Palace of one Pudentius (or Pudentia) a Roman Senator, and in which Palace they tell you S^t. Peter lived upon his comeing first to Rome. They shew you some antient mosaick pavement, they say part of the floor of the Roman Senators house. A tradition that does very well here to feed the Bigotry and Superstition of weak minds, but to which it is not necessary to add much faith, or worth examining one way, or another. – This is almost or quite the only remains of Antiquity, and the only thing worth observation on the Viminale hill, which is one of y^e. smallest of the Seven, and runs along between the Quirinale and the Esquiline. –

S^a. Maria Maggiore. We went from hence to S^a. Maria Maggiore, situated on the other side of the valley which divides the Viminile from the Esquiline, which last is one of the largest and most extensive of all the Hills. This is one of the four (a) most antient churches, and one of the four Basilicas that the Pope blesse's the people f^m. ev'ry year. It is very large and handsome both within & without, 'tho there are some considerable faults in the Architecture of y^e. Chief Front: The dividing it into so many parts and putting in so many windows &c, give a trifling and ugly appearance to y^e. whole front. The body of y^e. Church within is very long and large; It is supported by two rows of very large & handsome Granet Pillars, which make also two handsome Isles on each side: The cieling is flat and the best I have seen: Between y^e. body of y^e. Church & the Choir is a handsome Baldekhin, supported by four noble Porphiry Pillars: The Architect y^t. built it, thinking those Pillars at first too large, diminished y^m. so much that he thought y^y. looked too small, & therefore twisted a large wreath of Gilt brass round each of them. On each side the Church is a very handsome Chapel. On one side that of Paul the fifth, or the Borghese Chapel, which in point of fine and uncommon Marbles and stones, is much the ritchest and most beautiful I ever saw. The Pillars of the Great altar are of porphyry: Those of the other altars are chiefly verd-antique, none of y^m. encrusted, but entirely solid: Many very large Pillasters of Sicilian Jasper: In short the whole of y^e. Chapel is lined with verd-antique, Porphiry, gall antique, Oriental Alabaster, Sicilian Jasper, the finest black & white, and other the most uncommon Marbles &c. The cieling and many other parts were painted by Guido: Some are damaged, whilst others retain there beauty. Opposite this is y^e. Chapel of Sestus 5. It is much ornamented wth. fine Marbles, but more remarkable for y^e. Relicks kept there.

(a) The other three are S^t. Peters, S^t. Jean de Lateran, and S^t. Pauls without y^e. Gates, but to this last y^e. pope seldom goes

On one side of this Church stands one of those noble, Fluted Corinthian Pillars that supported the Body of the Temple of Peace: It is a very beautiful Pillar, but much dissighted by being placed upon a very high pedestal, and by the Statue of y^e. Virgin Mary which stands on Top upon a very large flat stone, which forms a part of a Cornish and Frise. – On the other side the Church is an Egyptian Obelisk.

Temple of Diana. Near this Church we saw some very small remains of a Temple of Diana, where we had an opportunity of observing y^e. manner in wch. they encrusted their walls. They put first a layer of very thin, bricks, upon this they put a Coat of a Scement composed chiefly of rosin, upon which they laid their marble about ½ or ¾ of an Inch thick: They use likewise some few Iron nails or kind of hooks.

We went next to the Church of S^t. Eusebius where there is a most beautiful Cieling painted by Minx [Mengs].

We passed by the Arch of Gallienus, which is so plain or raither coarse a building, that it hardly stoped us a minuit.

M^r. Gibbon and myself dined to day with M^r. Martin. From thence we went to Pompeo Battoni, one of the best painters at Rome; and from thence to Seg^a: Angelica [Angelica Kauffman], a German Girl, who paints very well.

Fig 14 Pompeo Batoni, 1774-87

Wednesday 24th October – Rome

Popes Palace on Monte Cavallo. The weather being bad this Morning we did not return to the Esquiline hill, but went to the Pope's Palace at Monte Cavallo (a); – The Popes haveing found the Air at the Vatican unhealthy, removed their residence to this place where the Air is very fine. The Palace is large, and not ill built: There is a very large Quadrangle with a Colonade round it. In the inside is a very long Gallery, and many large rooms; The furniture not very fine, and raither old; indeed we might not see the best, as the Pope is at present in the Country. There are many pretty good paintings, and some Capital pieces, such as, A Madonna, wth. our Saviour and Infant; by Guido. She is standing and holding up a Sheet with both hands; our Saviour is laying a Sleep on y[e]. Sheet: It is finely done. – The Martyrdom of S[t]. Erasmus by Nic: Poussin: The body of Erasmus whom they are emboweling is finely executed. The Colouring raither dark, & black. – S[t]. John in y[e]. Wilderness, by Raphael. It is just like that in y[e]. Tribune at Florence, but not so well painted (b) – I beleive a Copy. – The Popes private Chapel entirely painted, by Guido: The Cieling, walls, &c done by him are very beautiful; but an Annunciation over the Altar is admirable: The Angel is there represented kneeling before y[e]. Virgin.

(a) Upon y[e]. Quirinal
(b) This is painted on board.

Thursday 25th October – Rome

The fine weather encouraged us to day to return to the Esquiline hill. We first went to the Church of Sancta Bibiana. This is raither a Small Church, and not any way very remarkable: The Architecture was by Bernini, and is tolerably good. – In y[e]. Inside is a Statue of S[a]. Bibiana by the same hand: The drapery is pretty good, but the figure we all agreed is, like most of those done by Bernini, in a very trifling, stiff, affected stile of Sculpture. This figure is over the great Altar, and under it is a kind of Sarcophagus of one entire piece of Oriental Alabaster, which is above nine feet in length, & proportionably broad. –

S. Lorenzo F: de Mura. From hence we went to S[t]. Lorenzo fuori della Mura, a very antient Church. There are, a great many Antique Granet Pillars, with archetrives & Cornishes &c: but very ill put to gether: Some very indifferent pieces in Mosaick: The most remarkable thing I remember is a very large marble Sarcophagus on which the Ceremony of y[e]. Antient Marrigges is very perfectly represented: You see the young man & woman wth. their hands joined, a priestess standing behind them & holding her arms round them.

The Priest close to y^e. young man, & a boy leading a Sheep to be sacrificed. – Several other attendants, & emblematical figures of Industry, Plenty, Increase &c an odd subject for a Sarcophagus.

There are some Catacombs under this Church, but as there are others more perfect, we did not go into them. This Church is about ½ a mile out of Rome, on y^e. Tivoli road. S^a. Croce in Gerusalemme, where we went next is more remarkable for y^e. great number of relicks kept there, than for any thing else (a). – This last Church is near the Porta Maggiore where we saw some remains of the Claudian Aqueduct, which took its rise near 40 Miles from Rome. On one side the Gate you see the Monument of y^e. Aqueduct, on which are three Inscriptions relateing to its being began by Caligula, and finished by Claudius; and some addition being made by Nero. Sextus Quintus has made use of some part of this, to bring the Aqua felice. See Nardini p. 517. – I never saw brick-work so well done, or so solidly, as some y^t. is remaining here, which tho built so long ago, is still in ev'ry respect as perfect as if just finished. – Just by the Gate are some remains of the Theatrum Castrense, supposed to have been for the use of the Soldiers of y^e. Pretorian Camp. It is beleived to have been composed of three Rows of Pillars above each other, and of y^e. Corinthian order: Part of y^e. outward wall near y^e. heigth of the lower Pillars is still standing. It was of an elyptical Form, and pretty large. – This Church is said to have been built by Constantine: See Nardini: P. 155.

(a) It is nearer the Church of S^a. Croce

Minerva Medica. In a vineyard to y^e. right hand of Porta Maggiore, are the remains of a Temple, thought to have been that of Minerva Medica. Nothing but the bare outside walls as high as where the vault began, is now standing, – with the ribs of the Vault, or Roof. The form of the Temple was a decagong, and one sees that it was encrusted, with Porphiry. In the same vineyard, & not far from the Temple are two Buriing places under Ground. By an Inscription over the door, as well as several within it is plain that one of them was given to one Aruntius. The inside is chiefly kind of narrow passages; the sides built up with brick; In these walls are square, and round holes big enough to admit of a smallish round vase in which the Ashes were deposited. The manner of these holes in the walls, can be compared to nothing more exactly than the sides of a Pigeon house; They may be something larger, otherwise appear just like them. – There are many vases never yet opened.

Fig 15 View of St John Lateran, 1749

Friday 26ᵗʰ October – Rome

S ᵗ. John Lateran. We went this Morning to Sᵗ. Giovanni Laterano which is finely situated on the Monte Celio. The front of this Church is handsome, tho it appears too high for its breadth: The Balustrade, and Statues on the Top are certainly too high & large for the building. It was built by Borromino. The Portico is very large, & handsome. The Church is very large; The body of it support'd by four rows of Columns. On each side of the Middle Isle, wᶜʰ. is very wide, stand the Statues of the 12 Apostles: On each side each Apostle is a Column of Verd Antique, Solid, and yᵉ. most beautiful I ever saw: There are 32 of these Columns in this Church, 6 very large Gall Antique, and many of Porphiry. Before one of the Altars is a very handsome Pediment of Brass Gilt supported by two Noble Bronze, fluted Pillars, which are likewise Gilded. They are said to be cast out of the brazen Rostra of Antoʸ. & Cleopatra's ship's taken at yᵉ. Bat: of Actium. The Chapel belonging to the Corsini family is the most elegant one can see: It is beautifully adorned with different Marbles: There is a Sarcophagus of one entire piece of Porphiry, measuring near 9 feet long, by 4 broad and 4 high: – We were shewn yᵉ. Table on wᶜʰ. Our Saviour is said to have eat yᵉ. last Supper, It is two pieces of plain board, I beleive about 2 feet long each. They shew a great number of other relicks: We saw the two remarkable Chairs with holes in y^e. bottom; One of them is pretty entire: It is made of a red marble: The hole in y^e. bottom may be about 6 Inches diameter. The Chapel of S^t. Jean the Baptist is close to y^e. Church: Over the great font is a kind of Roof supported by eight very large Porphiry Columns; Over which are as many very small of white Marble. It is y^e. ugliest piece of Architecture I ever saw. – – – – -

Near this Church is likewise the Scala Santa, or a flight of Steps, six of wch. are said to be brought from Jerusalem. You see at all hours of y^e. day, numbers of people going up these Steps on their knees, stoping on each step to say an Ave Maria: When they come to the top, they kiss a Cross, which is cut in y^e. upper step.

What an Excess of Bigotry, and enormity of Superstition.

Before this Church stands a most noble Egyptian Obelisk, which some suppose to have been one of those erected in the Circus Maximus by Augustus; Others say that it was one that was brought by Constantius.

Saturday 27th October – Rome.

We began to day with the little Farnese Palace which belongs to the King of Naples. The cieling of the Hall is painted in Fresco by Raphael: It is divided into two parts – One represents a Council of the Gods, and the other a Feast of the Gods (a). The figures in both are admirable, but it might be wished that the Colours had not been so dark, indeed Coarse, and that the Ground had not been of so dark a blue. This last was the work of Carlo Moratti. On the end of the room, and the Top of the Sides, are painted different Story's relateing to the Wedding, &c of Psiche & Cupid. – In a room within this are several fine pieces of Scupture: An Agrappina setting in a Chair, without arms. She is here represented at full length, with her arms laid before her, and her feet crossed. She has a melancholy, composed, thoughtful countenance, and an air that suits more the good, but unfortunate wife of Germanicus, than the infamous mother of Nero. It is a most excellent piece of scupture, and finer than the Agrippina, at Florence. – The much admired Venus, known by the name of, Belles Tresses, which name she highly deserves, as those parts are executed in the most perfect manner. The head, and y^e. rest of the body are not wanting in beauty. – Here are besides three good heads, of a Gladiator, a Vestal, & Homer. You see in the same room the incomparable Galatea, by Raphael; She is painted standing in a Shell, to which two Dolfins are fastened.

At S^a. Maria Transtivere we saw a most beautiful Assumption by Domenichino: It is painted in fresco on the ceiling: The Virgin is represented flying up to heaven, and several angels round her: It is a very fine piece of painting, and well preserved. – In a Chapel at S[t]. Fransesco a Ripa, we saw a Dead Christ, with the Virgin, and Mary Magdalane and S[t]. François most beautifully painted by Anibal Caracci. – It is esteemed one of y[e]. best at Rome, done by him.

(a) The nuptials of Psiche & Cupid very near the Top of the vault, slanting, and in y[e]. side

Sunday 28th October – Rome

This Being Sunday, affords very little matter, for my Journal. I forgot to mention yesterday that, Mess[rs]: Ponsonby, Coll: Scot: Major Abercrombie, Baron Wolfe, and Moula dined with us. Mess[rs]: Holroyd, Bolton & Major Ridley arrived here to day.

Monday 29th October – Rome

Baths of Titus, &c. We returned this Morning to the Esquiline Hill and went first to S[t]. Pietro in Vincola, where there are several, middling Pictures, but nothing very extraordinary. – Near this Church are the remains of Titus's Baths, which it is plain were very large, 'tho at present there is but very little of them remaining: There are two large Semicircular Buildings, not far from each other, but which do not correspond. – At a little distance f[m]. these, after descending considerably, you see several pieces of vaults, supposed to have been under the others, and for the use of the Common People. A little farther is a very long and wide vaulted Gallery, which was used for a walking place in Summer. The windows were made towards y[e]. north, and none at the other Side.

Septizonium. Within a little way of all these, is a vaulted building which Nardini calls a Septizonium, and was undoubtedly a reservoir for water to supply, some of the Baths, the swimming Places, and very likely sometimes for the Naumachia in the Amphitheatre of Flavius, w[ch]. is not far distant. The outside wall on one side of this Reservoir was circular: The building was considerably longer than, it was broad: The inside is divided into nine Gallery's; Each Gallery above 100 ft: long, 17 wide, and high: In each partition wall are four doors placed Diagonally from one wall to the other, with a design probably of rend'ring the beating of y[e]. water less violent, than it would have been, if the doors had been opposite each other. The water brought here by an aqueduct came in through the Circular wall: The walls are very much encrusted by the waters. Under this building, were other passages, which might possibly be used to give the water a certain degree of heat. – From hence we went to S:

Gregorio, upon Monte Celio: In a Chapel on one side of the Church, there is an admirable Picture by An: Caracci: S[t]. Gregory is represented on his knees, praying to the Virgin, with several Angels &c. It is painted with more softness than common to that master; very beautiful, and well preserved. – In another Chapel, you see two walls painted in Fresco by, one by Domenichino, and the other by Guido. The latter has painted S[t]. Andrew, whom they are leading to be martyr'd, and he perceiveing the cross as he is going falls down, & worships it. Admirably done, but much damaged. In y[e]. other Dominichino has given the scourging of S[t]. Andrew: the Executioner is one of the finest & best drawn figures I ever saw, there are many more in it, very good, but likewise damaged.

Fig 16   Ruins of the Caracalla Baths, c.1766

Tuesday 30th October – Rome

We went to Monte Celio, and saw the Vivarii of Domitian just by the Church of S[t]. John & Paul: small remains; a building 4 stories high upon it. Arch of Dolabella: Arches of Neros Aqueduct, a vast height. Villa Mattei: a great many Statues & Busts: none fine. Temple of Claudius: Bad.

Wednesday 31st October – Rome

Thermae Antonina. The Baths of Antoninus Caracalla, commonly called Thermæ Antoninianæ (a): – They are situated on the rise of the Aventine between Porta S[s]. Paolo, and Sebastiano. – This may be reckoned amongst the most considerable, and magnificent works of the Romans, both for its extent, and the beauty and expensiveness of the materials: Spertianus speaking of y^e. Emperor says Thermae nominis sui eximias, quorum cellam soliarum architecti negant posse ulla imitatione, qua jacta est, fieri, nam & ex are, nel cupro cancelli superpositi esse dicuntur, quibus cameratis tota coperedita est; A tantum est spatii, ut id ipsum fieri negent potuisse docti mechanici. Of these Superb Baths nothing is now to be seen but the bare walls, but most of which are still standing, so y^t. the number, and size of the rooms may be very exactly known: – But there is still y^e. same deficiency in these, as in those of Diocletian, in respect to the places necessary for bathing (b): – Only six rooms are alotted for that purpose; three on each side the Hippocostum: Hot Bath, Cold Bath, and The other rooms are imagined to be for walking, swimming, and different kinds of Exercises: It appears very plain f^m. pieces of marble remaining, and many other marks in the walls, that they were encrusted wth. marble. Many of the rooms were of a very great size: – We took notice of one in particular wch. must have been in respect to size and ornaments very magnificent: – Its length is about 190 ft: the breadth above 80: and heigth I beleive near as much: On each side were four Marble Columns: In the walls between the Columns alternatively niches and basso-relievos: The niches, one round, between two square ones: At each end was a row of Columns formeing recesses, wch. if included, the room was near 300 ft long. The walls of this as well as the other parts, are the most substantial, & close brickwork I ever saw, except by y^e. antient Romans: The room described is a side room; in the middle is one near the same dimensions: – The extent of the outwards walls of these baths are very great: The length of the front wall above 1180 feet: Where the wall run out circular in the side above 1400; both measureing f^m. outside to outside: the greatest breadth measured the same, about 1120. The clear length within y^e. walls 1010: Ditto, breadth 980. – There is a difficulty wth. respect to the way into these Baths. It does not appear at present: It is supposed to have been over arches raised over the vaults now to be seen on the lower side: For what these vaults served is also uncertain. Perhaps for Baths for the common people; perhaps only to support the hill: Continued.[1]

I have procured a very exact plan of these baths taken by M^r. Byers.

(a) Built about y^e. year of Rome 966.

(b) There are vaults under the whole Baths wch. perhaps served for Baths likewise.

1   This is the end of the second volume of the diaries. There seems little doubt that Guise continued with the diaries, but their location is unknown, or they are lost – see the enigmatic first page of these diaries where an unknown donor gave the diaries to Sir William V Guise.

List of Illustrations

The publishers are grateful to the following people and organisations for permission to reproduce the illustrations. All possible care has been taken to trace and acknowledge the owners of the illustrations. If any errors have occurred, we shall be happy upon notification to correct them in any future editions of this book. The modern photo from Rome was taken when Paul & Jane Butler retraced Guise's and Gibbon's steps in January 2020.

Book cover: Allan Ramsay, *Preparatory sketch for William Guise portrait*, 1761. Credit: Yale Center for British Art, Paul Mellon Collection

Frontispiece: Allan Ramsay, *William Guise,* 1761. Credit: Private collection, courtesy of the Richard Green Gallery, London.

Fig 1 Thomas Patch, 'Portrait of a Man, called Edward Gibbon' from *Sketchbook of Portrait Studies 1760s.* Credit: Yale Center for British Art, Paul Mellon Collection. Described (as being of Gibbon) as 'doubtful' by the National Portrait Gallery. However, used as the frontispiece to Bonnard's edition of Gibbon's Journey from Geneva to Rome, with the caption "Gibbon at Florence in 1764 by Thomas Patch".

Fig 2   Elmore Court, Gloucestershire, seat of the Guise family, 2021. Credit: photograph Paul Butler 14.12.2021

Fig 3   Typical page from diary. Credit: photograph Paul Butler

Fig 4   George Keate, *The Manner of Passing Mount Cenis*, August 1755. Credit: British Museum. Keate was a draughtsman, painter, poet, naturalist and antiquary.

Fig 5 *Historical Map of Northern Italy 1796-1805 for the campaigns of 1796 – 1805.* Credit: University of Texas at Austin, Historical Atlas by William Shepherd (1911).

Fig 6   Giovanni Michele Graneri, *The Teatro Regio in Turin*, 1752. Credit: Museo Civico d'Arte Antica, Palazzo Madama, Turin.

Fig 7 John Harris, 'A Prospect of the City of Genoa', in *'Navigantium atque iterantium bibliotheca'*. Revised John Campbell, 1744. Credit: Simon Hunter, Antique Maps

Fig 8 Thomas Patch, *British Gentlemen at Sir Horace Mann's*, 1763-65. Credit: Yale Center for British Art, Paul Mellon Collection

Fig 9 Johann Zoffany, *La Tribuna degli Uffizi*, 1772 – 78. Credit: Royal Collection Trust/© Her Majesty Queen Elizabeth II 2022

Fig 10   Thomas Patch, *The Cognoscenti, Captain Walcot, Mr Apthorp and Thomas Patch*. 1764-65. In the North Gallery at Petworth House. Photo credit ©National Trust Images/Matthew Hollow

Fig 11 Giovanni Battista Piranesi 'Veduta della Piazza del Popolo', c. 1750. In *Le Vedute di Roma*. Credit: Harris Brisbane Dick Fund, 1937, Metropolitan Museum of Art, New York

Fig 12 Giovanni Battista Piranesi 'View of the Campo Vaccino, the Forum Romanum from the Capitoline Hill', 1748. In *Le Vedute di Roma*. Credit: Scottish National Gallery of Modern Art.

Fig 13 *The Niobe Group*, Villa Medici, Rome. In 1775 the original statues (last century BCE – 1st century CE; formerly thought be late 5th/early 4th century BCE) were transferred to the Uffizi. The present statues are copies. Credit: photograph Paul Butler 04.02.2020

Fig 14 Pompeo Batoni, *Self Portrait*, 1774-87. Credit: Museo di Roma, Palazzo Braschi, Rome

Fig 15 Giovanni Battista Piranesi 'Veduta della Basilica di S. Giovanni Laterano', 1749. *Le Vedute di Roma*. Credit: Yale University Art Gallery.

Fig 16 Giovanni Battista Piranesi 'Rovine delle Terme Antoniniane' [Baths of Caracalla], c.1766 in '*Le Vedute di Roma*'. Credit: Le Gallerie degli Uffizi, Florence.

Select Bibliography

Jeremy Black, *The British Abroad: The Grand Tour in the Eighteenth Century*, (1992)
Georges A Bonnard, ed., *Gibbon's Journey from Geneva to Rome: His Journal from 20 April to 2 October 1764* (1961)
Georges A. Bonnard, ed., *Edward Gibbon Memoirs of My Life* (1996)
Edward Chaney, *The Evolution of the Grand Tour: Anglo-Italian Cultural Relations since the Renaissance* (1998)
Edward Chaney, 'Gibbon, Beckford and the Interpretation of "Dreams, Waking Thoughts, and Incidents"', *Beckford Society Annual Lectures 2000-2003* (2004)
J Ingamells, ed, *A Dictionary of British and Irish travellers in Italy 1701–1800* (1997)
R.S.Pine-Coffin, *Bibliography of British and American Travel in Italy to 1860*, (Florence, 1974)

INDEX

Note: named churches, gardens, libraries, palazzi, temples, theatres and villas have been grouped under these headings (q.v.)

Carriages, 1, 4, 9, 79, 81
Castel San Giovanni, 59
Catacombs, 177
Celesia, Dorothea, 47-8
Celesia, Giuseppe, 48, 50, 54-5, 57
Celesia, Pietro Paolo, 44–8, 52, 54-5, 57, 58
Cenis, Mont, 3, 4, 6, 183
Chablais, Duke of, 20
Chaise, 33, 42–44, 59, 81, 152, 156
Chaloner, Mr, 2
Chambéry, 3
Chaney, Edward, x, xvii
Charles Emmanuel III, Duke of Savoy, King of Sardinia, 5, 9-12, 15, 18, 20, 22-4, 26-7, 30
Chivasso, 26
Churches, chapels, basilicas, cathedrals, convents, monasteries
    Florence
Basilica della Santissima Annunziata, 145-6
S. Croce, 139
S. Gaetano, 146
S.Lorenzo, 132-3
S. Maria del Fiore, cathedral, 141-2
S. Maria Novella, 146
S. Spirito, 142
S. Trinita, 146
    Genoa
Basilica della Santissima Annunziata, 46
Basilica di S. Caterina, 55
S. Filippo Neri, 52
S. Lorenzo, cathedral, 49
S. Stefano, 56
    Milan
S. Alessandro in Velabro, 32
S. Maria della Vittoria, 32
S. Maria Nascente, cathedral, 27
S. Maria presso S. Celso, 32
    Modena
SS. Maria Assunta e Geminiano, cathedral, 73
    Parma
S. Maria Assunta, cathedral, 63, 67
S, Sepolcro, 67
    Pavia
Certosa di Pavia, 40-1
SS. Stefano e Maria Assunta, cathedral, 43
    Piacenza
Convent of Roquelins, 61
S. Agostino, 61
SS. Maria Assunta e Giustina, cathedral, 60
    Pisa
S. Maria Assunta, cathedral, 152

    Reggio Emilia
Basilica della Madonna della Ghiara, 70
Oratorio di S. Stefano, 70
S. Maria Assunta, cathedral, 69
    Rome
S. Andrea al Quirinale, 169
S. Bernardo alle Terme, 170
S. Bibiana, 176
S. Eusebio, 175
S. Francesco a Ripa, 180
S. Giorgio in Velabro, 159
S. Giuseppe dei Falegnami, 161
S. John Lateran, 174, 179
S. Lorenzo fuori le Mura, 176
S. Maria degli Angeli, 170
S. Maria della Vittoria, 170
S. Maria in Aracoeli, 159
S. Maria Maggiore, 174
S. Maria Nuova, 161
S. Maria Trastevere, 179
S. Paolo fuori le Mura, 174
S. Peter's, 157, 161, 174
S. Pietro in Vincola, 180
S. Pudenziana, 173
S. Silvestro, 168
SS. Giovanni e Paolo, 181
    Siena
S. Maria Assunta, cathedral, 155
    Turin
Basilica di Superga, 10, 50
S. Uberto, Venaria Reale, 12
Santuario della Consolata, 10
SS. Martiri, 10
cicerone, 157, 162
cicisbei, 24
Cigoli, 137
Cimabue, 94
Clavering-Cowper, George Nassau, Lord Fordwich, 75, 137
Clementina, 82, 99
Cocchi, Raimondo, 125, 129
Cochin, Charles-Nicholas, 70, 102, 107, 121, 124
Conca, Sebastiano, 12
Corci, Marchesa di, 75, 143
Corregio, Antonio Allegri, 47, 63, 64, 67, 70, 83, 86, 121, 162
Corsa dei Barberi, 78-9, 81
Corsica, 45, 54, 57, 58, 153
Cortona, Pietro da, 18, 125-6, 161
Crousaz de Mézery, Henri, xii, 1, 6
Cruseilles, 2
Curchod, Jean-Jacob, 19, 24

Damer, John & George, 139, 142-8, 150-1

www.ingramcontent.com/pod-product-compliance
Lightning Source LLC
Chambersburg PA
CBHW051120300726
48981CB00002B/199